EXTENDING ECONOMICS WITHIN
THE CURRICULUM

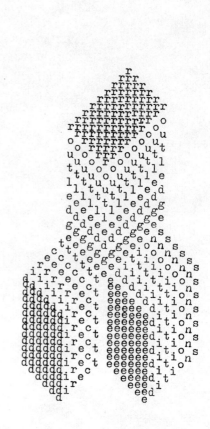

EXTENDING ECONOMICS WITHIN THE CURRICULUM

Edited by

Keith Robinson

and

Robert Wilson

on behalf of the Economics Association

ROUTLEDGE DIRECT EDITIONS

ROUTLEDGE & KEGAN PAUL
London, Henley and Boston

First published in 1977
by Routledge & Kegan Paul Ltd
39 Store Street
London WC1E 7DD,
Broadway House,
Newtown Road,
Henley-on-Thames,
Oxon RG9 1EN and
9 Park Street,
Boston, Mass. 02108, USA
Printed in Great Britain by
Thomson Litho Ltd,
East Kilbride, Scotland
© Economics Association 1977

British Library Cataloguing in Publication Data

Extending economics within the curriculum.
    1. Economics - Study and teaching (Secondary) -
    Great Britain - Congresses
    I. Robinson, Keith II. Wilson, Robert
    III. Economics Association
    330'.07'1241   H62.5.G7   77-30107

    ISBN 0 7100 8629 6

CONTENTS

NOTES ON CONTRIBUTORS

Mrs LINDA THOMAS - Deputy Head, Pollards Hill High School, Mitcham; and formerly Schools Council Field Officer in Wales.

DAVID J.WHITEHEAD - Lecturer in Education at the University of London Institute of Education; a member of the Council and Executive, and General Editor of 'Economics', the journal of the Economics Association.

DAVID CHRISTIE - Lecturer in Economics at Moray House College of Education, Edinburgh; and committee member of the Scottish Branch of the Economics Association.

ANGUS TAYLOR - Headmaster of Cramlington High School, Northumberland; formerly Deputy Headmaster, Wyndham School, Cumbria; member of the Council and the External Relations Committee of the Economics Association.

J.R.HOUGH - Lecturer in Education and Economics at Loughborough University.

JOHN McCAFFERTY - Adviser in Business Studies and Economics for the Lanark Division of Strathclyde Region; a former member of the Scottish Central Committee on Social Subjects; and a committee member of the Scottish Branch of the Economics Association.

LUIS MACIVER - Principal Lecturer in Education and Psychology at Dundee College of Education.

R.T.WINSOR - Head of Economics at King Edward VI Grammar School, Retford; and Press Officer for the Economics Association.

Miss DOROTHY DAVIDSON - Principal Teacher of Business Studies and Economics at Leith Academy, Edinburgh.

BRIAN ROBINSON - Senior Lecturer in Economics at Worcester College of Education; a member of the Council and Executive and Chairman of the Teacher Training Committee of the Economics Association.

Mrs PAMELA M.MORRISON - Teacher in charge of Economics, Townfield
School, London Borough of Hillingdon; examiner for the Middlesex
Regional Examining Board.

Mrs JENNIFER H.WALES - Head of Economics at Passmores School,
Harlow.

D.LYNE - County Adviser for Business Studies, Staffordshire.

H.A.RAMSAY - Lecturer in Economics at Jordanhill College of Education, Glasgow; formerly Lecturer in Business Studies at Philippa
Fawcett College.

F.S.SMITH - Lecturer in Education, Brunel University; Chief
Examiner in Economics for Middlesex Regional Examining Board, Metropolitan Regional Examinations Board, and Associated Examining Board.

LESLIE W.ORTON - Principal Teacher of Economics at Dunfermline High
School; Secretary of the Scottish Branch of the Economics Association.

Mrs PAT NOBLE - Senior Lecturer in the Media Resources Unit at
Garnett College; member of the Publications and Research and
Curriculum Development Committees of the Economics Association.

THE EDITORS

KEITH ROBINSON - Director of the Scottish Centre for Social
Subjects, Jordanhill College of Education, Glasgow; member of
Council and Executive, and Chairman of the Research and Curriculum
Development Committee of the Economics Association.

ROBERT WILSON - Lecturer in Economics at Aberdeen College of Education; committee member of the Scottish Branch of the Economics
Association.

OTHER PARTICIPANTS AT THE SEPTEMBER 1975 SEMINAR

Mr B.ATKINSON, Preston Polytechnic.
Mr J.BUTEL, Preston Polytechnic.
Mr C.DIMMOCK, Madeley College of Education.
Mr J.NIXON, Worcester College of Education.
Mrs E.RICHARD, Adviser in Business Studies, Leeds Education
Authority.
Mr F.ROBERTS, College Cartrefle, Wrexham.
Mr A.THRELFALL, Dudley College of Education.
Mrs P.TILLEY, Coventry College of Education.
Mr H.TRAVIS, Dundee College of Education.
Mr J.WALKER, Loughborough University.
Mr A.WALMSLEY, HMI.

INTRODUCTION
Keith Robinson

In June 1973 the Economics Association sponsored its first seminar in curriculum development. It was organised by Keith Drake of the Department of Education of Manchester University and the discussion was based on sixteen papers dealing with important issues of aims and objectives, methodology and assessment in economics teaching, and of the place of social sciences and, in particular, of economics in the school curriculum. The publication (1) of the seminar papers together with a summary of the discussion at the seminar and an indication of future research needs was of great value to teachers and lecturers wishing to keep abreast of the latest developments in economics education. The papers bore eloquent testimony to the advance of the subject in the curriculum of the secondary school since the days in the 1950s when Lord Robbins and others doubted whether it should have any place in school education at all.

The main emphasis at the seminar was on the teaching of the subject at 'O' and 'A' levels and on links between economics at school and further education. During the previous twenty years, there had been a remarkable expansion in these aspects of education, and the publication of an influential report of a joint committee of the Royal Economic Society, the Association of University Teachers of Economics, and the Economics Association (2) in the same year as the seminar amply demonstrated the much closer affinity of thinking between university, further education and school teachers on the nature and contribution of the subject at these levels.

A natural progression from this stage was an assessment of the contribution which the subject might make to the education of younger and less academic pupils, and a small number of papers at the 1973 seminar dealt with this issue. Already, in the columns of 'Economics' (the journal of the Economics Association) a series of articles had appeared which considered the possible extension of the economics curriculum below 'O' and 'A' levels so that a much larger number (perhaps even all) of secondary school pupils would have some acquaintance with the key ideas and principles of the subject.

Professor H.Entwistle's paper on Educational Theory and the Teaching of Economics (3) was seminal in that it attempted to apply pertinent educational theory to the question of whether economics is a fit subject for schools, especially below the sixth-form level.

He recognised the importance of the work of Piaget and Bruner in
demonstrating that learning is a developmental process and that
teachers must seek simplification of material by identifying the
key concepts and principles of any subject and illustrating them by
examples related to the level of thinking (in concrete or abstract
terms) of the learner. Entwistle argued that the fundamental
concepts and propositions of economics are themselves quite simple
but that in order to determine at what age these principles might
realistically be taught, it would be necessary to examine both the
logical structure of economics as a discipline and also the manner
in which its principles are manifest in the behaviour of learners
of different ages, intelligence and cultural background. Only then
might it be possible to substantiate in respect of economics
Bruner's hypothesis that any subject can be taught effectively in
some intellectually honest form to any child at any stage of development.

In two articles, The Organic Curriculum: an Experiment in
Primary Education (4) and Economics in the Primary School, (5)
A.Clarke discussed a full trial of material prepared by Professor
L.Senesh and his colleagues at Purdue University and intended for
use with children from six years of age upwards. He came to the
conclusion that the introduction of economic concepts even in the
simplest and most unsophisticated form to the child in the infant
school would be repugnant to most teachers at this level and that
it would be extremely unwise to introduce any form of economics
teaching below the age of eight. When introduced, he felt that it
should form part of a wider-ranging course concerned with social and
human relationships.

Professor Senesh contributed a chapter on Teaching Economic
Concepts in the Primary Grades (6) to the first edition of 'Teaching
Economics', which appeared in 1967, and he argued that to develop a
meaningful economics course in schools especially related to the
needs of younger children it was necessary to define the fundamental
ideas of economic knowledge; relate these ideas to children's experience; relate economics to other areas of the social sciences;
and relate the social sciences to social problems thus developing a
problem-solving awareness and ability in children.

The teaching of economics to less academic pupils was also considered in the first edition of 'Teaching Economics' in the context
of Certificate of Secondary Education courses which at that time
were beginning to appear in the curriculum. F.Davies doubted
whether it was desirable to defer the introduction of the subject
until this relatively late stage of a pupil's full-time education
and urged that any CSE courses 'should be sufficiently ambitious to
develop an understanding of the economic society in which we live
whilst guarding against the over-simplification of economic concepts
to the point where they destroyed that understanding'. (7) He believed that the teaching of economic concepts and the teaching of
institutional economics necessary to show the significance of the
concepts in their real-world setting should proceed simultaneously.

Working Paper No.2 of the Schools Council on 'The Raising of the
School Leaving Age' stated that 'everyone these days needs some
contact with the language and ideas of elementary economics; what
we do not know is how far they can be pursued with pupils at 15-16

of widely differing abilities'. (8) K.Dunning (9) described in 1967
an experiment in teaching economics to the whole ability range, including the remedial group, in a school in Manchester, which sought
to discover how the economic literacy of the Newsom-type child could
be improved. He accepted Bruner's spiral theory of learning and a
developmental approach to the teaching of economics which recognises
that pupils need to know those fundamental principles of the subject
which will be as relevant and useful at the end of the century as at
the time of the first teaching of the course. He stressed the
importance for young pupils of simple and concrete situations em-
bodying such principles as specialisation, mechanisation, risk-
bearing and demand, and of the need to return to these principles
with more complex and abstract examples at later stages in the
course.

This approach was broadly in line with the views expressed by
N.Lee in Economics Education for the Newsom Child. From a discussion of the 'structure' of economics in terms of the basic
concepts and key mechanisms which underline all analysis - concepts
such as opportunity cost, supply and demand relationships in the
market and spending and saving as determinants of the level of
income and employment in the economy at large - he reached the conclusion that 'the level of understanding of the Newsom child is
therefore to be measured in terms of the economic concepts he has
understood, the level of sophistication in his understanding, and
the range of real situations in which he can meaningfully apply the
concepts'. (10)

In an important and more wide-ranging contribution to this debate
than his paper of 1967, Dunning (11) in 1970 asked how economics
teachers who wish to teach the subject to less academic pupils can
justify its inclusion in an already overcrowded curriculum.
Statements such as 'we all need to know economics' should be re-
phrased as 'I think we all ought to know economics' in order to
bring out their essentially normative character. Support for such
value judgments is usually couched in terms of the supposed 'relevance' of courses in descriptive economics intended to prepare the
pupil for his role as a future consumer and worker, and Dunning accepted that such courses can help to make some sense of the world
into which the pupil will shortly move. He believed, however, that
the most worthwhile contribution of economics education at this
stage is in the fostering of reasoned judgments in economic issues
essential to the future citizen.

This inevitably brief survey of a lively debate lasting over the
past decade on the role of economics in the education of younger and
less academic pupils has highlighted two main issues

1 Should economics be taught at all to these pupils or should the
   subject be reserved for the later stages of the secondary school
   and exclusively for more academic pupils?
2 Should economics be taught as a single discipline to these
   pupils or should it form part of a more broad-ranging social
   science course?

It is in relation to these two questions that the title 'Extending
Economics Within the Curriculum' has been chosen for the papers presented at the second curriculum development seminar held by the Economics Association in September 1975 at Worcester College of Edu-

cation. The opening papers explore these questions in terms of general philosophical and psychological considerations, and they might, with advantage, be read in conjunction with some articles in 'Economics' and some chapters in the second edition of 'Teaching Economics', which have appeared since the first curriculum development seminar was held. (12) The remaining papers examine a number of different approaches to the teaching of younger and of less academic pupils involving economics as a single subject and as a component in a variety of multi-disciplinary courses: these papers, in particular, give much practical information and guidance to teachers who may wish to extend the economics curriculum in their own schools. It is hoped that the publication of the papers together with the discussions at the seminar will make a further significant contribution to the evolution of economics education in the secondary school.

I would like to thank all those who prepared papers for the seminar and who have so willingly undertaken the revision of them necessary for publication, and also all who took part in the stimulating discussions at the seminar. I am most grateful to Robert Wilson who taped all the discussions and has skilfully edited them; they appear at the end of single chapters or groups of chapters in accordance with the way in which they took place at the seminar. Unfortunately, David Christie and Leslie Orton were unable to be present at Worcester and so there was no discussion on their contributions. Finally, my thanks to Mrs Anne Wylie of the Scottish Centre for Social Subjects, who most efficiently typed the various drafts of the papers and the discussions for publication.

REFERENCES

1 WHITEHEAD, D. (ed.), 'Curriculum Development in Economics', Heinemann, London, 1974.
2 The Royal Economic Society, The Association of University Teachers of Economics, The Economics Association, 'The Teaching of Economics in Schools', Macmillan, London, 1973.
3 ENTWISTLE, H., Educational Theory and the Teaching of Economics, 'Economics', Autumn 1966 (vol.6, pt 4).
4 CLARKE, A., The Organic Curriculum: an Experiment in Primary Education, 'Economics', Autumn 1966 (vol.6, pt 4).
5 CLARKE, A., Economics in the Primary School, 'Economics', Autumn 1967 (vol.7, pt 3).
6 SENESH, L., Teaching Economic Concepts in the Primary Grades in LEE, N. (ed.), 'Teaching Economics', 1st edn, Economics Association, London, 1967.
7 DAVIES, F., CSE Economics in LEE, N. (ed.), 'Teaching Economics', 1st edn, Economics Association, London, 1967.
8 Schools Council Working Paper No.2, 'The Raising of the School Leaving Age', HMSO, London, 1965.
9 DUNNING, K., A Developmental Course in the Teaching of Economics for the Average Young Citizen, 'Economics', Autumn 1967 (vol.7, pt 3).
10 LEE, N., Economics Education for the Newsom Child, 'Economics', Spring/Summer 1969 (vol.8, pt 1).

11 DUNNING, K., What Economics Should we Teach?, 'Economics',
    Summer 1970 (vol.8, pt 4).
12 See particularly
    SUMNER, H., Economics in Schools: the Case for an Inter-related
    Approach, 'Economics', Winter 1974 (vol.10, pt 6).
    ATKINSON, B., Classroom Curriculum Development in Economics,
    'Economics', Winter 1974 (vol.10, pt 6).
    SCOTT, A. and STRAKER-COOK, D., Economics Pupils, 'Economics',
    Spring 1976 (vol.12, pt 1).
    CHRISTIE, D., Economics in the Early Stages of Secondary Edu-
    cation, SUMNER, H., Economics in the Context of Social Studies
    (8-13 age range), ROBINSON, T.K., Economics for the 16-year-old
    School Leaver, all in LEE, N. (ed.), 'Teaching Economics', 2nd
    edn, Heinemann, London, 1975.

Part one

GENERAL CURRICULUM ISSUES

Chapter 1

CONCEPTUAL THINKING IN ECONOMICS AND THE HUMANITIES

Linda Thomas

INTRODUCTION

During the period 1971-4, a small group of teachers in a Welsh industrial seaside town, aware of the demand created by the introduction of comprehensive education in 1970, set in motion a process
of curriculum development. The section of the curriculum with which
they were concerned covered the group of subjects known as humanities. The group of teachers set itself the task, in 1971, of providing an integrated humanities course for fourth and fifth form
pupils in the comprehensive school. The economics specialist was
asked to take responsibility for the economics content of this
integrated course. As a result of the developmental work which occurred during the three years, certain conclusions were reached and
certain lessons were learnt. These can be conveniently grouped
under two broad headings - lessons concerning the nature of integrated courses and lessons concerning the processes involved in
curriculum development.

This paper contains a description of this attempt to design a new
integrated humanities course for fourth and fifth form pupils.
Section 1 contains a description of some of the research work undertaken by the team. Section 2 contains the application - experiment
and evaluation - process which occurred concurrently with the
research work described in section 1. This is conveniently handled
in historical form. Section 3 presents the conclusions.

1 RATIONALE FOR INTEGRATION

Early discussion between team members exposed the universally-held
belief that the main trap which the integrator must avoid is that of
propagating a 'scissors and paste' approach in which bits and pieces
from various subjects are stuck together to form a haphazard collection of interest based topics, and in which no attention is paid
to mastering the logically distinct conceptual structures of the
separate disciplines. The major theme which emerged from a study
of relevant literature was that knowledge is differentiated into
distinct autonomous forms and that the development of understanding

is only possible through the mastery of these distinct, if inter-connected, conceptual schemes.

B.Bernstein (1971) (1) distinguishes the 'integrated' approach from the 'focused' approach, where different subjects focus on a common problem. He claims that the way to ensure that conceptual structures are safeguarded is to organise integration by the use of 'relational ideas' or 'supra-content concepts' which focus on general principles at high levels of abstraction, rather than to use a thematic approach. In the terminology used in this paper it would mean integrating at the conceptual stage rather than at the content stage. This is an idea which has recently also gained popularity in America (Taba, 1962). (2) Bernstein and Taba challenge conventional subject structures which emphasise the need to acquire structures of knowledge organised in hierarchical fashion such that the ultimate mystery of the subject is revealed only very late in the educational life of the select few. But Bernstein confuses the issue by suggesting that the study of such highly abstracted general principles will in some magical way reveal the ultimate mysteries, that is, the 'potential for creating new realities' and the deep structures of the subject to the greenest novice. He treats the internal problem of creating a coherent sequence of learning inside separate subjects in a rather cavalier fashion. The problem of matching the conceptual development of child and subject certainly does not disappear merely by the use of abstract principles as a means of organising integrated schemes of work.

On the other hand, Hazel Sumner (3) over-reacts against the excessive Bernstein claims by rejecting completely the idea of a general principle as anything more than an organisational tool. Describing the high-level concepts as embracing concepts derived from the contributing disciplines, she writes

where these concepts are used to locate significant or rewarding content there may be something to be said for them, but where they are used as a teaching objective there is doubt on the grounds that they are too general to be useful to the pupils in helping them to understand their social environment.

If this argument is accepted, it is difficult to distinguish between such concepts and the discredited themes and topics which they are to replace, since the concepts are used purely as a means of selecting content.

Beyer (1971) (4) analyses different types of concepts. He shows that some are so narrow that they are hardly more than definitions. Others are so broad and all-embracing that they may best be used to store information and/or to structure courses of study in the Sumner way. But other concepts are more useful since they make sense out of experiences and these are the objectives and tools of learning.

Selected analytical concepts

GEOGRAPHY	ECONOMICS	POLITICAL SCIENCE	SOCIOLOGY AND ANTHROPOLOGY

I

GEOGRAPHY	ECONOMICS	POLITICAL SCIENCE	SOCIOLOGY AND ANTHROPOLOGY
Site	Price	State	Role
Situation	Cost	Law	Status
Scale	Money	Sanctions	Norm
Boundary	Producer	Legislative	Family
Resource	Consumer	Executive	Group
Landscape	Goods	Judicial	Class
Link	Services		
Node			

II

Areal distribution	Scarcity	Decision making	Culture change
Areal association	Market	Leadership	Acculturation
Spatial interaction	Allocation	Citizenship	Assimilation
	Production		

MULTI-DISCIPLINARY

Change	Comparative advantage
Institution	Interdependence
System	Conflict
Ideology	Multiple causation

The remainder of this section undertakes the task of proving that it is possible to construct a middle road between the Taba and Bernstein claims that use of key concepts supplants the need to construct a developmental structure for each subject and Sumner's implied claim that key concepts are meaningless generalisations once they are viewed as teaching objectives.

First of all, the epistemological case rests on the team's basic philosophy taken to its logical conclusion. If knowledge is differentiated into distinct disciplines, realms of meaning or forms of knowledge, each with its own conceptual structure, then it must be possible to take an overall view inside each form or discipline. The area of concern here is what is named the humanities - Hirst's (1972) 'History and the human sciences' (5) (the form involving propositions connected with intentions) and Phenix's (1958) 'synnoetics' (relational insight between the other person and the self). (6) If the existence of this form of knowing with its own conceptual framework is accepted it must be possible to expose it. Researchers working on the problem have developed a set of basic principles or key ideas as Bernstein advocated. The objectives of education become understanding and mastery of this conceptual structure. It is the last step which proves difficult - the one which Bernstein is able to take so glibly in theory - the task of delineating the actual process of conceptual development so that a coherent sequence is obtained. The discredited social studies of the 1940s and 1950s provide evidence of the failure to expose the logical structure inside the conceptual framework of each discipline.

Blyth (1972), (7) when he uses subjects as resource areas to illustrate basic key concepts, is able to ignore the problem by assuming that the subject areas reflect an underlying unified and common conceptual structure. If this assumption is justified, then the subject areas are merely resource areas to be used to illustrate basic concepts and are merely convenient tools to be used to make areas of work manageable. The problem is that the assumption is difficult to justify both in terms of recognisable humanities courses and in terms of the various mixes of subjects to which the title humanities is conveniently applied. Even within the discipline, as defined by Hirst and Phenix, subjects are not simple structures but mutations. Hirst calls some of these 'fields of knowledge'. Instead of being concerned with the straightforward development of the underlying conceptual structure of the form of knowledge in their own particular area, these subjects are concerned with specific theoretical and practical questions. Each one has therefore developed its own conceptual structure based on secondary concepts which are only indirectly reducible to the basic concepts of the discipline. It is impossible to turn the clock back and insist that the development of knowledge in the humanities be rerouted in a more efficient manner. Development has already occurred in a mutated way and although it makes the task of demolishing subject boundaries difficult, it is not impossible.

This argument is strengthened when considering courses which mix subjects from different disciplines. In these cases, the overarching set of key concepts, used as an integratory tool, in no way represents the conceptual framework of a form of knowing or a realm of meaning.

In each of these cases, the logical structures of each subject must be accepted as they are, but Hazel Sumner is wrong in implying that this is all that can be done, when she claims that the existence of hybrids inside the humanities makes it impossible to integrate at the conceptual stage. The integrator must carry out the task of relating the conceptual structure of each individual subject to the basic concepts which have no developmental structure of their own. It is then meaningful to talk of making the gaining of knowledge and understanding of the key concepts through mastery of the individually distinct conceptual structures of each subject, an educational objective.

(a) The key concepts of the humanities form of knowing

The first task is to identify the basic principles or generalisations which form the basic constructs of the area of knowledge known as the humanities. Taba suggests the following focusing ideas:

1 All people have basic needs which are met in different ways.

2 People differ in their degree of dependence on their environment.
3 Certain social institutions such as the family and education are
   universal but differently organised.
4 Some processes and institutions are influenced by tradition;
   others change quickly and easily.
5 One of the major characteristics of the modern world is dependence between people.
6 Institutions develop to support a way of life.
Blyth and his colleagues list the following key concepts: ◄
1 Communication.
   The significant movement of individuals, groups or resources or
   the significant transmission of information.
2 Power.
   The purposive exercise of power over individuals, groups or
   resources.
3 Values and Beliefs.
   The conscious or unconscious systems by which individuals and
   societies organise their response to nature, social and super-
   natural orders.
4 Conflict/Consensus.
   The ways in which individuals and groups adjust their behaviour
   to natural and social circumstances.
5 Similarity/Difference.
   Classification of phenomena according to relevant criteria.
6 Continuity/Change.
   Distinction of phenomena along this essentially historical
   dimension.
7 Causality.
   The notion that change in a state of affairs can be attributed
   to the phenomena preceding it.
8 Specialisation/Interdependence.

(b) The key concepts of each subject field

It has been previously argued that the key concepts of each individual subject are logically reducible to the key concepts of the
humanities form of knowing but that they are mutations to the extent
that they are also concerned with particular theoretical or practical questions relating to their own field of knowledge. Each set is
therefore distinct and autonomous. (See Appendix 1.1 Key Concepts
for Economics.)

(c) The developmental structure of each subject

To enable the teacher to match the learning experience with the
child's development, the developmental structure of each subject
should be exposed.
   Very little work has been done in the humanities to apply
Bruner's 'spiral' approach, which entails applying first principles
to more difficult and complex material rather than introducing the
learner to distinctly new concepts and principles. The ritualism

and formalism of the old 'logical structures' of the subject per-
sists in practice. Systematisation is essential if learning is to
make sense but the teacher should relate the logical progression of
the substantive concepts of the subjects to the child's spontaneous
conceptual development. (Appendix 1.2 illustrates the application
of the spiral approach to the key concepts stated in Appendix 1.1.)

(d) Objectives: the conceptual structures of individual subject
fields related to the key concepts of the humanities form of knowing

Before attempting to set out the objectives for such an integrated
course, one important point must be reiterated. Much American and
some British work is based on the assumption that the development of
what Bruner (1960) (8) calls 'methodological techniques' is
something which occurs (or does not occur) separately from concept
development. But cognitive development subsumes the development of
mental abilities and intellectual skills, being both a necessary and
sufficient condition for such development. Therefore, to state
behavioural objectives as teaching or learning objectives is unnecessary since their growth is an inevitable component of conceptual development. For example, it is impossible to conceive that
knowledge and understanding of the conceptual structure of economics
could proceed without the development of the intellectual skills
delineated in 'The Teaching of Economics in Schools' (1973). (9) It
is also impossible to conceive that the development of these skills
could occur except through the understanding of economic concepts.
1 A capacity to follow and sustain an economic argument and to
   make logical inferences from given information;
2 a capacity to set out and communicate to others a logical
   argument in economics;
3 a capacity to be aware of assumptions made implicitly in the use
   of an economic model to assist a process of reasoning, and a
   capacity to perceive how a modification of the assumptions might
   affect the conclusions;
4 a capacity to understand the mutual interrelations and interde-
   pendencies of the various elements in an economic system and to
   take account of them in handling economic problems;
5 a capacity to understand and explain the economic effects of
   important economic institutions on economic policies;
6 a capacity to make appropriate inferences from quantitative
   data;
7 a capacity to apply to an economic problem the models of economic analysis that are most appropriate to it.
Such a list is necessary only as a check list to be used to counteract the tendency to treat concepts in the same way as information,
that is, as inert packages to be accumulated uncritically.
   Taba goes further and applies the strict behavioural objectives
model to the affective domain as well. When this occurs, the exercise becomes not only unnecessary but unacceptable. First, it
implies that the affective and cognitive domains are separate enti-
ties, and that a child can comprehend without feeling involvement.
Second, the process is a gross oversimplification of what actually
happens in schools. The pupil is expected to display precise and

measurable behaviour changes at the end of specific educational experiences tellingly referred to as 'treatments'. Third, the process trivialises the nature of the educational experience. One totally unexpected effect of ploughing through the narrowly prescribed, heavily structured American humanities course is a far greater feeling of restriction and pedagogic control than is achieved by most conventional subject presentations. Perspective is narrowed, not widened, as a result and the image of education as training is not an inappropriate one.

The only possible statement of objectives is one involving the development of the conceptual structures of the subjects and the relationship between these and the key concepts of the humanities way of knowing.

A detailed breakdown of economics objectives related to an integrated scheme using a categorisation of concepts similar to that advocated by Blyth and his colleagues is given in Appendix 1.3.

2 APPLICATION

The first attempt: the humanities course in 1972-3

Background: philosophy   In order to highlight in as dramatic and effective a way as possible some important analytical points, many educational philosophers draw caricatures of two extreme forms of educational enterprise – the traditional and the progressive. The traditional school curriculum is usually depicted as content-bound. Hirst (1967) (10) writes

> Objectives are limited to mastery of certain areas of very well established knowledge, the acquisition of certain widely held beliefs, the learning of a number of skills, and the development of a very limited range of qualities of mind. The matter or content used to achieve these objectives is largely, if not entirely, a body of propositions to be learnt, together with material for the practice of related skills, organised into a structure of distinct 'subjects'. The methods or activities employed are largely confined to the formal procedures of 'chalk and talk'.

The teacher is a specialist and as such an authority on all matters concerned with the imparting of knowledge, but he neglects and ignores the facts of development and motivation, preferring to deploy punishment techniques in the indiscriminate manner deplored by such writers as Skinner, for example. While admitting the obvious exaggeration of this account, nevertheless it is a more effective indication and a truer picture of the traditional grammar school philosophy, than a progressive framework would be.

During the 1960s and early 1970s two events occurred which precipitated curriculum change, in general, and the development described in this paper, in particular. First, the educational mood prevailing in the early 1970s and the consequent external pressures affecting teachers' perceptions of their role and function played an important motivational part in the initiation of this school-based curriculum development model. In 1971, the kind of statements which were having an effect on curriculum builders included the following:

1   The Newsom Report (1963) (11) emphasised that in order to let
    the least able boys and girls enter into an educational experi-
    ence which is genuinely secondary, schools required a curriculum
    built around the keystones represented by four words: practi-
    cal, realistic, vocational, choice.

2   The Newsom Report also stated that the last years at school need
    a unifying theme to give them coherence and purpose at a stage
    when the pupils themselves are growing restive. Such a theme
    can be found in the idea of preparation for adult life, and the
    school programme, in the last year especially, ought to be de-
    liberately outgoing.

3   Schools Council Working Paper No.2, 'Raising the School Leaving
    Age' (1965) (12) stated (p.12)
       The view of the curriculum put forward in this paper is
       therefore holistic. It is suggested that it should possess
       organic unity, and that the organising principle most likely
       to provide a sound basis for development is the study of Man,
       and of human society, needs and purposes.

4   The Schools Council publication Enquiry 1 (1968) (13) noted
    amongst the views of teachers that in most subjects and not just
    the traditional practical ones teachers should aim to have
    pupils doing things actively rather than sitting at their desks.
    Subjects should, when possible, be linked to pupils' lives
    outside school so that they could see the value of what they are
    learning.

Second, in September 1971 one particular girls' grammar school in an
industrial seaside city was reorganised and became a comprehensive
girls' school. Previously it drew its pupils from among 11+ successes throughout the whole of a city. To facilitate reorganisation, during 1971-2 the previous first form grammar school entry
was allowed to continue into the second form. The new entry for
1971-2 consisted of three third forms (ex-second forms at the
secondary modern), three fourth forms (ex-third forms at the
secondary modern), and one fifth form. These were grafted on to
the existing four grammar school streams, at each year. However
appropriate the traditional curricular framework had been in the
context of a girls' grammar school, it proved to be less effective
in a comprehensive school environment, and some members of staff
were impelled to reconsider their approach to their pupils both
personally and through their subjects.

   The curricular concessions made by the school to take account of
the changes described above were implemented during 1972-3. For
fourth year ex-secondary modern pupils these included the desig-
nation of a whole afternoon for an integrated humanities course, the
provision of money to enable any necessary field work to be carried
out, the provision of a high staffing ratio, and the provision of
the large hall plus six other classrooms for use by the humanities
team. The pupils were also allowed to choose from a range of
leisure/vocational/interest activities during two other afternoons
in the week. The traditional subject structure was maintained
during the remainder of the school week. No funds were made automatically available for servicing the humanities team. Any resources used (apart from stationery and travel) had to be provided
by the heads of the departments concerned.

Six teachers formed the teaching team. The heads of history, business studies and PE departments and two science and one geography teacher were involved. All members of staff who expressed an interest in this work (evidenced by attendance at a general meeting called to discuss the project) were offered the opportunity to join the team. In addition, it was felt that some major departments such as history and geography must be represented. It was therefore realistic to assume a certain commitment to the new approach and to working with this group of pupils, from each member of the team. Skills and knowledge of educational principles varied among team members. One was a subject specialist, with no professional educational training. Others had pursued broader courses of study at colleges of education.

Seventy girls, normally divided into three streams on the basis of ability, were involved in the humanities course. With very few exceptions these pupils lived in the school's new comprehensive catchment area in one of the oldest working-class areas of the city. There is no doubt that the pupils' attitudes to school were, at least, utilitarian or apathetic and, at worst, implied complete rejection of the educational system. This is borne out by the high rate of truancy and absenteeism, by the behaviour and demeanour of the girls, and by their hostility, which was expressed verbally and in actions. The only evidence which can be produced to support this belief is anecdotal and subjective but, nevertheless, belief in its existence had a potent influence on the design of the course. Holly (1973) (14) suggests that for teachers faced with such a problem there are only two alternatives: to continue directing pupils in mindless but undemanding activities or, in the tradition of Stenhouse (1969; 1970), (15) to give up the attempt in favour of a policy of neutral chairmanship, thereby not only rejecting the practice of setting educational objectives, but also attempting to provide a rational alternative to the rigidity of traditional structures. (16) In a devastatingly perceptive attack on middle-class educational reformers, Holly suggests that to take the first way out is by far the more common practice.

Research   The humanities team made a serious attempt to evade the first alternative. The members carried out some research which put them on guard against the scissors and paste approaches employed by the discredited social studies schemes of the 1950s, in which bits and pieces from various disciplines were stuck together to form a haphazard collection of interest-based topics. The members also considered one other approach to integrated work - Schools Council Humanities Project. (17)   But this approach was rejected for financial reasons and an individual system was developed by the team.

Application: Experiment   In essence, the team's philosophical and practical background, plus the rather haphazard research programme accomplished by the members, became concentrated into two major principles which underpinned course preparation and syllabus construction. These were, first, a commitment to a holistic, relevant, thematic approach; and second, a commitment to the avoidance of the dangers of trivialisation. At this stage very little serious epistemological research had been undertaken and little discussion of the importance of objectives or of structure and sequence had occurred. Therefore the team attempted to reconcile the two major principles by the use of a particular method of teaching and the approach they used was a team teaching one. The subject specialists introduced a section of work on the town which consisted of a lead lesson followed by some weeks of follow-up work. In this way, the history, geography, economy and cultural and leisure life of the city was covered in turn. It was hoped that this would safeguard academic standards and also provide a purposeful, relevant and interesting course.

Application: Evaluation   In the school-based model, evaluation is inevitably a subjective process. As such it is a blunt instrument but it does represent a serious attempt to match actual practice with stated objectives.

The team during the first trial considered the effect of the newly introduced course under three headings; the effect on the pupils, the effect on the staff, and the effect on the content of the course. The behaviour of the pupils at best reflected little more than boredom. At worst, behaviour became disruptive and unco-operative. Increasingly, during the year, the team had to reconcile themselves to an abnormally high absenteeism rate on Friday afternoons.

The staff recognised the danger inherent in carrying out such a subjective evaluation, namely that the result would be merely to reinforce their own entrenched attitudes. To check this tendency the research programme, put in motion before the inception of the trial, was extended into a continuous process. This not only enabled the staff to recognise the degeneration of the course into an attempt merely to fill time as painlessly as possible by keeping classes amused and occupied but also helped them to attempt a cause/effect analysis. The analysis identified the following reasons which formed the base for the course restructuring which eventually led to the second trial.

First, the team concluded that the aims of the course were narrow and restrictive. They suspected that they had been over-impressed by the Newsom philosophy, and had set aims which sought to socialise rather than educate. Unable to express their dissatisfaction in a coherent, rational form, the pupils merely abandoned any attempt to co-operate.

Second, the child-centredness of the course was ruthlessly exposed as quasi and artificial. Pupil needs were translated into the needs of pupils as viewed through teacher eyes, interest and relevance was interpreted from a teacher perspective, and learning experiences were not related to past experience.

Third, the course content was, in essence, still subject-based, with the artificially imposed theme merely serving to add a further constraint to an already lengthy list.

Last, Hirst's image of a tail wagging a dog was recognised as an appropriate one for the situation in which methods such as team teaching and enquiry-based learning were strictly adhered to and elevated into objectives.

A second attempt - the humanities course in 1973-4

Aims and objectives   Both the practical experience gained during the first trial and the continuous research programme undertaken by some team members helped to inform and clarify subsequent discussion and analysis of appropriate aims and objectives. Two major influences were easily discernible in the team's work at this stage.

First the team was impressed by American-based work which emphasised the importance of framing precise educational objectives in terms of the development of global cognitive skills. When the team considered the ideal product of the American educational system - a person possessing the ability to apply critical judgment, to analyse, to create, to synthesise and to understand, and possessing the habit of reflective thought - it seemed to match the vision of the rational educated man. The Newsom Report added weight to this when it stated that all boys and girls need to develop, as well as skills, capacities for thought, judgment, enjoyment, curiosity, and that they need to develop a sense of responsibility for their work and towards other people, and to begin to arrive at some code of moral and social behaviour which is self-imposed.

Only one problem remained - a vague feeling of unease at the complete absence of conceptual analysis within separate subjects in the American models which were often thematic in approach. The second influence on the team was Bernstein's approach, which seemed to provide a possible answer by claiming that one way of ensuring that individual conceptual structures were safeguarded, while developing global abilities, was to organise integration by means of relational ideas or supra-content concepts to focus on general principles at high levels of abstraction.

Research   In addition to general epistemological research, several other practical approaches were reviewed. The Schools Council Sixth Form General Studies Project was analysed, but of greater interest was Taba et al. (1967) (18) primary school programme, the Schools Council History, Geography, Social Studies 8-13 Project (1971-5) and the example of a probationary teacher's approach to environmental work contained in the Schools Council 'Boon Kit' (1970) (details of all three projects are obtainable from the Schools Council's 'Project Profiles' and 'Publications Leaflet'). The work undertaken by these schemes was directed at a younger age group and the content was inappropriate, but the carefully argued philosophical background reinforced the team's theoretical research conclusions. In each case general supra-content concepts rather than themes or topics were used to effect integration.

Application: Experiment   The stated aim of the team was to develop global abilities and cognitive skills. Objectives were framed in terms of the achievement of skills of analysis, discrimination, synthesis, evaluation, rationality, criticism, and creativity.

Objectives were classified under the following headings adapted from Bloom's (1956) (19) taxonomy of educational objectives in the cognitive domain.

Knowledge	Recall of learned material. Ability to recall and remember facts, definitions, generalisation, methods, etc.
Comprehension	The basic level of understanding which gives meaning to learned material. Ability to understand and interpret information presented in verbal, graphical or symbolic form in documents of various kinds and to translate such information from one form to another.
Application	Use of knowledge which is comprehended to solve problems not previously encountered or which are structured in a novel way. Ability to assess observations, to check that hypotheses are consistent with given information, to make new predictions. Ability to collect relevant information, to sift out irrelevant, to assess the reliability of observations and information, to make a reasoned case, to recognise value judgments, to test decisions and judgments.

The classification is a hierarchical one since it is recognised that the ability to apply depends on complete mastery of the content matter and that this itself subsumes some measure of recall of information.

The objectives were confined to the cognitive domain despite American arguments that courses should be structured to develop both cognitive and affective abilities and skills. The team argued on the basis of some considerable experience of teaching and influencing children and on the basis of the research work described in section 1 that attitude change was far too complex and uncharted an area to be attempted in a systematic way. Furthermore they felt that the most effective approach in this area was a very subtle one based on a combination of good example, free discussion, tolerance and occasional highlighting of alternative aspects and perspectives.

The team chose to highlight two key concepts during the first term - Communication/Cultural change, defined as the significant movement of individuals, groups or resources or the significant transmission of information, and Continuity/Change defined as the distinction of phenomena along an essentially historical dimension.

A range of resources and teaching methods was used, for example films on the developments in coal and steel and on life in a consumer society, posters depicting aspects of the coal and electricity industries, filmstrips, appropriate television programmes, work cards. The work cards were less strictly structured than American examples, owing to the traditional British reluctance to accept a full-blown behavioural model. However, care was taken to introduce new facts, to allow opportunity for complete understanding and to create application situations (to foster development of cognitive skills) at each stage of the content presentation process.

At the end of the term an assessment procedure was devised so as to enable diagnosis of pupil difficulties and also to provide rather more objective material on which to base course evaluation. Small discussion groups were formed and the article 'Life Sentence for the Soul' by Peter Brown (20) was studied by each group. Any word definitions and routine explanations of superficial queries were carried out. The remainder of the assessment consisted of two stages. First, to test understanding, an attempt was made to obtain a consensus opinion of the message contained in the article. As group members made a contribution to the discussion the point was noted and a precis of the article was laboriously constructed. Second, to test for the presence of the cognitive skills which should have been fostered and developed by the term's work, members of staff conducted discussion sessions based on the article. For example, team members (in retrospect optimistically) expected to find an appreciation of the partisan nature of the writer's arguments, and a recognition of the fact that the writer, in order to strengthen his case, deliberately ignored any of the benefits or opportunities provided in a modern industrial society for the working man. They expected to find an ability to recognise the emotive language and to disregard it. They expected to find an ability to discriminate between factual evidence and value judgments. Instead, each team member reported that the response, in general, to the article was highly superficial and frivolous. No group was able to appreciate and understand the point, made in the article, that the four pillars were underpinned by a kind of protestant ethic. No group could grasp that Peter Brown intended his analysis of this ethic to be as condemnatory as his analysis of the pillars. The pupils, without exception, were unable to penetrate the concrete statements, describing the working man's attitude to hard work, to reach an understanding of the subtle attack contained in the statements. When their attention was drawn to this, reactions ranged from bewildered astonishment to incredulity, disbelief and rejection.

In these circumstances, the attempt to assess the development of cognitive abilities highlighted, with even greater clarity, pupil inadequacies. As long as discussion was allowed to remain at a concrete 'chat' level; as long as pupils were allowed to use any points raised as a springboard for relating personal experience; as long as evidence was confined to the level of subjective opinion; and as long as the combination of old wives' tales, undigested mass media pronouncements and superstition which passed as their beliefs and views was tolerated, pupils remained alert and interested. On the other hand the overwhelming impression was of inability and unwillingness to tolerate any kind of challenge of their lives, their behaviour, and their views.

Evaluation   Team members were now faced with the realisation that it was impossible to judge what pupils had gained from the course. Faced with the overwhelming evidence of the discussion groups, all other evidence - that is, the improvement in attendance, the reported interest in course content, the reported willingness to co-operate - became insignificant and even false indicators of the success/failure of the course. Team members reluctantly concluded that the approach based on defining objectives in terms of global cognitive abilities and organising content by means of key concepts failed to achieve the stated aims of the course - the development of rationality.

The continuous research programme was now used to focus on the two independent aspects of the second trial. Team members undertook

to subject global abilities to rather closer scrutiny and to try
and identify more precisely the steps involved in their acquisition.
The team also compared the key concepts approach to organisation of
content, with the discredited topic or theme approach and were
forced to conclude that the former was also a 'focused' approach,
however subtly camouflaged. Although opportunities for 'understanding' and 'application' were studiously provided these were indis-
tinguishable, for the pupils, from statements of facts since they
were not related to any coherent conceptual structure.

3 CONCLUSION - THE NATURE OF INTEGRATED SCHEMES

During the research programme set in motion to analyse the compo-
sition of intellectual abilities, three other schemes of work were
also considered. The Schools Council 'Integrated Studies' project's
rationale substantiated conclusions reached independently by the
team. Bruner's work influenced the spiral approach finally advocated by the team. The pattern advocated by the Schools Council
'History, Geography, Social Studies 8-13' project was also influential since it allowed for the infusion of the situational variables - teachers, pupils, schools, environment (details of the
Schools Council projects are obtainable from School Council's
'Project Profiles' and 'Publications Leaflet').

At one stage the team returned to first principles, in order to
counteract the tendency to allow the momentum of the development
process to turn into a self-generating and self-perpetuating force.
The possibility of replacing an integrated scheme by an inter-
disciplinary scheme, in which each specialist works as a specialist-
plus, was considered. One example of such an inter-related approach, described by Moore and Nicholson (1973) (21) used topics and
themes to organise material but also ensured that there was a recognisable English contribution, history contribution and so on.
Groups of students rotated between teachers of each discipline to
obtain experience of that subject specialist's contribution to the
theme. Subject specialists brought their own specialist experiences
to bear, but they also took cognisance of the ideas of colleagues in
planning and working. Lead lessons served as integratory tools and
specialists ranged over a wider area than with their own specialisms. The authors noted that the success of this scheme was dependent on two conditions, first the success of lead lessons in realigning the different perspectives by providing an over-view or
global picture, and, second, success in the task of making links
between subjects apparent at every opportunity.

The team rejected this inter-disciplinary scheme, basing their
decision first on the experience of the first trial, where the deficiencies of such an approach were ruthlessly exposed, and, second,
on a belief that the possible reification and formalisation of
subjects is too big a risk to justify; third, on the growing conviction that the realigning process cannot be artificially imposed
from outside.

The culmination of the two-year research/application process into
the nature of integration is the set of conclusions outlined below.
The members of this particular team of curriculum developers were

concerned to ensure that any integrated scheme of work advocated and implemented by them should conform to their criteria of worthwhileness. These conclusions provide practical answers to the questions posed by the team.

Aims and objectives: criteria of worthwhileness

The aim of any integrated course should be the development of rationality, redefined as dependent on cognition or the mastery of conceptual structures. The supra-content general principles of the second trial can be retained but must be linked to the conceptual structures of the individual subjects.

Furthermore it becomes important to order material so that concepts may be acquired systematically and in a balanced way.

By refusing to accept slavishly and automatically the traditional structures of conventional school subjects, opportunity can be provided to relate pupil development to the conceptual structure of the subjects.

Stages in course preparation

The first stage involves deriving the basic concepts of the individual subjects. The second stage is concerned with ordering subject matter so that the concepts are acquired in a balanced way. If Bruner's 'spiral' thesis is accepted, progression means treating each concept at every stage but in a gradually more sophisticated form as levels of understanding advance. Rather than progression from simple to difficult concepts, the Bruner thesis advocates progression for all concepts from simple to more sophisticated content. In this way the integrity of the subject is safeguarded and learning is also related to the child's development.

The third stage relates the conceptual structures of individual subjects, exposed in the first two stages, to the key concepts of an integrated scheme. This is the stage commonly ignored by other schemes, e.g. the Schools Council History, Geography, Social Science 8-13 project. It may be argued that at the 8-13 stage such emphasis on concept development is misplaced, although Bruner (22) argues that any subject may be taught in an intellectually honest form at any level. Certainly by the time pupils have reached the last years of a secondary school they must have access to the substantive conceptual structures of the disciplines.

The fourth stage entails slotting the pupil in at the correct developmental point. Continuous assessment of a diagnostic kind plus the preparation of individualised learning packages enables the teacher to provide remedial attention for some and greater variety for others.

Last, the course planner must continually check material and results against the cognitive abilities check list to ensure that the development of understanding and of the intellectual skills is safeguarded and that the schemes do not degenerate into a formal presentation of information.

An example of a scheme of work based on this model is given. It

is intended for use with pupils who have some considerable experience of this approach, who have already progressed through one or
more of the stages of development and who have already met the key
concepts with less sophisticated contents. Each key concept is
treated at two levels, and unit II demands more sophisticated application of concepts than unit I.

A SCHEME OF WORK FOR AN INTEGRATED HUMANITIES COURSE

Communication/Cultural Change

UNIT I   Technological change contributes to the nature and extent
of cultural change.
  (a) During the last two centuries drastic changes have
       occurred in the methods of production of goods and
       services.
  (b) These changes affected the lives of the people and
       resulted in changes in other areas of living.

UNIT II   Cultural change is accelerated by increased knowledge, mobility and communication.
  (a) Dissemination of new knowledge often leads rapidly to
       new discoveries.
  (b) The development of the teenage pop subculture is
       fostered by the mass media.
  (c) The speed of communication/cultural change depends on
       the remoteness of areas.

Continuity/Change

UNIT I   Changes that occur in one part of society often produce
changes in other parts of society.
  (a) Economic changes may effect changes in other insti-
       tutions (education).
  (b) Some change may be unplanned (middle-class; shop-
       floor organisations in the trade union movement).
  (c) Many people in society oppose change (Railways
       nineteenth century; Maplin twentieth century).

UNIT II   Certain institutions in society change very slowly despite
the inappropriateness of traditional behaviour.
  (a) Institutions closely linked with technological change
       tend to change rapidly.
  (b) Judicial, parliamentary, royal, religious and edu-
       cational institutions resist change.

Conflict/Consensus

UNIT I   Prosperity depends on natural resources, worker know-how,
values and technological development.
  (a) A developed society has many institutions to foster

prosperity (education, banks, transport, money, insurance).

(b) Trade is a means societies use to acquire goods they lack (trade blocs).

(c) The industrial institutions of a prosperous society are large and specialised.

UNIT II   The interaction of man with his environment raises problems.

(a) Man has often exploited the environment to his own detriment (land use; urban problems, water supply; pollution; transport).

(b) Unemployment of resources may occur.

UNIT III   Conflict may develop when the subgroups of a culture differ in goals and expectations and each tries to maintain its own way of life.

(a) Movement of people into areas occupied by others may result in conflict (ethnic groups; women's lib).

(b) The resolution of conflict may result in physical and ideological changes (brain drain; world war).

(c) Conflict may never be satisfactorily resolved without presence of institutions to maintain order (laws, police).

Causality

UNIT I   Change in a state of affairs is attributable to phenomena preceding it.

(a) The causes of inflation may be illustrated by reference to the price of food and houses.

(b) Many social advances occur because of political change.

UNIT II   One case study (Northern Ireland; poverty).

Power/Societal Control

UNIT I   Technological development gives man greater power over resources.

(a) Man can adapt and control his environment to a certain extent (mass production; agriculture; water supply; transport systems; Channel tunnel (bridges)).

(b) Environment is still a powerful influence (agriculture; transport).

UNIT II   Individuals and groups vary in the amount of influence they can exert in making and carrying out decisions which affect people's lives significantly.

(a) Large firms exercise considerable power over markets (monopolies) and over people (working conditions; location).

(b)   Large trade union organisations exercise considerable control over their members and society.

(c)   The government has power invested in it on our behalf (safety;   child labour;   incomes).

Values and Beliefs

UNIT I   A society's values and beliefs help to explain the kinds of choices it makes.

(a)   A society's values affect the rate of economic development (rat race;   planners v. people).

(b)   A society's values affect the role of government (democracy).

(c)   A society's values determine its welfare provisions.

UNIT II   The greater the variety of values in a society, the greater the likelihood of conflict.

(a)   People entering an established society make many modifications in their behaviour. If these modifications are unacceptable further conflict may result.

(b)   People of different ethnic backgrounds contribute to both the cultural and economic growth of a country.

Co-operation/Interdependence

UNIT I   The existence of problems common to all individuals leads to co-operation.

(a)   The efficient use of resources necessitates some degree of pooling of resources (taxation).

(b)   The more complex the society, the more co-operation is required.

UNIT II   The behaviour of each individual affects other persons and groups because everyone depends on others for the satisfaction of needs.

(a)   The development of an interdependent society brings many advantages.

(b)   The development of an interdependent society creates many problems (strikes;   regional unemployment;   war).

Similarity/Difference

UNIT I   The physical social and biological environments show important differences.

(a)   The physical resources of an area encourage specialisation in the use of land.

(b)   The diversity of a nation's people is often reflected in its institutions and forms of expression (language idioms;   music;   drama;   art;   religion).

UNIT II   The social environment in particular is both similar to, and distant from, the immediate past.
   (a)   Each generation has certain distinctive ways of doing things.
   (b)   The growth of the welfare state is a significant difference in twentieth-century Britain.

CONCLUSION - PROCEDURES IN CURRICULUM DEVELOPMENT

Purpose v. worthwhileness

The first major conclusion suggests that the curriculum development process is composed of two distinct parts, one concerned with the purpose and the other with the worthwhileness of courses. These parts may be differentiated because they pose different problems and make different demands on curriculum planners. An evaluation of the first attempt shows that the team, when they introduced the integrated course into the curriculum, were largely influenced by external pressures. They therefore had no internal yardstick in the form of criteria to assist in constructing a worthwhile course or in evaluating such a course.

Sources of external pressure on the secondary school curriculum include parental expectations, society's needs, the knowledge explosion, and economic factors. Since the curriculum must be designed so as to take account of so many diverse elements, and resources used to do this are limited, one stage in any curriculum development process must concentrate on the purpose of any particular curriculum change, in order to ensure optimum use of curriculum space. That is, any curriculum change must be evaluated against the philosophy of the school, presented as a set of aims and objectives.

However, consideration of purpose alone is not sufficient to ensure a worthwhile curriculum. Two reasons account for this. First, mistakes may be made, since curriculum development in practice is not easily confined into a tight, elegant schedule. It may be possible to set the curriculum development process in motion without being able to articulate precisely the school's philosophy, especially in times of rapid change. It may also be possible to articulate a set of aims and objectives which eventually prove to be unacceptable when later research and development work help to inform such statements of intent. For example, with hindsight, it is relatively easy to rule out some of the integrated schemes described in this paper purely by considering their purpose and matching the aims and objectives of such schemes against a better informed and more rational school philosophy.

Integration purely to provide watered-down courses suitable for the less-able pupil must eventually be ruled out. Similarly, integration for reasons of 'relevance' or 'usefulness' must become suspect since it counts as socialisation rather than education. Integration which emphasises the wholeness of knowledge and which seeks to promote the development of global abilities such as 'problem-solving' and 'enquiry' is also ruled out, since knowledge is not a whole but is differentiated into distinct ways of knowing, mastery of which is a necessary condition for achieving intellectual

skills. Holly argues that integration, per se, does not necessarily
provide a truer, more comprehensive picture of reality:

>it is better that pupils should do meaningful work in history and
>geography separately than that they should perform historical
>rituals under the guise of humanities or enquiry. Unstructured
>learning has a way of becoming perfunctory activity, mere per-
>formance. Grand thematic titles are no guarantee that anything
>significant is going on. (23)

Consideration of their aims and objectives alone should lead,
eventually, to rejection of such schemes. Meantime, unless another
safeguard is used it is possible to persevere with such courses
since they articulate the school's philosophy, however misguided or
uninformed.

Second, in cases where the introduction of an integrated scheme
is justifiable in relation to a more rationally articulated school
philosophy, it is still necessary to demonstrate the worthwhileness
of the scheme by reference to criteria in which purpose plays no
part. For example, it is obviously tempting for curriculum planners
who wish to build a balanced curriculum to consider integration as
an alternative to the present organisation in terms of school
subjects, that is, to adopt an integrated approach because the
school subject approach is uneconomic of space and time. Some
people argue that integration is a possible way of streamlining the
curriculum for it offers a more economic way of offering a general
education. Alternatively integration may be regarded as an antidote
to the empire-building tendencies of subjects. F.Musgrove (1968)
(24) comments in his article on Curriculum Objectives that subjects
are 'highly organised, hierarchical, bureaucratic. They are busy
discerning reasons for their existence and their importance. They
develop their own defence systems against encroachment.' In these
cases the introduction of an integrated scheme is justifiable in
relation to the stated aims and objectives of the school. But there
is no built-in guarantee that the scheme itself will be worthwhile.
As Richard Pring (1970) (25) points out, integration raises
important questions of epistemology and ethics which are all too
often ignored. Furthermore, it is an exceedingly complex process
demanding a rigorous objectivity on the part of the educationalists
concerned and the most laudable purpose does not guarantee this.

In conclusion it can reasonably be stated that any scheme must be
subjected to evaluation against criteria of worthwhileness. If it
meets the criteria it can then take its place in the curriculum
planning process.

A school-based model

The second major conclusion reached in this work is that although
much of the analysis of curriculum development contained in this
paper emphasises the importance of viewing the curriculum as a set
of aims and of intentions, plus a body of content and range of
methods, the curriculum is also something which has to take root and
develop in actual school settings. It is realised in the day to day
life of a school which embodies organisation, social relationships,
the ethos of the school and its relationship to the outside world.

The kind of issues raised in this analysis finally have to be confronted, deliberated and acted upon in the schools. Cunningham (1969) (26) highlighted this issue in his report 'Starting from Cold' when he described how a school began to introduce changes into the curriculum of its fourth year pupils. The second attempt was more successful than the first one (admittedly success was subjectively evaluated), and Cunningham gave the following explanation.

First, the second scheme began to involve teachers in the rethinking of aims and objectives by starting from the strength of their particular subject expertise. They were not asked to surrender their subject areas in order to move into the unfamiliar territory of an inter-disciplinary or integrated course. The work took place within the reassuring framework of the normal timetable.

Second, the emphasis, so far as the teachers were concerned, was upon sharing the stimulus of a piece of first-hand experience, and upon co-ordinating their work so as to develop further the pupils' understanding of the experience. Such organisational arrangements can be of value within all schools wishing to gain experience in enquiry work; they can be of particular value within small schools which, faced with the demands of setting or option arrangements to allow for examinations, may find organisational difficulty in also arranging for integrated courses taught by teams of teachers.

Third, careful preparation is essential, but so too is the art of the opportunist. The planning must not impose rigidity: the teacher must be free to seize opportunities, must be able to change the direction of the work, and must be sensitive to the demands coming from the pupils. An example of this is the way the home economics teacher rapidly switched the major visit to the carpet factory but then used the aluminium factory as a contrast out of which came discussion on what could be expected of the men in household routine bearing in mind their working conditions. Such opportunism is essential to enquiry work carried out through discussion. The more thorough the planning and the preparation of material, the more confidence the teacher will have in allowing pupils 'their head'.

Fourth, the expertise of the subject specialist is of particular importance to the exploration of an experience. It must move from the immediate and narrowly personal reactions into a more general understanding if the adolescent is to gain in maturity and self-discovery. The experience of the history teacher is of particular relevance here. Quite correctly he pointed to the limitations of the follow-up visit to the old iron-works. Change and its implications for the adolescent becomes real when it is in terms of people and their lives. Then the imagination can seize on the monuments of the past and recreate them in terms of their meaning to living people. This is a guide to the ordering of material and approaches in the comparative studies, the studies that lead from the immediate to its general significance. The enquiry must start from and must at all its stages relate to the human condition. In this case profiles showing in vivid detail how people worked and how it affected their lives would have been of great use as a telescope into the past. The comparison with the present could then have provided evidence on which to base judgments, which may have been looking towards the future. Such an examination of the lives of the

people could possibly have made the visit to the iron-works more
relevant.

A practical model of curriculum development cannot ignore the
capacities, attitudes, knowledge and beliefs of the individual
teacher. These, in turn, are influenced by social norms, by the
environment, by the school and by the children. These are the situational variables which, unless catered for, can cause the breakdown
and abandonment of any curriculum development model. It is for this
reason that the content of such teacher-proof schemes as Bruner's
'Man: A Course of Study' is not acceptable to the team.

Evaluation

The third major conclusion concerns evaluation and assessment.
Pupil assessment may no longer be relevant for the purpose of pre-
diction, but it cannot be abandoned since it is an essential part of
the diagnostic process. It may have a different form and may
involve no formal testing but it must exist.

It may be unrealistic to attempt any kind of systematic evaluation especially in conditions noticeably at variance with even the
loosest educational research model standards, but it should still be
possible to study the procedures employed by educational researchers
in order to improve the subjective evaluation undertaken in school.

A distinction is made between formative and summative evaluation.
Formative evaluation takes place during the lifetime of the developmental work and is designed to improve the work in as many ways as
possible. This involves organising and analysing feedback of information so that consequent changes in materials and teaching methods
may take place. This form of evaluation is also known as concurrent
or on-going evaluation. It is essentially evaluation by trial and
revision in the school situation.

Summative evaluation tends to occur in the post-trial situation;
it attempts to find out whether the final effects of the project are
those which were intended. Although there is a clear philosophical
distinction between formative and summative evaluation, nevertheless
most evaluations have a dual aspect.

A model of evaluation which is very prevalent in the USA is the
behavioural objectives model. It begins with the aims of a scheme
stated in general terms and translates these into specific behavioural objectives so that tests and instruments may be designed
to measure attainment of these, hoping thereby to make exact evaluations. This methodology owes much to psychometrics and a research
and development approach to curriculum development.

This behavioural objectives-based model of evaluation is,
however, very restricting in that it does not allow evaluators to
assess other than overt changes in the affective domain nor does it
supply teachers with information which would help them to adapt
materials and methods. The interactive model supplements the evidence of objective testing with a wide range of information gathered
from teacher and pupil opinion, observation of classroom behaviours,
and such devices as attitude scales and classroom diaries. Evaluators attempt to provide information in the round, case studies are
prepared, and attempts are made to illustrate the interactions which

occur within schools when the curriculum is undergoing change.
Teachers evaluating their own courses become participant-observers
of what occurred in the classroom.

This all round, interactive approach to the problems of evaluation is much in line with Parlett's (1974) (27) recently described
model of evaluation called illuminative evaluation. Illuminative
evaluation does not reject the measurement of behaviourally specified objectives where this is appropriate. Rather it sees this approach as being but one part of a wider attempt to identify the key
issues and analyse them in the most fitting way possible.

The model of school-based curriculum development developed in
this paper suggests that final and crucial evaluative judgments of
their work should be made by teachers in the schools. This leads to
an emphasis upon on-going evaluation of new materials and new
methods of teaching, so that in their final form they are well
founded and tested against criteria of worthwhileness. But evaluation is also concerned with the obtaining, providing and delineating of useful information for decision-makers, since it is impossible to undertake research to provide criteria for judging worthwhileness without also providing sounder information on which to
base implementation decisions.

APPENDIX 1.1

KEY CONCEPTS FOR ECONOMICS

The joint authors (1973) of 'The Teaching of Economics in Schools'
classify the principles under which a modern economy works as
follows:
  1 the logic of choice in terms of opportunity cost and the margin-
     al principle;
  2 the logic of specialisation and trade in terms of comparative
     advantage;
  3 the partial analysis of supply and demand in a single market;
  4 the determination of the rewards of factors of production;
  5 the general analysis of aggregate national income, expenditure
     and activity.
The main preoccupation of the authors is with the content of the
material used at sixth form level, and with examination structures.
Therefore the analysis is differently orientated from the one undertaken in this chapter which is designed to uncover the conceptual
structure of the subject. Lumsden and Attiyeh (1971) (28) developed
a set of fundamental economic concepts:
  1 Scarcity and choice
     (a) Needs and wants
     (b) Resource allocation
     (c) Value systems
  2 Economic efficiency
  3 Income distribution
  4 Aggregate output and income.
The set used in this analysis is similar to the two described above.
Where differences exist, these reflect personal preference rather
than ideological difference.

1 The economic problem (scarcity, choice, economic efficiency, opportunity cost).
2 The existence of markets and their economic purpose and function.
3 The operation of the price system and other allocative mecha-nisms.
4 The role and effects of specialisation.
5 Income distribution - methods and criteria.
6 The nature of aggregate equations.

APPENDIX 1.2.1

	Stage I	Stage II	Stage III
THE ECONOMIC PROBLEM (scarcity; choice; economic efficiency; op-portunity cost)	Family needs depend on: number of children number of dependents choices made Family needs are met by earning, etc. Child's needs are met by parents, etc. Needs change and grow with time Resources are scarce: time, money. Thus families: budget (deep freezers, bulk buying, do-it-yourself) + choose (income/leisure, spending/saving, gambling) + share + + borrow	Local needs depend on the area concerned. A farming community, a town, a tourist area, in winter and summer, all require different services. Community needs are met: by producing and by local authority services in developed communities Resources are scarce: raw materials are not evenly distributed Thus communities: trade + use local resources efficiently + choose (local examples) Some resources are wasted	National needs depend on: population size and structure + choices made The needs of a consumer society change over time. National needs are met: by producing (note technological change) by government by volunteer bodies Resources are scarce: land, capital, labour, enterprise, know-how, raw materials especially in certain areas. Thus the nation: experiences high prices (rents, interest rates, house prices) + makes best use of resources (water, energy, fuel, transport) + trades (common market membership) + chooses + shares (co-operative retail society) + emphasizes capital formation The nation also aids less developed countries

APPENDIX 1.2.2

	Stage I	Stage II	Stage III
THE EXISTENCE OF MARKETS AND THEIR ECONOMIC PURPOSE AND FUNCTIONS	The determinants of demand. The effect of price on demand. Shopping. Retail and Wholesale Trades. Large and small scale business. Advertising. Consumer Protection. Resale Price Maintenance Buying: use of money, credit, banks, building societies. Supplying by working: who works? where do they work? and by owning: who owns industries?	The determinants of supply. Effect of price on supply. Local markets in physical sense + concept. Producing: illustrations of mass production in local industry illustrations of different organisational structures and of size by comparative studies illustrations of meaning of cost of production and of social costs in local industry illustrations of finance of small local firms (local savings, banks, trade credit) Importance of insurance and local financial institutions. Illustration by comparative studies of barter v. money. Labour supply and migration.	Price determined by demand and supply. Changes in demand and supply. National and international markets. Exchange rates. Firms grow by expansion and merger. Examples of national and multinational companies. Effect of monopolies on prices. Finance of industry - the national capital markets. Marine insurance and banking. The working population: immigration, population and brain drain; trade unions. Effect of goods market on factor market

APPENDIX 1.2.3 and 4

	Stage I	Stage II	Stage III
THE OPERATION OF THE PRICE SYSTEM AND OTHER ALLOCATIVE MECHANISMS	Provision of 'free' goods. Effect on families of prices policy and VAT. Effect on families of rationing and black markets. 'Fair wages'. Skill and sex differentials in wages in the family. Effect of trade unions on wages.	Local subsidies for council house rents. Provision of: local transport systems; local parks; local car parks. Location policy attempts to deal with the problem of the underuse of local resources. Agricultural subsidies.	Prices are determined by demand and supply. Perfect markets, free competition and the optimum allocation of resources. Communist/capitalist systems. Causes of government intervention: war-rationing, maxima/minima, free goods, natural monopolies, imperfect market, etc. Kinds of government intervention: laws, market policy (location, monopoly), nationalisation, taxation, subsidies, tariffs. Effect of trade unions on wages.
THE ROLE AND EFFECTS OF SPECIALISATION	Specialisation in the family: role specialisation, job specialisation, hobbies. Importance of acquisition of skill for vertical mobility. Chain effects. Advantages of specialisation at family level. Increasing need for services (offices, commerce, transport) and machines.	Regional specialisation. Growth of urban societies. Importance of transport and money (comparative studies). Chain effects - strikes, structural changes. Advantages of specialisation at local level.	Occupational structure of nation (primary, secondary, tertiary industry). International specialisation depends on raw materials, technology, workers. Importance of transport. Chain effects - war, natural disasters. Specialisation and comparative costs.

APPENDIX 1.2.5 and 6

	Stage I	Stage II	Stage III
INCOME DISTRIBUTION METHODS AND CRITERIA	Wages, salaries, profits. Rich and poor families. Workers and non-workers (welfare payments). Skilled and non-skilled (two parents, for example)	Rates. Rich and poor in the local community and in an underdeveloped community. Local welfare agencies and institutions. Skill differentials in local industries.	Taxes. Wealth tax. Change in favour of poorer, wage earner, borrower. Welfare payments. Effect of inflation. Power of enterprise and trade unions. World income distribution: rich and poor countries.
THE NATURE OF AGGREGATE EQUATIONS	Families can spend only what they earn or borrow. Children can spend pocket money (not earned). Real wages depend on: cost of living and government action (prices and incomes). Saving is prerequisite for borrowing.	Local examples to show income as a flow (e.g. local shopkeepers at Christmas). Comparative study of regions of over and under employment to isolate features. Comparative study of stagnant community with fast growth community to isolate features. Comparative studies of cost of living in different areas (as per 'Nationwide').	People in a nation can consume only what is produced and traded. The income round. Capital formation. Connection between savings and investment. Causes of inflation, growth, underdevelopment, unemployment (elementary treatment). Standard of living and cost of living. League table of growth. Effects of international trade (elementary treatment). Effects of government intervention.

APPENDIX 1.3.1 Objectives for economics related to an integrated scheme

RELATIONSHIPS BETWEEN SUBJECT CONCEPTS AND HUMANITIES CONCEPTS

STAGE I

STAGE I	Communication and cultural change	Power and societal control
THE ECONOMIC PROBLEM	Effects of technological changes on the range of alternative goods available: colour television holidays cars/caravans consumer goods etc. Change in consumption habits: convenience foods man-made fibres the deep freeze Change in numbers of children per family	Saving as a means of control over resources.
MARKETS	Effects of changes in the workforce: working wives rosla in terms of both quantity and quality.	Advertising: effect on the teenage market and on families. Consumer protection
PRICE AND THE ALLOCATIVE MECHANISM		The effect of prices and incomes policy on families.
SPECIAL-ISATION	Emphasis on skills and education: rosla. Greater use of machines at work.	Specialisation confers power over resources.
INCOME DISTRIBUTION		
AGGREGATE EQUATIONS	Real wages: standard of living cost of living	

APPENDIX 1.3.2

STAGE I	Conflict/consensus	Continuity/change
THE ECONOMIC PROBLEM	Family needs are met by: earning (by both or one parent) borrowing gifts/legacies/pools wins Budgeting: at adolescence young marrieds families Each choice made may be expressed in opportunity cost terms: borrowing saving income/leisure Scarcity leads to high prices.	Change in consumption patterns. Change in leisure time. Change in attitude to the question of the relative importance of wages/net advantages.
MARKETS	Money as a tool in modern society. Phenomenon of resale price maintenance.	Change in shopping habits. Change in the position of the wholesaler.
PRICE AND THE ALLOCATIVE MECHANISM	'Free goods' note their existence. Examples of black markets and rationing. Effect of trade unions on family's wages.	Introduction of VAT to replace purchase tax.
SPECIAL-ISATION	Housewife/breadwinner; role specialisation in families. Occupational specialisation: description advantages and disadvantages Vertical mobility/immobility	Administration/ bureaucracy/office systems
INCOME DISTRIBUTION	Effect of inflation (simple treatment) on family incomes.	
AGGREGATE EQUATIONS	Child's pocket money as an example of income not earned.	

APPENDIX 1.3.3

STAGE I	Interdependence and co-operation	Causality
THE ECONOMIC PROBLEM	A child's needs are met by his parents. Sharing in a family.	Scarcity and a high demand results in higher prices.
MARKETS	Financial institutions survive because of co-operation: banks building societies. The retail co-operative	How demand is determined. Effect of high prices on demand.
PRICE AND THE ALLOCATIVE MECHANISM		
SPECIAL-ISATION	Individuals do jobs within the family and at work, which they do best. This leads to interdependence.	Chain effects Need for: transport commerce
INCOME DISTRIBUTION	Welfare state payments	
AGGREGATE EQUATIONS	Spending = income + borrowing in the family	Saving necessary for borrowing.

APPENDIX 1.3.4

STAGE I	Similarity/difference	Values and beliefs
THE ECONOMIC PROBLEM	Families receive different incomes. Families make different choices. Families have different numbers of dependents. Families have different needs, in comparison with other families and with families in the past.	Taste and the individual's scale of preference will affect the choices he makes. Gambling.
MARKETS	Different kinds of retail store. Retailing and wholesaling. Large and small shops and businesses. Workers and owners.	Use of credit Child labour
PRICE AND THE ALLOCATIVE MECHANISM	Skill and sex differentials in wages. Illustrate.	Idea of fair wages
SPECIAL-ISATION	Different hobbies Different family roles Different jobs	
INCOME DISTRIBUTION	Non-competing groups Wages, salaries, profits (workers and non-workers) Rich and poor families	
AGGREGATE EQUATIONS		

APPENDIX 1.3.5

STAGE II ✓	Communication and cultural change	Power and societal control
STAGE II THE ECONOMIC PROBLEM	Regional resource patterns. Use of examples of the South Wales coal mining valleys to highlight depopulation and pollution and the run-down of social capital.	The importance of capital in the coal and steel industries. Examples of the use of power over the environment: Port Talbot harbour Milford Haven Llyn Brianne Severn Bridge
MARKETS	Effects of depopulation: the Rhondda Swansea valley	Local examples of trade union power
PRICES AND THE ALLOCATIVE MECHANISM	The effect of decline of the industries of South Wales coalfield on unemployment.	Location policy as the use of government power to redress effect of regional changes.
SPECIAL-ISATION	In a mining community, the extent and degree of specialisation results in gradual rate of diversification. Growth of towns and cities.	
INCOME DISTRIBUTION		Local government raises part of its revenue by levying rates.
AGGREGATE EQUATIONS		

APPENDIX 1.3.6

STAGE II	Conflict/consensus	Continuity/change
THE ECONOMIC PROBLEM	The pattern of local industry depends on: environment (resources) + local needs + climate Thus regions trade. Regional unemployment may occur.	Changes in local consumption patterns: restaurants, entertainment.
MARKETS	Problem of social cost of industry - pollution. Use of money in developed communities as opposed to barter in primitive ones. Development of local financial institutions - Bank of Wales.	Development of new industries in South Wales - description.
PRICES AND THE ALLOCATIVE MECHANISM	Local government rent subsidies to council house tenants. Provision by local authorities of local parks, car parks, transport free in some cases. Local examples to illustrate interference by government when social costs are high e.g. lower Swansea valley project.	
SPECIAL-ISATION	Regional specialisation and the diversification of industry. Urban problems	
INCOME DISTRIBUTION		Some areas benefit at the expense of other areas.
AGGREGATE EQUATIONS	Some regions suffer unemployment. Other regions have excess demand for labour. The comparative study to isolate some of the reasons.	

APPENDIX 1.3.7

STAGE II	Interdependence and co-operation	Causality
THE ECONOMIC PROBLEM	Some needs are met by local government. Comparative study of primitive community.	Prices of goods which are scarce in locality are high. Comparative studies of communities where prices of such goods are low
MARKETS	Local small firms depend for finance on: trade credit local banks local financial institutions	Study of local markets to illustrate the determinants of supply. Effect of price on supply. Causes of costs of production.
PRICES AND THE ALLOCATIVE MECHANISM		
SPECIAL-ISATION		Creates a need for: transport illustrate money by means of a comparative study Chain effects of strikes and structural changes.
INCOME DISTRIBUTION	Local welfare associations and agencies	
AGGREGATE EQUATIONS	Income as a flow illustrated by means of local examples, e.g. local shopkeepers at Christmas; holiday trade.	

APPENDIX 1.3.8

STAGE II	Similarity/difference	Values and beliefs
THE ECONOMIC PROBLEM	Consumption patterns in South Wales and elsewhere. Resource patterns in South Wales and elsewhere. Different areas need different services (compare different communities, e.g. tourist, farming, town).	Use local examples of the way local values (as expressed e.g. in voting for local parties) affect choices made.
MARKETS	All firms, locally, have common features. Firms differ in: organisation size cost structures	
PRICES AND THE ALLOCATIVE MECHANISM		Agricultural subsidies benefit farming area. 'Fair rents'
SPECIAL-ISATION	Regions specialise in different goods.	
INCOME DISTRIBUTION	Skill differentials in local industries. Rich and poor locally.	
AGGREGATE EQUATIONS	Growth of various regions - isolate some relevant features. Use comparative studies to illustrate differences in the cost of living in different communities.	

APPENDIX 1.3.9

STAGE III		Communication and cultural change	Power and societal control
STAGE III	THE ECONOMIC PROBLEM	Characteristics of a consumer society. Classification of resources: land, capital workers, know-how enterprise raw materials technology Aid to underdeveloped nations	Power over resources: water supply energy and fuel transport Channel tunnel Importance of capital formation.
	MARKETS	Changes in the working population: migration internally immigration the brain drain the common market Emergence of competitors, e.g. Japan.	Power of large scale institutions: monopolies trade unions Growth of firms: by expansion merger Multinational companies
	PRICES AND THE ALLOCATIVE MECHANISM	Interference by government significantly changed in twentieth century. Decline of laissez-faire.	Government control: child labour location policy monopoly policy prices and incomes import and export restrictions
	SPECIAL-ISATION	Occupational structure has changed: tertiary production migration use of machines	
	INCOME DISTRIBUTION	Disappearance of the stately home because of taxation, or its modification.	Power of: enterprise trade unions government (taxes)
	AGGREGATE EQUATIONS	Standards of living significantly higher.	Incomes policy as one example of government tools to regulate the economy.

APPENDIX 1.3.10

STAGE III	Conflict/consensus	Continuity/change
THE ECONOMIC PROBLEM	National needs are met by production. Thus nations: use resources efficiently (specialisation) + trade (common market) Some unemployment of resources occurs. Prices are high for scarce goods	Change in consumption patterns because of changes in the structure of the population. Single most important change in use of resources - industrial revolution.
MARKETS	Examples of institutions which facilitate production and distribution: banks marine insurance international institutions	Growth of firms and industry.
PRICES AND THE ALLOCATIVE MECHANISM	Concept of free enterprise and the optimum allocation of resources. Discussion of reasons for government interference: rationing/black markets minima, maxima free goods Some effects: smuggling black markets Power of trade unions.	Role of government has changed over time. Some functions remain static.
SPECIAL-ISATION	International specialisation and comparative advantage. Specialisation necessitates transport.	Development from primary to secondary to tertiary production
INCOME DISTRIBUTION	Effect of inflation: fixed incomes lenders weak bargaining positions Rich and poor nations	Redistribution: in favour of poorer in favour of wage-earner
AGGREGATE EQUATIONS	Government has developed tools to regulate economy. Unemployment. Importance of savings and investment. Importance of international trade.	League table of comparative growth of nations.

APPENDIX 1.3.11

STAGE III	Interdependence and co-operation	Causality
THE ECONOMIC PROBLEM	Some needs are met by: voluntary bodies by the government Sharing as a nation Common market entry	Consumption succeeds production. Prices are high for scarce goods: interest rents house prices
MARKETS	Capital market: pooling savings banks etc.	Cause of changes in demand, supply, costs. Interaction between markets, e.g. goods and factor markets Monopolies can control prices
PRICES AND THE ALLOCATIVE MECHANISM	Reason for government interference in free enterprise: existence of natural monopolies.	Price is determined by supply and demand in the free market. Causes of government intervention.
SPECIAL-ISATION	Effects of	Pattern of specialisation depends on: technology workers raw materials Specialisation - lower costs: chain effects.
INCOME DISTRIBUTION	Provision of welfare payments	
AGGREGATE EQUATIONS	The income round	Income as a flow Causes of: inflation growth unemployment underdevelopment (elementary treatment)

APPENDIX 1.3.12

STAGE III	Similarity/difference	Values and beliefs

THE ECONOMIC PROBLEM	Economic problem universal
	Needs vary: geographically
	            (education, health)
	            overtime
	            (population)
	Resources vary.
	Interest rates; rents vary.
		Compare a consumer society with less materialistic one to show effects on choices made.

MARKETS	All markets have common features, national and international. Markets also differ, e.g. international markets involve exchange rates.	
PRICES AND THE ALLOCATIVE MECHANISM	Private ownership and public ownership Skill and sex differentials	Taxation system and question of subsidies influenced by value systems. Communist and capitalist systems.
SPECIAL-ISATION	Different countries specialise in different goods.	
INCOME DISTRIBUTION	Comparison of nineteenth and twentieth centuries. Skill differentials	Taxation affects the rate of redistribution of incomes.
AGGREGATE EQUATIONS	Savings/investment Capital formation as a part of national income, in developed and underdeveloped countries.	

REFERENCES

1   BERNSTEIN, B., On the Classification and Framing of Educational
    Knowledge in YOUNG, M., 'Knowledge and Control', Collier
    Macmillan, New York, 1971.
2   TABA, H., 'Curriculum Development - Theory and Practice',
    Harcourt, Brace & World, New York, 1962.
3   SUMNER, H., 'Integration and Sequence in Economics for 8-13
    Year-olds', Unpublished Paper, Schools Council History,
    Geography and Social Science 8-13 Project.
4   BEYER, B.K., 'Inquiry in the Social Studies Classroom: A
    Strategy for Teaching', Charles E.Merrill, Englewood Cliffs,
    1971.
5   HIRST, P.H., Liberal Education and the Nature of Knowledge in
    DEARDEN, R.F., HIRST, P.H. and PETERS, R.S., 'Education and the
    Development of Reason', Routledge & Kegan Paul, London, 1972.
6   PHENIX, P.H., 'Philosophy of Education', Holt, Rinehart &
    Winston, New York, 1958.
7   BLYTH, W.A.L. et al., 'History, Geography and Social Science
    8-13 - An Interim Statement', Schools Council Publications,
    1972.
8   BRUNER, J.S., 'The Process of Education', Harvard University
    Press, Cambridge, Mass., 1960.
9   Report of a Joint Committee of the Royal Economics Society, the
    Association of University Teachers of Economics, and the
    Economics Association, 'The Teaching of Economics in Schools',
    Macmillan, London, 1973.
10 HIRST, P.H., The Curriculum, in Schools Council Working Paper
    12, 'The Educational Implications of Social and Economic
    Change', HMSO, London, 1967.
11 NEWSOM REPORT, 'Half our Future', Report of the Central Advisory
    Council for Education (England), HMSO, London, 1963.
12 SCHOOLS COUNCIL, Working Paper No.2, 'Raising the School Leaving
    Age', HMSO, London, 1965.
    SCHOOLS COUNCIL, Working Paper No.12, 'The Educational Impli-
    cations of Social and Economic Change', HMSO, London, 1967.
    BOON, G. and CUNNINGHAM, H., 'Enquiry Work in an Urban Setting',
    Schools Council, London, 1970.
13 SCHOOLS COUNCIL, 'Enquiry One', HMSO, London, 1968.
14 HOLLY, D., 'Beyond Curriculum', Hart Davies, MacGibbon, London,
    1973.
15 STENHOUSE, L., Open Minded Teaching, 'New Society', 24 July
    1969, pp.126-8.
16 STENHOUSE, L., Some Limitations of the Use of Objectives in
    Curriculum Research and Planning, 'Paedagogica Europaea', vol.6,
    1970, pp.73-83.
17 STENHOUSE, L., The Humanities Curriculum Project, 'Journal of
    Curriculum Studies', vol.1, no.1, 1968, pp.26-33.
18 TABA, H. et al., 'A Teacher's Handbook to Elementary Social
    Studies', Addison-Wesley, Reading, Mass., 1967.
19 BLOOM, B.S. et al., 'Taxonomy of Educational Objectives',
    Longman, London, 1956.
20 BROWN, P.C., Life Sentence for the Soul, 'Twentieth Century',
    vol.176, no.1038, 3rd quarter 1968, pp.8-10.

21   MOORE, R.A. and NICHOLSON, R.J.F., Integrated Specialisms,
     'Times Educational Supplement', 22 June 1973, p.27.
22   BRUNER, J.S., op.cit.
23   HOLLY, D., op.cit., p.145.
24   MUSGROVE, F., Curriculum Objectives, 'Journal of Curriculum
     Studies', reprinted in HOOPER, R., 'The Curriculum - Context,
     Design and Development', Oliver & Boyd, Edinburgh, 1971, p.228.
25   PRING, R., Curriculum Integration, 'London Institute of Edu-
     cation Bulletin', Spring 1970, pp.4-8.
26   CUNNINGHAM, H., 'Starting from Cold', unpublished paper, 1969.
27   PARLETT, M., The New Evaluation, 'Trends', no.34, July 1974.
28   LUMSDEN, K.G. and ATTIYEH, R.E., The Core of Basic Economics,
     'Economics', Summer 1971.

DISCUSSION

Mrs Thomas acknowledged that 1975 was perhaps not the most pro-
pitious time to be directing attention towards the possible integration of subjects since, in her estimation, current opinion tends
to hold such schemes in fairly low regard. She found little support
at the seminar for her claim that there exists a distinctive
'humanities way of knowing'. Nobody was keen to define 'humanities'. In England the subjects it embraces appear to be somewhat
arbitrarily chosen: in Scotland the term is not used.

There was doubt expressed, too, over the claim that key or core
concepts can be identified convincingly, and certainly some of those
selected by Mrs Thomas are not peculiar to the humanities, as she
readily accepted. There was some support for the view that critical
faculties cannot be developed in pupils if teaching ignores
concepts, but not everybody accepted Mrs Thomas's contention that if
one develops the concepts of a subject then one automatically
teaches pupils to be critical in their thinking.

The assessment procedures at the end of both the 1972-3 stages of
the course and the 1973-4 course were the subject of some comment.
In particular, did not the high rate of truancy and absenteeism at
the first stage provide some evidence that critical faculties had
indeed been developed in these pupils? Again, evaluation of the
second stage was considered to be very ambitious. Were the results
not what most teachers might well have expected?

There was a general feeling that Mrs Thomas had tried in a most
commendable way to provide an intellectual underpinning for the
curriculum experiment discussed in her paper and that her analysis
would be of considerable value to those interested in exploring
further the relationship between conceptual thinking in single
disciplines and in integrated programmes.

Chapter 2

SHOULD ECONOMICS BE TAUGHT TO ALL SECONDARY PUPILS?*

David J. Whitehead

INTRODUCTION

The first part of this paper examines what light educational philosophy can throw on the issue of justifying the inclusion of
economics in the school curriculum. In the second section, a critical appraisal is made of the conventional arguments used by economists when advocating that their subject should be in the school
curriculum. Also some arguments against the inclusion of economics
are examined. Finally, in the third section, some of the problems
which may arise from teaching economics with other social sciences
are discussed and some examination syllabuses are scrutinised to
obtain evidence on what is being taught today in this curriculum
area.

DO EDUCATIONAL PHILOSOPHERS JUSTIFY THE INCLUSION OF ECONOMICS IN
THE CURRICULUM?

Let us examine what three fashionable educational philosophers have
to say about the curriculum. They are Hirst, in his article
Liberal Education and the Nature of Knowledge, written in 1965, (1)
Phenix in his book 'Realms of Meaning' published in 1964, (2) and
John White in his recent publication 'Towards a Compulsory Curriculum'. (3)
    Paul Hirst has attacked the problem of providing a definition of
liberal education in terms of the qualities of mind it ought to produce and the forms of knowledge with which it ought to be concerned.
He examines the view that liberal education means ability 'to think
effectively, to communicate thought, to make relevant judgments, to
discriminate among values'. (4) But, he argues, such mental qualities must have public criteria to mark them. That is, if there is

* My thanks are due to Denis Lawton, Keith Drake, Keith Robinson and
  Raymond Ryba for their most helpful and constructive comments on
  earlier drafts of this paper. Also for many of the principal
  ideas I am indebted to Nigel Wright. The views expressed and any
  stylistic infelicities remain my own.

no public way of showing that A is 'thinking effectively' and B is
not, then for all we know, the village idiot may be thinking effectively, in which case the term is meaningless. So, Hirst continues:

> if the public terms and criteria are logically necessary to
> specifying what the abilities are ... then no adequate account
> of liberal education in terms of these can be given without a
> full account in terms of the public features of the forms of
> knowledge with which it is concerned. (5)

Also, he argues, there are very real objective differences
between the modes of communication in, say, science and religion,
and therefore in the mental processes involved in these. In short,
Hirst deduces that there are a number of discrete forms of
knowledge, each form requiring the development of creative imagination, judgment, thinking, communicative skill and so forth, in
ways peculiar to that particular form of knowledge.

His main conclusion, which is scarcely value-free, is that everyone should have a liberal education based on the forms of knowledge,
which are 'the complex ways of understanding experience which man
has achieved, which are publicly specifiable and which are gained
through learning'. (6)

Distinct forms of knowledge are marked out by each having:

1 its own peculiar concepts,
2 a distinctive logical structure arising from a distinct conceptual framework within which experience can be understood,
3 tests against experience in accordance with particular criteria
   which are peculiar to that form, and
4 its own distinctive methodology.

Hirst proceeds to list these distinct forms of knowledge. The
nearest to economics is what he calls 'human sciences'. However,
even if one accepts 'human science' as a discrete form of knowledge,
and that therefore it should be part of a liberal education, it does
not follow that teaching economics is justified, for it is just one
amongst many human sciences competing for a place in the curriculum.
Although economics may have its own peculiar concepts and a distinctive logical structure, its tests against experience and its
methodology are not unique but shared by the other human (social)
sciences. So economics as a distinct curriculum discipline cannot
be justified on the ground that it develops some desirable ability
of a general nature; so might psychology or sociology. It can be
readily seen that an assumption of the Hirst model is that some sort
of transfer of learning is possible. Any evidence for this within
the social science field is not given. It follows that to justify
economics to the exclusion of other social sciences, it would need
to be shown that the concepts and logical structure of the subject
are intrinsically more educative than for example those of psychology or sociology. If this cannot be done, and if it is accepted that
pupils need to be made aware of the empirical testing procedures of
the human sciences (i.e. their methodology), and also need to be
introduced to the concepts of each human science, then some form of
interdisciplinary or integrated approach would seem to be necessary,
given the time constraint in a school curriculum. We shall return
to this theme later.

Phenix also has attempted to elaborate a philosophical theory of

the curriculum for general education based on the idea of logical
patterns in disciplined understanding. His central thesis is that
knowledge in the disciplines has patterns or structures and that an
understanding of these typical forms is essential for the guidance
of teaching and learning. 'The learning of these patterns is the
clue to effective realisation of essential humanness through the
curriculum of general education.' (7) Phenix distinguishes six
fundamental patterns of meaning, one of which he calls empirics.
Each realm of meaning may be described by reference to its typical
methods, leading ideas, and characteristic structures. He states
that empirical sciences express meanings as probable empirical
truths framed in accordance with certain rules of evidence and
verification and making use of specified systems of analytic abstraction. (8) And he proceeds to argue that empirics is one of the
basic competences that general education should develop in every
person.

Very briefly, he suggests four principles for selecting and
organising the content within each 'pattern of meaning'. The first
is that the content of instruction should be drawn entirely from the
fields of disciplined enquiry. Second, from the large resources of
material in any given discipline, those items should be chosen that
are particularly representative of the field as a whole. His third
point is that content should be chosen so as to exemplify the
methods of enquiry and the modes of understanding in the disciplines
studied. Finally, the materials chosen should be such as to arouse
imagination. (9)

Despite the numerous interesting insights thrown up by Phenix's
approach, it is important to stress that he makes no claim that the
principles he puts forward provide a complete basis for the construction of the curriculum even of general education. He does not
argue the case for economics, but presupposes that each of the
fundamental disciplines (economics included), no matter how technical it may be at the advanced levels, is pertinent to every person
as a person, and therefore that it is possible to present its human-
ly significant leading ideas for general educational use. (10) The
nearest he gets to justification is when he argues that no one realm
of meaning can be perfected without the aid of the others. All six
realms form a complex unity of inter-related yet relatively autonomous domains. (11) It follows that the curriculum should at least
provide for learnings in all six of the realms of meaning. But it
appears that Phenix is of no greater assistance than Hirst to those
seeking a philosophical justification for the presence of economics
in the curriculum.

Let us now consider John White's approach to curriculum planning.
He argues that any compulsory study is an intolerable infringement
of the child's liberty unless it can be shown that the study is essential in the interests of the child. (12) White then argues that
it is in the interest of the child to know what he wants, and there
is some knowledge which is essential if one is to be able to recognise one's wants and to choose wisely between the various options
open to the autonomous adult. He writes:

   some teachers pigeonhole 11 year-olds entering their secondary
   schools as future manual workers likely to be drawn into the
   familiar patterns of life associated with such occupations; in

making their courses 'relevant' to the lives these children 'will
lead', they do nothing to enlarge their vision of other possible
ways of life, but merely help unwittingly to create in them the
belief that the familiar working-class patterns are the ones they
should follow. (13)

First the child must be introduced to what White calls 'Category I'
activities - activities which it is 'logically impossible' to have
any understanding of until one has engaged in them. He mentions
communication skills, mathematics, physical sciences, and aesthetic
appreciation. All other (Category II) activities - for example,
foreign languages, cookery, mountain climbing and economics - he
claims can to some extent be understood without actually engaging
in them.

We shall pass over the problem of how operationally to distinguish between Category I and II activities, and move on to
White's second assertion. He maintains that children must be helped
to understand the different possible ways of life which they may
choose to lead. In order to present these various ways of life to
the child, the study of history, literature, philosophy and ethics
is recommended.

The third and final constituent of White's compulsory curriculum
is other education necessary to integrate what has been learnt according to the above two criteria, and to achieve the understanding
necessary to translate knowledge into practice. For, having obtained all the 'theoretical knowledge necessary to choose between
different activities and ways of life, the child needs some practical understanding of the world before going out and "doing it"'.
(14)

White contends that essential to this practical understanding is
some understanding of economic affairs, social and political institutions, and natural, geographical features relevant to socio-
economic matters. He will have to know something about 'industry,
domestic and international trade, taxation and income distribution'.
It is difficult to ascertain from where White has plucked these
topics; one certainty is that, given all the other subjects in his
compulsory curriculum, depth treatment will be possible in only a
very narrow sample of topics.

So much for the philosophers. Hirst cannot be used as a weapon
to justify economics to the curriculum mongers. White would
certainly admit it, but not because of the nature of the subject.
His approach to it as a Category II subject is much more pragmatic -
if it has instrumental value, then it may be included. This brings
us much closer to the arguments used by economists for the inclusion
of economics in the curriculum, which will now be considered.

WHAT CASE IS MADE BY THE ECONOMISTS FOR THE INCLUSION OF THEIR
SUBJECT IN THE SCHOOL CURRICULUM?

First I shall note the arguments advanced by various writers, and
then examine to what extent they can be instrumentally justified.
I shall exclude consideration of a specialist sixth form course in
economics.

The **AMA** declares that a course in economics will make all school

leavers good citizens, more efficient producers of goods and more judicious consumers of goods. (15) The syllabus of the Scottish 'O' grade in economics has the following aims:
(a)   to enable pupils to see economics as a dynamic social science of concern to everybody,
(b)   to provide pupils with an understanding of the basic economic problems which will increasingly face them, and
(c)   to develop in pupils a capacity for economic reasoning and for logical expression of ideas based on a study of the relevant data. (16)

K.Dunning argues that the most worthwhile contribution of economics education is the fostering of economic judgments on contemporary issues as a vital part of the education of the individual as a citizen and a member of society, and that the development of the skill of identifying and using economic concepts, even if it is severely limited by the intellectual capacity of the pupil, is preferable to no development at all. (17)

Let us now examine these justifications in turn. First, the 'good citizen' argument advanced by the AMA. It seems to me that this aim is embarrassingly naive and untenable. It presupposes that there is a general consensus of opinion defining what is meant by being a good citizen (which is doubtful) and that in some way the academic study of economics can change the behaviour of initiates in the desired direction. Concerning the argument that economics will make all school leavers more efficient producers of goods, it is hard to see how this hypothesis could ever be tested. If it were the case, it would presumably apply to the way that students deal with the economics course itself. Is there any evidence that economics students study more efficiently than others? And finally, quite apart from the absence of any evidence on the matter, the prospect of a course in economics turning pupils into saintly, dynamically efficient readers of 'Which?' does not attract me. Courses in morals, politics, decision-making and consumer protection may be magnificent - but they are not economics.

A second type of argument is exemplified by the first Scottish Certificate objective, namely that we should enable pupils to see economics as a dynamic social science of concern to everyone. This sort of aim presumably has the status of an asserted value judgment. The justification of any one subject cannot be considered in isolation. If the number of justifiable subjects exceeds the time and space available in the curriculum, then some sort of selection must be made, that is, the relative claims of the various subjects must be considered. As John White points out, the onus is on people to give reasons why their subject should be in the curriculum, and not upon everyone else to give reasons why it shouldn't. What special claims has economics over other social sciences such as anthropology, social psychology? Besides, the increasing complexity of society would also seem to call for the study of cybernetics, vegetable growing, industrial sabotage, psychoanalysis and karate. Why economics?

Then we come to the set of arguments associated, crudely speaking, with providing pupils with enough information to enable them to understand the newspapers and television news, and vote responsibly. Some knowledge of economics may well be necessary to achieve these aims, but I hope to show that such knowledge may not be as comprehensively useful as might initially be supposed. If teachers were to concern themselves with helping children to understand the newspapers, a knowledge of economics alone would be wildly insufficient. (For example, in a typical newspaper, the 'Daily Mirror' on Tuesday 10 June 1975, 49 column inches out of 2912, or 1.7 per cent were devoted to items remotely concerned with the economy. Or perhaps a course in economics would stop pupils reading the 'Mirror'?!) Some knowledge of foreign politics, the sexual proclivities of peers and pop stars, and historical and comparative studies in football would be essential. Wouldn't it be simpler to have the news explained in a way which a non-economist would not find misleading or incomprehensive? Much economics teaching at present has to offset the over-simplicities of economic journalists. How often do these commentators, when retailing the latest strike figures, put them into proportion, say in relation to the rate of strikes in comparable countries? How often, when bemoaning the latest balance of visible trade deficit, do they indicate (a) that we have had a visible surplus only three or four times since 1896 anyway, and (b) that the margin of statistical error is as great as the deficit (or at least has been so until recently)? How often when dealing with wage increases, do they distinguish between wage rates and average weekly earnings, and use a standard weekly, monthly or annual measure for all workers? As regards the 'responsible voter' argument, do we really think that an understanding of economics will enable voters to vote more rationally (whatever that means)? It certainly sounds good, but it is pie in the sky. Students coming up to voting age might benefit more from courses in investigative journalism, overlapping directorships, truth detection and personality assessment techniques.

The fourth common group of arguments may be summed up as 'economics is a discipline which imparts useful intellectual training'. I mentioned earlier the Scottish Certificate aim 'to develop in pupils a capacity for economic reasoning and for logical expression of ideas based on a study of the relevant data'. Since, as Hirst points out, a good number of subjects develop the intellect - mathematics, science and philosophy, for example, all require clear thinking and step-by-step reasoning - what is needed is a demonstration that either economics develops the intellect in a way in which no other subject can, or that economics develops the same mental qualities as some other subjects do, but that economics does it at least as well, and adds a useful substantive content by way of a bonus.

The first argument, that the skills and abilities developed by economics are in some sense unique, does not, at an intuitive level, hold water. Richard Szreter has distinguished the following characteristics of the 'economic way of thinking': (18) the capacity for logical step-by-step reasoning (which is also developed by mathematics and philosophy); the readiness to distinguish between fact and opinion, scientific statements and value judgments (science and history); the ability to see the many-sidedness of economic and social problems (history, literature and geography); thinking in terms of short and long run consequences of events (history, biology) and so on. My basic point here is that without showing that

economics itself is a worthwhile study, the claim that it brings
together a number of skills that are also developed elsewhere is
insufficient, unless it is held, as Dunning maintains, (19) that it
is the combination of such skills within one subject (economics)
which makes its inclusion in the curriculum so uniquely worthwhile.

But perhaps economics is at least as good as other subjects in
developing certain skills and abilities. This is an empirical
question which hasn't yet been answered. So the ground is still
shifting under our feet. Even if this were shown, it would still
be necessary to make a case for the substantive content of economics
vis-a-vis other subjects. For example, as already mentioned, the
Scottish Certificate syllabus has the third aim, 'to provide pupils
with an understanding of the basic economic problems which will increasingly face them'.

It may well be that the economist has a distinctive way of viewing events and problems, but even if this is so, it still needs to
be shown that this distinct viewpoint is in some way necessary to
everybody (and should be acquired at school). After all, there are
other unique ways of viewing the world, such as through Zen
Buddhism, Marxism, or an alcoholic haze, but this is not sufficient
to justify their inclusion in the curriculum.

Finally, on the question of how the inclusion of economics in the
curriculum can be justified, I want to examine briefly the vocational argument. It is said that economics is useful for pupils going
into banking, commerce, insurance, etc. Even this will not be the
case if the syllabuses do not reflect the kind of skills and
knowledge which these sort of occupations require. This is not to
touch on the important question of whether, given appropriate syllabuses, the vocational aim is actually realised in the learning
achievements of pupils. Also, this argument would presumably not be
sufficient to justify teaching the subject to all, but only to those
who think it might be useful vocationally. Moreover, some would
argue that vocational training should not take place at school.

Having been rather critical of some of the standard pro-economics
arguments, I want now to analyse two arguments used against its inclusion. Lord Robbins claimed in a now famous article (20) that
economics was too difficult for schoolchildren. Presumably, if it
were conclusively proved to be too difficult for schoolchildren, the
question of whether it ought to be taught would not arise. It is
usual at this point to cite Bruner's dictum as evidence against
Robbins, namely, 'We begin with the hypothesis that any subject can
be taught effectively in some intellectually honest form to any
child at any stage of development.' (21) It is rarely stated that
he proceeded to add: 'It is a bold hypothesis and an essential one
in thinking about the nature of a curriculum. No evidence exists to
contradict it; considerable evidence is being amassed that supports
it.' He then gives examples of scientific and mathematical concepts
being taught to young children. However, if we are honest with ourselves, we have to admit that although we may have some evidence
from the Economics Education Project (22) that economics of the
'A-level' or 'O-level' type may be learned by appropriate pupils,
there is precious little evidence concerning whether economics can
be taught to children of all abilities. Some American evidence may
be obtained from Senesh, in a lecture given at the London University

Institute of Education in 1974. (23) He reported that the most
recent research in the USA indicated that economics could not be
taught even to sophomores; he then paradoxically adduced this as
an argument for teaching economics to six-year-olds.

There is no kind of magical number which justifies our starting
to teach economics at the age of 11,12,13, or 14, etc. There is
no scientific validity for the selection of any particular age.
I have a more powerful argument, that the children are part of
the economic world and making economic decisions, little but po-
tentially very meaningful decisions, from a very, very early age.

A second argument is that economics is bristling with value
judgments and that pupils are not equipped to deal with teachers'
exposition of pet theories, dogmas and prejudices, which would be
ridiculed at any gathering of trained economists. Also, the content
of economics - that is, the absence of any Marxist economics, no
questions on the distribution of income or less developed countries,
the paradigm of the free market - to some extent misleads the pupil.
Economics as indoctrination? One answer to the first accusation
would be to say that the usefulness of economics is that it is a
subject in which such value judgments might be made explicit, and
discussed with the pupils. Perhaps a true story by Professor Senesh
may emphasise this point.

I was talking to a girl from our neighbourhood elementary school,
and I asked her what she had been doing at school. Elizabeth
said that they had that day discussed Cambodia, and one little
boy stood up during the story-telling and said, 'My father is for
bombing Cambodia because if we don't bomb Cambodia the government
will save money and would waste it on poor people.' And I asked
Elizabeth what the elementary school teacher said. She said,
'And now let's take the textbook and read Chapter 3.' As long as
we have this kind of fear of opening a discussion on the simple
question, what is more humane, to kill people or help people, as
long as we have such timid teachers, who don't pick it up on the
spot and make a teaching unit out of it, we do not have a social
science programme.

As far as the content of the economics curriculum is concerned,
it might be argued that teachers have it in their power to change
syllabuses. However, to say this is like saying that the Ritz is
open to all. If teachers lack the means (or are denied them, which
is more accurate) then the right to change syllabuses, put in alternatives and so forth, is only fraudulently described as an opportunity. In other words, how many teachers have access to the
reduced work load, resources and in-service facilities to work on
curriculum and syllabus reform, all of which would be necessary to
give them the power really to use the entitlement to change syllabuses? In the state of Victoria, Australia, economics teachers
teach 24 out of 40 periods per week. They have such an opportunity.

To summarise so far, I have suggested that few if any of the
arguments advanced by the protagonists of economics education for
all schoolchildren bear close examination, but that the conclusion
that one cannot 'prove' that economics should be on the curriculum
for all sixteen-year-olds is not a sufficient reason for not having
it there. But I have also maintained that the arguments marshalled
against economics are not easy to admit. It is not possible in this

short paper to examine the justifications by which other social
sciences seek admission to the school curriculum. If it may be assumed that they can all make cases equally as strong as economics,
and if further it may be assumed that there would be inadequate
space on the timetable for fully-fledged separate treatment of the
basic concepts of each social science, then some form of inter-
disciplinary or integrated course would be needed. This leads me
on to consideration of the question whether economics can be taught
as a constituent of such a course.

WHAT PROBLEMS MAY ARISE FROM THE TEACHING OF ECONOMICS WITH OTHER SOCIAL SCIENCES?

As Brian Holley graphically puts it:
    If the world of social phenomena can be regarded as an area, then
    we can regard economics as a beam of light focussed on a small
    part of the total area, but shedding some rays on surrounding
    areas; other disciplines focus on one or other of the surround-
    ing areas but shed light on the area which is of central concern
    to the economists. (24)
It is all very well for curriculum planners to suggest such
courses as integrated social sciences, but the problems of planning
such a course are immense. If pupils are pursuing a topic-centred
approach, drawing on the relevant social sciences when applicable,
it will be very difficult to ensure that the logical progression of
the substantive concepts of each social science is adhered to. A
possible solution, suggested by Hazel Sumner, is to emphasise the
contributing disciplines in turn, meanwhile using such concepts from
the other social sciences as are relevant and necessary to the topic
under consideration. (25) This is similar to Senesh's view of the
teacher as conductor, and the individual social sciences sometimes
as soloist, at other times, background orchestral noise. (26) However, his social science programme 'Our Working World' is not one in
which some concepts are presented at one level and others at the
next. Instead, all the fundamental ideas of the social sciences are
introduced at the earliest level and grow with the child as each
level calls on him to apply them in increasing depth and complexity.
No such polymath as Senesh has yet appeared in the UK to achieve
such a synthesis!
    Keith Robinson, who has written extensively in the field of eco-
nomics for less able pupils, makes the point that the single-
discipline approach reflects a judgment on the relative importance
of individual disciplines which may no longer be valid, and it may
mean that certain areas of knowledge are largely unexplored in the
school curriculum. (27) Hence, he argues, some form of integration
is essential if the curriculum is to be both more efficient in terms
of organisation of knowledge and more effective as a medium for preparing pupils to move into the world outside the school where daily
problems are multi-faceted.
    The experience of the Social Science Faculty of the Open Uni-
versity is pertinent here. For several years, their Foundation
Course entitled 'Understanding Society' used a discipline-centred
approach, with a few weeks being allotted to each social science

discipline to explain its fundamental concepts. (28) This was found
to be so confusing and apparently irrelevant (especially the economics component) to the students that the course had eventually to
be replaced. Also, the course emphasised disciplinary structure at
the cost of obscuring the links between individual disciplines and
the ways of thinking which are common to all social sciences. A
short analysis of the new course 'Making Sense of Society' (29) may
be illuminating, since it has evolved as a result of an enormous
amount of feedback from tutors and students on the earlier Foundation Course. First, students start by considering several phenomena which are commonly regarded as social problems (unemployment,
crime, immigration) and which seem to be more relevant to the
student as topics for study than do many of the concerns of social
science theory. Gradually the concepts and methods of social
science are introduced, as and when they are necessary to illuminate
the problems. Although this analysis of social problems has advantages in suggesting relevance and generating interest, it has the
disadvantage that it does not provide a systematic framework for the
study of society as a whole. So the course team rejected the
'problem' approach for the main body of the course. This is divided
into seven main parts, which attempt to provide a coherent structure
to some of the most important topics covered by the social sciences
without resorting to sections based on individual disciplines. The
topics are Communication, Production and Allocation, Work, Social
Relations, Attitudes and Beliefs, Power and Social Change. These
dimensions of society are used to introduce social science methods
and to demonstrate disciplinary ideas in an inter-disciplinary
context. (30) First indications are that this course is meeting
with considerable success. In my view, not only would this course
be a considerable improvement on most social science 'A' level
subjects taken by school students, but it also might lend itself to
adaptation for use with the 14-16 age group.

In the light of the Open University's experience with the inter-
disciplinary approach, it is perhaps unfortunate that the Scottish
Economics Curriculum Development Project for the first two years of
secondary education should be only economics, and justified as such
on the ground that it would as a single discipline be easier to
assess. (31) Simply to argue that any inter-disciplinary approach
would be extremely difficult to operate seems to me to shy away from
the problem. It also seems strange to me that, according to David
Christie, the assumption is made that this two-year course may be
terminal, that is, that the pupils will not proceed beyond the
course to any further formal study of economics. If so, why is it
geared to 12-to-14 year-olds rather than say 14-to-16 year olds?
One might think that some lessons could have been learnt from the
above-mentioned course devised by Senesh, a six-year integrated
social science course, from ages 6 to 12. This has been out-
standingly successful and has been taken up avidly by the elementary
schools.

It would be relevant to hear the experience of one school that
has tried to integrate the social sciences, namely Thomas Bennett
School, Crawley. Peter Mitchell has written of his Integrated Humanities Course for the fourth/fifth years:

We were determined to pursue the idea of the common curriculum

representing history, geography and social sciences and thus to
avoid a proliferation of single social science disciplines that
would be set against history and geography in a system of curriculum options.

An important reason for introducing curriculum innovation in
the 4th/5th years was our dissatisfaction with what pupils had
achieved at the completion of Mode I on history, geography and
commerce. This is achievement in terms of cognitive development
and not in terms of grades. The breadth of content to be covered
forced teachers to use an excessive degree of didactic teaching
thus stifling the pupils' initiative in the learning situation.
This is a generalisation which may be challenged but in schools
with pupils of less than the highest ability, who feel it their
responsibility to help their pupils to high grades it usually
holds true. It was clear to us that the humanities programme
would necessitate a wider range of modes of learning than our
previous teaching, our intention to be more explicit about attitudes and values, for example, draws attention to the need for
pupils to have the opportunity for discussion. (32)

This quotation raises the very real problem of whether what is
currently taught at CSE and 'O' level really has any connection with
economics. One might make the point about economics below 'A' level
similar to that which Gandhi is alleged to have made when asked what
he thought about Christianity: 'It sounds a very good idea; I
think it ought to be tried.' I have recently examined all 14 CSE
boards' commerce, social economics and economics Mode I syllabuses
and examination papers, and all 8 Examination Boards' 'O' level
commerce and economics syllabuses. It was a very depressing exercise. The typical CSE syllabus involves rote learning of large
numbers of facts about the economy, and seems to specialise in encouraging the learning of material with built-in obsolescence.
Little attempt is made to structure syllabuses analytically. Some
are patently vocational. For example, the East Anglian Commerce
syllabus includes: 'Documents: Letters of enquiry, price lists,
orders, invoices, statements, credit notes, receipt and despatch of
goods, receipts.' In the 1973 paper, Q6.C.b.iii asks the candidate
to explain the meaning of the Stock Exchange term 'contango'. To me
this is almost as sick as explaining how to get a mortgage and buy a
house to a majority of school leavers, in the London area at any
rate. The 1973 Social Economics examination paper of the East
Anglian Board requires the name of the Chancellor of the Exchequer,
the place where tea auctions are held (by the way, how many people
know that very recently most of the commodity markets moved from
Mincing Lane to new premises in Mark Lane), and that hardy perenni-
al, the name of the Consumer Association's publication. Are these
the sort of bits of information which will help the candidates to
negotiate their way through the world?

One or two CSE boards are trying to structure their courses more
analytically, however. For example, the East Midland Social Studies
syllabus has a Bloom-type breakdown of educational objectives (see
Appendix 2.1). So does the JMB 'O' level in Government, Economics
and Commerce paper, which is perhaps the most interesting syllabus
to appear at this level. The aims are divided into three parts:
knowledge, comprehension and application, and expression (see Ap-

pendix 2.2). At least some attempt is made to be explicit about the sort of skills the pupils are intended to develop, and some success is achieved in getting off the lowest domain of purely descriptive knowledge.

Is there any effort being made in the direction of an integrated social science course for the Certificate of Extended Education? There are very few developments in this field. The Metropolitan Board has introduced a CEE in economics from September 1974. The syllabus is outstanding in its tedium. It comprises four parts:

1   The Economic Problem
2   The Labour Market
3   Management of the Economy
4   The capital and money market

These subjects are assessed by a written paper. Part II will consist of an applied economic study, namely a project, for example, a study of a major industry, or one aspect of London's economy, e.g. City of London Transport, or of a growth centre, such as Croydon. This is a one-year course, aimed at students who have achieved grades 2-4 in CSE, and who wish, for whatever reason, to continue studying for a further year at school (see Appendix 2.3).

An example of a syllabus which is at least described in terms of the model of integration I have been developing, is that of the East Anglian Board's CSE in Social Studies syllabus B (see Appendix 2.4). The aim of this very interesting syllabus is to lead the pupils to an understanding of the interplay of man and society and towards an insight into the influence of social groups on his life and on others' lives. The main themes of Paper I are the family, the economic system, power, socialisation and education, social control and belief systems, and living in cities. Treatment of values is very definitely included, for example, mechanisation and its influence on work satisfaction; why some people are more powerful than others and the effect this has on the distribution of wealth and persistence of poverty; why some people do not keep to the rules of society; how this 'deviance' may bring about changes in the rules. The second part of the course involves study of one or more topics in depth, viz. population, crime, methods in social research, study of a foreign society or a local community, stratification, and women in society. Also a project is submitted. This could of course be a 'collection' of discrete subjects. But it also lends itself to the focused approach I mentioned earlier.

So much for the present state of play. Finally, we examine some of the problems implied by the analysis.

A first practical problem is that, even if an integrated social science course is regarded as worthwhile, can it be staffed? It may be possible for an economist (at present perhaps engaged only in 'A' level/'O' level work in his subject) to make his contribution to such courses in the context of team teaching. As Keith Robinson remarks, unless there is an economist in some way involved, it is unlikely that economic issues will be analysed satisfactorily, for teachers with only a limited acquaintance with the subject may either under- or over-assess its significance in relation to a particular problem or event. (33) But doesn't that argument hold for all the other social sciences too?! No wonder the Australians

call their integrated courses 'fused'! Moreover, any breaking down
of subject barriers will meet resistance from the fact that teacher
identity is often defined in terms of loyalty to a discipline's
social system.   As Raymond Ryba points out, any kind of integration
in which the teacher has not got the support of a discipline with
which he is thoroughly familiar, is likely to be faced with enormous
problems. I quote:

> Society is making increasing demands on the teacher, and today he
> is called upon to perform a vast number of tasks which in the
> past he was not expected to do. If we are expecting teachers to
> be almost superhuman already, are we not now expecting them to do
> an increasingly impossible job? If we add the need to be a
> polymath even if just within the social science field, it is an
> unrealistic hope. However, team teaching might go some ways
> towards solving some of these problems. (34)

However, some teachers will always find it difficult to work co-
operatively with other teachers or in a team situation. 'Social
science specialists should see each other as allies, not as enemies
making rival bids for one of the scarce resources in the school-
time.' (35) This need not mean that specialist teachers lose their
identity by this kind of co-operation.

Such problems have implications for the training of teachers for
the middle-secondary age group, and there appears to be a case for a
general social science education in colleges and universities backed
by specialisation in one of the contributing disciplines. The new
Open University integrated social science course would seem to be
more suitable for this type of curriculum.

A second controversial problem concerns what economic concepts
should be taught to all children within a social science course.
Norman Lee has suggested more a problem-based than a conceptual approach, with fuller and more critical examination of the ends of
economic systems and the development of the pupils' facility to
examine their own thinking in evaluating those ends; more study of
alternative economic systems, more time devoted to income distribution, and problems of poverty, conservation, housing, education,
etc.; and greater use of the contributions of other behavioural
sciences in studying consumer behaviour and greater attention to
more realistic market forms and their possible welfare implications.
(36)

Third, much work needs to be done, having isolated the core
concepts of economics (an awe-inspiring task), to determine the
length of time taken by pupils of varying abilities to learn them as
part of an integrated course. Only then can one make recommendations about when such a course should start and how many years it
should last. The so-called Yellow Book, namely the Report on the
Teaching of Economics in Schools, is really only concerned with 'A'
level economists and the needs of the universities. For example,
the report states that the committee concentrated on the problems of
the teaching of economics at the sixth form level, and did no attempt to deal with any possible repercussions on teaching at earlier
stages. (37) To my mind a rather heroic evasion of responsibility.

Another similar point is made by John White about some of the
young school leaver courses, which seem to be emergency final year

courses. There is nothing wrong with these in principle if they
are only very short-term expedients. But short-term expedients
often have a habit of growing into permanent institutions. The
Humanities Project, for instance, may enable the young school leaver
to express his own views and hear those of his classmates on war and
violence and poverty; but without a thorough grounding in relevant
information, in all the problems of fact and value which surround
these immense issues, it is hard to see that very much can be
achieved; it is like building a roof with no house to go beneath
it. (38)

A fourth obstacle is mentioned by Denis Lawton; the general reluctance of decision-makers (i.e. heads, curriculum co-ordinators,
directors of studies, etc.) to recognise that it is either desirable
or possible for all pupils to have a basic economic and social
understanding. He wonders if perhaps they are frightened of their
schools becoming subversive or perhaps they are merely imprisoned in
the usual situation of curriculum inertia. They may be confused by
the rival assertions of philosophers of education, and the general
confusion among economists as to what economics is. (39)

However, I do not think that this reflects the situation as it
is today. Increasing numbers of teachers are becoming aware of the
need to introduce some form of course to enable their school leavers
to appreciate the problems of the society in which we live. What we
must try to do is to work out the sort of programme which, while
satisfying the educationalists, will be seen by students as relevant
to their needs.

To sum up, what I have suggested is that the purpose of extending
economics teaching to all school pupils must be examined very
carefully. It is not possible to present a very strong case either
for a multi-disciplinary or for an inter-disciplinary approach,
though the latter is favoured by the present writer (whilst admitting that the proof of the pudding will be in the eating).
Nevertheless Phenix's caveat must be borne in mind:

The difficulty with non-disciplinary studies is that they offer
a temptation to shallow, non-disciplined thinking because of
the mixture of methods and concepts involved. They require more
knowledge and skill, greater care, and better mastery of materials than do studies within a particular discipline, where the
lines of productive thought may be kept more directly and continually in view.

Arguing the case for a particular curriculum is difficult in vacuo;
perhaps the next task is for a draft syllabus to be devised, so that
we can begin to discuss whether such proposals as I have outlined
are capable of being implemented.

APPENDIX 2.1

East Midland Regional Examinations Board

Social Studies CSE

Aim: 'to develop responsibility and initiative in individual
children, to increase their self-respect; to provide the incentive

and to foster the ability to be of some service to the Community and
to develop a critical faculty in relation to the environment'.
    'To develop:
1   A knowledge of facts in the chosen sections of the syllabus.
2   An understanding of the terminology used in the sections of
    the syllabus.
3   Simple research techniques.
4   A critical faculty.
5   An appreciation of social and moral issues taught, discussed
    and researched.'
    Syllabus: Has 6 sections, of which 3 are industry, Everyday Eco-
nomics and World Problems.
    Exam: 2 papers: 1 short-answer type 40 per cent, 1 essay type
30 per cent. Project work 30 per cent (strong emphasis on origi-
nality).
    The industry paper is highly descriptive. The Everyday Economics
is mainly macro, with sections on insurance and personal budgeting.
The purpose of the World Problems syllabus is to give an appreciation of the demands of World Citizenship.

APPENDIX 2.2

Joint Matriculation Board

'O' level in Government, Economics and Commerce

'Aims to enable schools to provide courses which will help in the
general education of candidates towards their future as citizens;
to encourage them to study human behaviour within the scope of
government, economics and commerce.'
    'The objectives of the exam. It is not intended that any one
question will exclusively examine any one particular ability.'
1   Knowledge:
    (a) of political, economic and commercial framework of the UK.
    (b) of basic political, economic and commercial concepts and
         terms.
2   Comprehension and Application:
    (a) ability to understand, interpret and apply information
         presented in writing and in the form of statistics and
         diagrams
    (b) ability to select and use ideas in the presentation of
         logical argument and reasoned comment.
3   Expression:
    the ability to organise and present material, and to express
    it in a clear and appropriate form.
The weighting of abilities is (1) 55 per cent (2) 45 per cent.
    Part 1   30 mins: objective questions on common core, stress
category (1)
30 per cent of marks.
    Part 2   2 hours: 1 compulsory question on core material =
$\frac{1}{2}$ hour; series of 3 essay questions on optional studies - 20 per
cent and 50 per cent of marks respectively. Optional studies
embrace 3 names in title.

APPENDIX 2.3

Metropolitan Regional Examinations Board for the Certificate of
Secondary Education

CEE Economic Studies

The examination will be in two sections
Part One - Written paper   70 per cent
          Time allowed - 2½ hours (Candidates may be allowed
                                    up to half an hour extra)
Part Two - An Applied Economic Study   30 per cent.
    The aim of the syllabus is to familiarise the pupils with the
economic basis of our society and to obtain some understanding of
the economic factors which help to determine the environment in
which they live as producers and consumers.
    A great emphasis is placed on the major developments in the
British economy since 1945 (including changes in industrial
structures and the growth of the public sector) and Britain's position in the EEC. The treatment is to be descriptive and analytical as appropriate.

Part One - Developments in the British Economy since 1945

Part One will be divided into two sections.
Section A - Short answer type questions.
          There will be no choice.   30 marks.
Section B - Essay type questions. Candidates
          will answer 4 out of 7. The
          questions may or may not be structured.   40 marks.
The syllabus for Part One will be as follows:
 1 The Economic Problem
    Allocation of scarce resources to alternative ends; choice;
    scarcity; opportunity cost; the exchange of goods and
    services - banking and money, various economic systems.
 2 The Labour Market
    Population - statistics and trends - education and training -
    mobility; trade unions - collective bargaining and wages.
 3 Management of the Economy
    Aims of government economic policy:
    (a) National Income and Government Finance (detailed analysis
         of National Income Accounts not required); the Budget.
    (b) Full employment and Regional Planning.
    (c) The Balance of Payments.
 4 The Capital and Money Market
    Sources of finance; the value of money - index of retail prices
    and inflation. Banking.

Part Two - Applied Economic Study

The Applied Economic Study should be chosen from either (a) or (b)
below

(a)   One aspect of London's economy such as:
      The City of London
      Your neighbourhood
      Transport
      Tourism
      A growth centre, e.g. Croydon, Thamesmead.
(b)   A study of one major industry.

APPENDIX 2.4

East Anglian Examinations Board

B/18/-/B   Social Studies

(a)   Paper I, of 2 hours duration plus 10 minutes reading time
      40 per cent.
(b)   Paper II, of 1¼ hours duration 30 per cent.
(c)   Three Topics 30 per cent.

Aim of the syllabus

The pupil is to be led to an understanding of the interplay of man
and society towards an insight into the influence of social groups
on his life and on others' lives.

Syllabus

Note
Comparisons with Western and other cultures, past and present,
should be made whenever possible.

Paper I
  1   The Family
      (a)   The nature of the family (extended and nuclear families);
            roles within the family.
      (b)   The changing role of the family during the past 100 years
            and the social reasons for this.
      (c)   The functions of the family within·society, and its re-
            lationship with other social groups and institutions,
            including those of the economic system.
      (d)   Influence of stages of family life on roles and functions.
  2   The Economic System
      (a)   The meaning of work; non-work; leisure.
      (b)   Influence of occupation on leisure.
      (c)   Levels of wages and salaries, and factors which might
            affect them.
      (d)   Size of firm and method of production (noting especially
            mechanisation and automation), and their influence on work
            satisfaction.
  3   Power
      (a)   Why some people and groups in society are more powerful

than others and the effect this has on the distribution of wealth and the persistence of poverty.
(b)   What use the government is to the people; how it decides on the aims of society and gets them carried out; and how it regulates conflict between persons and groups.
(c)   The ways in which governments are chosen and changed in different societies. What part political parties and pressure groups play in this.
4   Socialisation and Education
(a)   How heredity and learning influence a person's life.
(b)   How a person learns from his family, friends, workmates and other people he comes into contact with throughout his life.
(c)   The type and length of formal education received by different sorts of people and why the type and length differ.
(d)   How the mass media and advertising influence people.
5   Social Control and Relief Systems
(a)   The different sorts of social rules, and why people obey them.
(b)   The influence of religious belief and humanist belief on behaviour.
(c)   Why some people do not keep to the rules of society; how this 'deviance' may bring about changes in the rules.
6   Living in Cities
(a)   Evolution of the Modern City.
(b)   Physical effects of living in cities (overcrowding, congestion, pollution).
(c)   How and why people live in different parts of the city according to their income, social class, and minority group.
(d)   How far the community continues to exist in the city, and the influence of both local community and the city on the individual.

Paper II   (themes to be studied in greater depth than those in section A) One or more of these to be chosen for examination in 1974 and 1975.
7   Population
(a)   Size of population
Birth rate - influence of ideology and values of the society; birth control.
Death rate - life expectancy, infantile and adult death rate, medical advances.
Migration - reasons for; restrictions on.
(b)   Class variations in birth rate, death rate, migration.
(c)   Changes in age, sex, and geographical distribution of British population, and social consequences of changes.
(d)   Population, characteristics of different societies (pre-industrial, agrarian, industrial); relation to resources (under-population, over-population, optimum population).
8   Crime
(a)   Types of crime - social and geographical distribution.
(b)   Patterns and trends in crime.

(c)   Causes of crime.
(d)   Treatment of law-breakers;   aims and methods.
(e)   Organisations connected with the prevention of crime and with detection, trial and treatment of law-breakers.

9   Methods
(a)   How information in the study of society is obtained (i.e. by surveys, interviews, observation, comparative studies).
(b)   How information is interpreted (understanding of information gathered).
(c)   Design of research into society (forming and testing hypotheses).

10   Study of a Society outside Great Britain or any Local Community
(a)   World views values and norms of the society/community.
(b)   Social control, e.g. legal, customary, moral and religious rules.
(c)   Relation to physical environment and to other societies/communities.
(d)   Aspects of culture, and their contribution to cohesion.
(e)   Minorities and treatment.
(f)   Changes taking place.

11   Stratification (Social Divisions)
(a)   Primitive societies, age-groups, rank.
(b)   Agrarian societies, the estate system of feudal Europe, caste.
(c)   Industrial societies, class, status groups, power groups.
(d)   Social mobility.
(e)   Cultural, religious, ethnic and national minorities.

12   Women in Society
(a)   Historical changes in status and role of women in Britain.
(b)   Relation of status of women to valuation of their role in different societies (primitive, agrarian, industrial).

Examination

(a)   Paper I   Two questions will be set on each of the six sections of the syllabus. Candidates will attempt five questions, not more than one from each section.

(b)   Paper II   Two questions will be set on each of the six sections of the syllabus. Candidates will attempt two questions, one from each of two of these syllabus items.

(c)   Three topics are to be chosen by each candidate from the list below. Resource guidance should be provided by the teacher, who will also mark the completed work. It is expected that the length of each topic will be about 1,000 words or the equivalent in graphical form.

1   A social survey
2   An historical subject, studied from the viewpoint of social studies, e.g. working-class education in nineteenth century Britain.
3   A report on community work.

4   Interpretation of social statistics in graphical or other
    form.
5   Study of a trade union.
6   Study of an occupation.
7   Study of an industrial or commercial organisation.
8   Study of a social service.
9   Study of the work of a social worker.
10 Study of the work of a social reformer.
11 Study of a world religion.
12 Study of a political ideology.
13 Report on work opportunities in the local area.
14 Report on a social studies topic of the pupil's own choice.

REFERENCES

1   HIRST, P., Liberal Education and the Nature of Knowledge, in
    'Knowledge and the Curriculum', Routledge & Kegan Paul, London,
    1974, pp.30-53.
2   PHENIX, P.H., 'Realms of Meaning', McGraw Hill, Chicago, 1964.
3   WHITE, J.P., 'Towards a Compulsory Curriculum', Routledge &
    Kegan Paul, London, 1973.
4   HIRST, P., op.cit., p.34.
5   Ibid., p.35.
6   Ibid., p.38.
7   PHENIX, P.H., op.cit., p.x.
8   Ibid., p.8.
9   Ibid., pp.10-11.
10 Ibid., p.54.
11 Ibid., p.270.
12 WHITE, J.P., op.cit., pp.5-24.
13 Ibid., p.45.
14 Ibid., pp.50-60.
15 ASSISTANT MASTERS' ASSOCIATION, 'The Teaching of Economics in
    Secondary Schools', Cambridge, 1971, ch.1.
16 SCOTTISH CERTIFICATE OF EDUCATION EXAMINATION BOARD, Scottish
    Certificate of Education, New Syllabus in Economics at the
    Ordinary Grade.
17 DUNNING, K., What Economics Should We Teach?, in 'Economics',
    vol.8, pt 4, Summer 1970, pp.199-206.
18 SZRETER, R., Economics in Secondary Education, in LEE, N. (ed.),
    'Teaching Economics', 1st edn, Economics Association, London,
    1967, p.17.
19 DUNNING, K., op.cit.
20 ROBBINS, L., The Teaching of Economics in School and Universi-
    ties, in 'Economic Journal', 1955, LXV/260.
21 BRUNER, J.S., 'The Process of Education', Vintage, Chicago,
    1963, p.33.
22 See Economics Education Project; Papers 1 and 2: Interpretive
    Manuals for the Advanced and Intermediate Level Tests of Eco-
    nomics Comprehension, Heriot-Watt University, 1970.
23 Unpublished. Tape of lecture held by Institute of Education.
24 HOLLEY, B., The Place of Economics in the Secondary School
    Curriculum, in WHITEHEAD, D. (ed.), 'Curriculum Development in
    Economics', Heinemann, London, 1974, p.89.

25 SUMNER, H., Integration and Sequence in Economics for 8-13
    year-olds, in WHITEHEAD, D. (ed.), op.cit., p.101.
26 SENESH, L., 'New Paths in Social Science Curriculum Design',
    Science Research Associates, Palo Alto, Calif., 1973, pp.18-19.
27 ROBINSON, T.K., Economics for the Less Able Student, in
    WHITEHEAD, D. (ed.), op.cit., p.124.
28 See the D100 Foundation Course: 'Understanding Society'.
29 See the D101 Foundation Course: 'Making Sense of Society', The
    Open University Press, Milton Keynes, 1974.
30 POTTER, D. and SARRE, P. (eds), 'Dimension of Society', The Open
    University Press, Milton Keynes, 1974, p.3.
31 CHRISTIE, D., Economics in the Early Stages of the Secondary
    School, in WHITEHEAD, D. (ed.), op.cit., p.107.
32 MITCHELL, P., in CANNON, C., 'Social Sciences in the Sixth
    Form - an Approach through Integration', Schools Council
    Pamphlet 11, 1973.
33 ROBINSON, T.K., op.cit.
34 RYBA, R., quoted by WHITEHEAD, D., Digest of Discussions, in
    WHITEHEAD, D. (ed.), op.cit., p.228.
35 LAWTON, D., Economics in Relation to Other Subjects within the
    Curriculum, in WHITEHEAD, D., op.cit., p.92.
36 LEE, N., Concealed Values in Economics Teaching, in
    WHITEHEAD, D. (ed.), op.cit., p.62.
37 Joint Committee of the Royal Economic Society, Association of
    University Teachers of Economics, and Economics Association,
    'The Teaching of Economics in Schools', Macmillan, London, 1973,
    paragraph 6.
38 WHITE, J.P., op.cit., pp.101-2.
39 LAWTON, D., op.cit.

ACKNOWLEDGMENTS

Acknowledgments are due to the following for permission to quote
from examination syllabuses: Joint Matriculation Board; East
Midland Regional Examination Board; Metropolitan Regional Examinations Board; East Anglia Examinations Board.

DISCUSSION

Whitehead was criticised for what several speakers considered to be
his cavalier treatment of the arguments put forward by economists
in favour of the teaching of economics to all pupils in secondary
schools. One speaker described Whitehead's account of the economists' case as a caricature. Various speakers then proceeded to
defend the teaching of economics to all pupils. Among the
arguments used were:
  1 Economics has a role to play in consumer education, and all
     pupils are consumers. Moreover, local authorities are committed
     to the cause of consumer education.
  2 A more 'economics literate' electorate will demand a better
     quality of economic argument in political speeches, political
     party propaganda, newspaper articles and television and radio
     commentaries.

3   Economics need not make any unique claims for itself since many
    subjects already taught in schools make no unique contribution
    either.
4   Economics makes a worthwhile contribution to an education for
    all pupils which helps in the understanding of the world in
    which they live: every pupil is entitled to this education.
5   Economics has a part to play in the handing on of our culture
    to the next generation.

All this plainly delighted Whitehead, who subsequently explained
that the particular part of his paper to which exception had been
taken was intended to provoke economists into reassessing, restating
and revitalising their case, which he considered to be in danger of
ossification.

There was criticism of Whitehead for seeming to want to draw too
many conclusions from examination syllabuses. It was suggested to
him that a syllabus generally provides few clues to the nature of
the work it allows teachers and pupils to undertake in the
classroom, and that just as much valuable work is done by many
teachers despite the syllabus as is done by them perhaps because
of it.

There was general disappointment that the paper had little to say
about proposed content, although this is clearly an area of dispute.
Nobody favoured a diluted form of the current typical 'O' level
syllabus. Several speakers were in favour of finding room in a
teaching syllabus for the acquisition of specific useful social
skills of an economic nature, e.g. how to open and operate a bank
account, how to make an income tax return, how to obtain a mortgage.
Others stressed the danger of economics courses becoming a form of
justification for capitalism and an instrument of social control.
Opinion was divided on the desirability of making such courses
subject to public examination, but the majority seemed to favour
this. Nobody considered a value-free course to be remotely feasi-
ble. Some speakers wanted teachers to declare their prejudices
openly; another reminded us that other persuasive forces in society
do not share our concern for objectivity, and a number of speakers
argued the merits of a deliberately contentious approach by teachers
as a means of developing critical faculties in senior pupils.
Nobody seemed keen to exemplify where teaching ends and indoctrination begins. Several speakers objected to occasional hints that we
might consider offering 'different sorts of economics for different
sorts of pupils', hoping to see the establishment of a common
course, even though this would make examining a very difficult task.

The general feeling was that if 'economics for all' is to become
a reality, then it will most likely be as part of an integrated
course, and that herein lies a variety of problems. First, much
economics teaching will be undertaken by non-specialists, and this
will have implications for teacher training, and in-service training
in particular. Second, there will be a great need for teaching
materials and learning materials of all sorts to support teachers.
Third, such courses presuppose a willingness on the part of staff
in schools to co-operate in planning and executing them, and such
co-operation frequently depends as much on personal friendships as
on intellectual conviction, the former being particularly at risk
in times of rapid staff turnover.

Such courses may therefore be unable to sustain a consistency of commitment to them, but, as one speaker pointed out, many of the above arguments apply equally to the teaching of economics as a separate discipline within schools at the present time. One speaker saw a Schools Council project as probably the best means of making progress towards a target of 'economics for all'.

Chapter 3

THE CONTRIBUTION OF ECONOMICS TO THE CURRICULUM OF YOUNGER AND LESS ACADEMIC PUPILS

David Christie

INTRODUCTION

This paper begins by briefly examining contributions capable of being made by economics to the curriculum of younger and less academic pupils. It then considers the central role of the teacher in determining the format of the economics education to be adopted to meet the needs of these pupils.

ECONOMICS AND EDUCATION - SOME PRELIMINARIES

The first task which concerns us is to discover the contribution of economics education to the all-round development of younger and less academic pupils. As a starting point we should distinguish between the needs of younger pupils on the one hand and those of less academic pupils on the other. These terms are, of course, relative: all that can be done is to provide working definitions which will act as guide-posts to the territories in which we are interested. By 'younger' pupils is meant those in the common course years. In Scotland, these years are SI/SII (age group of pupils 12-14). 'Less academic' is a more problematic term, which, for the purpose of this paper, is taken to cover those pupils who have left the common course but who are not pursuing courses leading to certificate examinations. (This is in many ways an unsatisfactory definition and it should be noted that there is room for a great deal of research into the meaning of 'less academic' in relation to economics education. It is earnestly to be hoped that the seminar, of which this paper is a part, will provide guidelines for such research.)

We must bear in mind that the needs of a bright 12-year-old from a supportive background are likely to be different from those of a less academic 16-year-old from a deprived background. One pupil is starting off his secondary education with high hopes of achieving the conventional successes to be expected of someone of his endowments and background. The other is leaving an education system which has not yet learned to cope successfully with his needs and those of his peers. Any economics education that these individuals encounter must reflect their different needs. This must seem

68

painfully obvious to most people concerned with schools, but it is
included to remind enthusiasts for widespread economics education
(including the present writer) that the actual effects on individuals of following economics courses must depend on a wide range of
variables, including pupils' abilities, social background, class
size, teachers' qualifications and motivations, school type, number
of periods per week, and materials available. These actual effects
may not quite match the possible effects hoped for by those making
claims for the inclusion of the subject in the curriculum.

It is certainly possible to produce a list of desirable outcomes
on individuals of education - e.g. literacy, numeracy, oral and
aural abilities, ability to work alone and harmoniously in groups,
initiative, sensitivity, and good citizenship - and also to indicate
how the study of economics is capable of assisting younger and less
academic pupils to acquire more of them. There is no doubt that
many pupils following well constructed economics courses, organised
by highly motivated and skilled teachers will acquire more of many
or all of the desiderata listed. The snag is that the same list of
achievements could be drawn up by every subject specialist from the
artist to the zoologist, and given the same conditions, similar
results would emerge.

I am not prepared to argue that some years of study of economics
at any stage will do more for an individual than some years of study
of English literature or a course in moral education or car maintenance, even although I take it for granted that economics education
has much to contribute to the curriculum in general and the education of many individuals in particular, and that there is increasing agreement on this. Ultimately, it is a matter for curriculum
decision-takers to decide what to include and it remains an open
question whether, in fact, it is strong claims for a particular
subject that result in change in the curriculum, or if more subtle
influences are at work.

The setting of a list of the educational needs of 'younger' and
'less academic' pupils is an awesome task which has been undertaken,
consciously and unconsciously, by a vast army of people including
teachers, headmasters, ministers of education, planners, philosophers and taxpayers. The resulting curriculum reflects this list -
explicit or implicit - and it is within this given framework that
individual teachers have to operate, albeit with some degree of
freedom.

A major theme of this paper is that the teacher of economics has
a central role to play in marrying up his perceptions of the needs
of the younger and less academic pupils, which the system sends to
his class, with an appropriate form of economics education. It is
in these areas that most opportunity exists for teacher initiative
in the development of the curriculum, since there are no public
syllabuses and examinations which might largely direct his efforts
due to the constraints they impose.

SOME THOUGHTS ON CURRICULUM DEVELOPMENT

In the late 1960s and in the 1970s there has been a great drive for
curriculum development in the United Kingdom through such agencies

as the Schools Council in England and Wales, the Consultative
Committee on the Curriculum in Scotland, HMI's, Colleges of Education, local authority advisers, teachers' centres and examination
boards. To a great extent these have been the pace-makers, and although a number of teachers have been much involved in the development work, there is evidence to suggest that the vast majority of
classroom teachers have been cast in the role of followers rather
than leaders. The present economic climate calls into question the
amount of spearheading that can be expected of the agencies listed
above, and it seems likely that much more curriculum innovation -
including economics for younger and less academic pupils - will have
to come from individual classroom teachers than in recent years.
Clearly the agencies listed above will retain a vitally important
role in the process and the change is likely to be one of emphasis
rather than of principle. However, it is as well to remember that
curriculum development can, and does, take place without the need
for expensive and much-publicised projects, and that there are clear
advantages in active teacher involvement in very small scale developments.

All curriculum development projects have to make some assumptions
about conditions in schools upon which to base their approach.
Stated and hidden assumptions are made about all sorts of factors,
e.g. the number of periods a week to be devoted to the project, and
the availability of equipment. A major difficulty is that if assumptions are made about minimum provisions of staff, time and
equipment in the schools which are to use the materials developed,
then the 'better endowed' schools may be faced with insufficiently
developed materials; similarly, over-generous assumptions about
provision can lead to the production of too rich a diet for some
schools. In one economics project it was assumed that each class
would have two periods per week devoted to the course, and that the
teacher had access to a blackboard, slide projector, overhead projector, tape recorder and kit of objects to be used in building up
models of selected aspects of the economy. However, in one school
which used the materials, only one 30-minute period per week was
allocated. In another, the teacher was peripatetic and did not use
the kit on the grounds that it was too inconvenient to carry it
around. In a third school, there were fully equipped close circuit
television facilities which could have been used but which were not,
in fact, exploited by the project. In another project - on integrated science - key assumptions related to the close co-operation
of members of staff and the availability of a sizeable slice of a
technician's time. Tales were told of colleagues who did not talk
to each other and of the inability of the technicians to give adequate time to the project because of other work which seemed at
least as important. In a third project, some years were spent by
the development team in designing tasks which required the use of
specialised stationery. The increased costs of paper, combined with
the current financial stringency, have contributed to thwarting at
least some of the developers' intentions.

There are many other examples which could be cited of discrepancies between the assumptions of projects and the realities of the
school situation. These points are not being made to attack the
'agency led' curriculum development movement - which has many fine

achievements to its credit - but rather to provide encouragement to those who would, or who will have to, launch their own piece of development within their own local conditions. The experience of some large-scale projects, combined with the fact that every economics department is different from all the others and that every class is different from all the others, leads to the conclusion that there is a very great deal to be said for letting the conditions on the ground determine what will happen in respect of economics education for the younger and less academic pupil. In any case teachers are not cut off from the undoubted expertise which lies with agencies listed above and these have a responsibility to support the individual classroom teacher in his efforts to make the most of the situation in which he operates. It may be the case that more initiative will have to come from individual teachers who can call on the specialised skills to be found in those groups which formerly took the lead. The result could be a truly collaborative effort involving teachers, curriculum developers and evaluators, and also educational researchers. (1) It must be admitted that all this places a burden on the classroom teacher and that it requires him to be well motivated and highly skilled in a number of areas including the identification of his pupils' needs and the organisation of resources to meet these needs. (2)

Having implied that it is largely a matter for the teacher to judge the needs, abilities and interests of his class, and to judge the extent of possible co-operation with other teachers, what choices face him in respect of the alternative approaches to economics education?

APPROACHES TO THE TEACHING* OF ECONOMICS TO YOUNGER AND LESS ACADEMIC PUPILS

There are a number of possible approaches to the teaching of economics to younger and less academic pupils. Considerable attention has been focused on the format that economics education should take at these stages - 'single' subject, or a more 'plural' approach such as multi-disciplinary, inter-disciplinary, co-ordinated or integrated social science (or studies). Major curriculum development projects have reflected both the 'single subject' approach (e.g. the Scottish Central Committee on Social Subjects SI and SII project in Scotland) and a 'plural' approach (e.g. the Schools Council Project - History, Geography and Social Studies 8-13). (3) Care has to be exercised, however, when examining the 'single subject versus the rest' debate to obtain a clear view of what is meant by 'economics'. There is not much doubt that for many people inside the debate, the term 'economics' conjures up a vision of the largely positive neo-classical model which dominated (and still does) economics teaching in the upper reaches of the secondary school and almost all of higher education in the 1960s and early 1970s. In spite of its success, this model has been under sustained attack

---

* 'Teaching' is shorthand for 'the form in which economics is included in the curriculum and the teaching and learning strategies employed'.

both from within and without the economics profession. (4) However, it has to be pointed out that this is only one model of economics, and it is not necessarily proposed by anyone as being suitable for the curriculum of younger and less academic pupils. If a much broader view of economics is taken, then some proposals for a 'plural' approach could look narrower than proposals for a single subject approach. It's a game of words, and for that reason it is necessary to look at the content of the packet rather than its label. For the purposes of this paper, the word 'economics' is to be taken to include any attempt to describe, analyse, or explain economic phenomena, relations between them, changes in them and consequences of these changes. This very broad view seems appropriate given the nature of the pupils under discussion. It means that there is no embargo on historical or geographical perspectives, that individual differences may be discussed (i.e. psychological questions may be dealt with), that class differences or power structures may enter the arena of debate (i.e.sociological and political aspects may be dealt with). In any case, there is a fundamental sense in which all knowledge is unified and it is disturbing to contemplate a curriculum for these pupils which erects artificial divisions between what are merely different aspects of enquiry into human life and behaviour. Additionally, it can be argued that the question of integration or inter-relatedness with other subjects is a matter best settled by the local conditions within particular schools. One possible result of such an approach is that there may be thrown up a number of very interesting and unexpected possibilities, which would never have been the subject of a major curriculum development project. One example which can be cited is an experiment with a non-certificate class in Scotland which involved very close co-operation between teachers of economics, business studies and art in the production for sale of leather goods. (5) This serves to remind us that although it seems natural for economics to combine with other social subjects, it is perfectly possible for combinations with a whole range of other subjects to take place. Indeed, for less academic pupils, there may be a strong case for combining economics with vocational subjects, or in a more general approach to life in industrial society.

Fortunately, one of the advantages of the open-ended nature of economics as described above is that it permits of a variety of approaches, and the subject matter can be dealt with at various levels of sophistication. Economics will always be concerned with matters such as the allocation of resources, the behaviour of prices, employment, output, standard of living, externalities and the provision of public goods. This involves the student of these matters in a number of activities - the collection of facts (e.g. what is the distribution of wealth in the UK? how many people get on a number 11 bus at 9.00 a.m., 11.00 a.m., 1.00 p.m. and 5.00 p.m.?), the formulation of explanations of economic phenomena (e.g. why does the demand for money vary? why does the price of apples fall in late summer?), the testing of hypotheses (e.g. that an increase in the subsidy on labour has little effect on the level of regional unemployment; that bus fares are too low if there are queues for buses at 5.00 p.m.). In addition, the student must constantly be on guard against a failure to identify his own value judgments or

to make explicit those hidden assumptions which would not stand up
to any scientific scrutiny.

Within this wide canvas there are many possible approaches from
which the professional teacher will select the most appropriate for
his younger or less academic class. Some of these approaches are
discussed briefly below. Each has strengths and weaknesses and in
the absence of a clear statement of needs no attempt is made to
match approaches with classes of particular ages or abilities. For
some classes, an appropriate approach might lay particular emphasis
on the structure and institutions of the UK economy, with particular
reference to how they might be experienced by the pupils in their
particular environment. One strength of this factual descriptive
approach is that it is likely to inform pupils about their environment, but it may be criticised on the grounds that it fails to develop higher intellectual skills, because most of the time is spent
pursuing its chief aim of providing an information network. An
oft-heard criticism is that this approach is likely to be boring.
In fact, this criticism may be true of any approach, and care has
to be taken to distinguish between unjustified criticisms of approaches and justifiable attacks on unimaginative syllabuses, im-
poverished teaching materials and plain bad teaching.

An alternative approach is to lay stress on the 'concepts' of
economics. The so-called conceptual approach purports to lay bare
the structure of the subject and so provide the pupil with a toolkit
to examine the real world. This approach, adopted by the Scottish
Curriculum Project, has had some success with both younger and less
academic pupils. It tends to place a fair amount of reliance on the
analysis of suitably structured hypothetical situations, and for
that reason it is open to the criticism that it may fail to take
much notice of the actualities of life in a complex economy.

A third alternative is to lay stress on 'current issues and
problem-solving'. This approach involves selecting a number of key
issues and contemporary events and subjecting them to some form of
analysis or scrutiny. One merit of this approach is its seeming
attractiveness in terms of topicality and 'social relevance', but
criticisms may be levelled against it on the grounds that a superficial view may be taken and that at the end of the course the pupil
may not have built up any significant framework to use in future
analysis.

A fourth alternative might be to admit that we live in a mixed
economy and to examine the manner in which some carefully selected
goods and services become available for our use. Comparisons could
be made of the supply and demand forces at work in relation to, say,
pencils and education, roads and cars, chocolate and milk. This approach is capable of being flexible in that some classes may take a
more descriptive line while others may lay greater stress on a more
analytical approach of the market and planning forces at work,
possibly some paying attention to a wide range of related political
and even sociological considerations. Some international comparisons can be made.

There are doubtless many other approaches which can be taken.
They may validly be regarded as 'economics' if they contain aspects
of the characteristics listed above. Other chapters in this book
provide detailed syllabuses which might be followed and there is now

a much wider repertoire of methods and strategies available to the teacher of economics. (6) However, the main problem lies in the selecting of an appropriate approach for the class under consideration, and this remains an area in which the teacher has to deploy his professional skills in order to develop the most suitable curriculum for his own pupils.

CONCLUSION

As far as most subjects are concerned, there are serious difficulties in justifying their inclusion in the curriculum, if this justification is to be based on scientific (including empirical) evidence. Many 'justifications' are, in fact, rationalised prejudice, sometimes passed off as 'common sense'. It seems to be 'common sense' that pupils should leave school knowing something worthwhile about the way in which the economy operates, and being able to think (albeit imperfectly) about some of the economic problems which beset us all. It would be difficult to produce incontrovertible evidence that existing economics courses achieve these ends and as yet many of the claims made for the subject cannot be sustained. However, such lack of evidence does not necessarily invalidate support for the subject. Ultimately, it may boil down to the fact that a group of professionals honestly hold the belief that economics education is a worthwhile addition to the curriculum of the young and less academic pupil, and, on that basis, they press for the implementation of suitable courses.

REFERENCES

1   A similar point, expressed from a different standpoint, is made by A.Morrison in his chapter in 'Frontiers of Classroom Research', ed. G.Chanan, NFER, 1975.
2   Classroom Curriculum Development in Economics by Brian Atkinson in 'Economics', Winter 1974, gives a useful survey of literature which will prove helpful to the teacher.
3   These projects are well documented. See chapters 6 and 7 in this book and 'Teaching Economics' (ed. N.Lee, Economics Association, London, 1967) and 'Curriculum Development in Economics' (ed. D.Whitehead, Heinemann, London, 1974). Detailed reports are issued through the Scottish Centre for Social Subjects at Jordanhill College of Education, Glasgow, and through the Schools Council.
4   The attacks are well known - e.g. see the articles by G.D.N.Worswick and E.H.Phelps-Brown in 'Economic Journal' for March 1972. One attempt at defence is Sir David MacDougall's In Praise of Economics in 'Economic Journal' for December 1974.
5   See the short article by J.Bisset in the 1976 Scottish Branch 'Bulletin' of the Economics Association.
6   'Teaching Economics', ed. N.Lee, part 4, provides a useful survey of these.

DISCUSSION

There was no discussion of this paper because Mr Christie was unable to be present at the seminar.

Chapter 4

EXTENDING ECONOMICS EDUCATION IN SECONDARY SCHOOLS, AND THE POLITICS OF THE CURRICULUM

Angus Taylor

The premise that provides the starting point for this paper is that economics education can and should be a part of the curriculum followed by all young people for some part of their secondary, and perhaps primary or middle school, education. The main purpose of the paper is to discuss the implementing of the extension of economics education in the context of the changing structure of the secondary school curriculum, and the changing style of secondary school management. It is addressed to teachers of economics, be they heads of large departments or one man departments, or be they simply assistant teachers of economics. In a state of change, they have power, and are in a position to use the politics of curriculum management to achieve an aim which, I argue, is in the best interests of the community and its young people.

The main aim of economics education in secondary schools has been, and probably still is, the initiation of relatively able, distinctly mature students into what Brian Holley (1) has called 'a sort of society' of economists. Many teachers will have seen a group of 'A' level economists thrive among their sixth form peers on the exclusiveness the mystery of their subject provides. Extension of the subject within the curriculum has included forays into year four, among those dropping Latin in year three, and into sixth form general studies.

Economics will continue to contribute to the curriculum in this way, but it has a much broader contribution to make as well. This contribution results from seeing the curriculum, with Denis Lawton, (2) as 'a selection from the culture of a society'. In making the selection, Lawton argues, 'economics and the other social sciences score very highly in a list of priorities derived from a situational analysis: all adults are involved in a vast number of activities which are social, political or economic'. All students should have the opportunity of acquiring the basic general principles necessary for elementary economic and social understanding.

Two further preliminary points need to be made. The first is that I am not necessarily arguing that economics as a discrete subject should increase its hold on the curriculum. In his stimulating article (3) on the place of economics in the curriculum, Brian Holley seems to me to be missing the point when he argues that

any attempt to bring about a substantial increase in the number of
pupils studying economics, 'qua economics', will and should fail.
He argues that schools should be less concerned with sanctified
knowledge, more with abilities and skills. But economics has no
unique skills and abilities and so should not survive as a separate
school subject. However, I would argue that there are substantive
generalisations belonging to economics (4,5,6) which are a vital
part of any selection from our culture. It is not important that
they may be accommodated in the curriculum under a different
'title', for that is all that it is. Pupils introduced to these
generalisations will be studying the essence of economics, although
not necessarily the range of the subject, which would give them
access to the exclusive society of economists. As Hazel Sumner
points out, we now feel far less that our subject will be mutilated
if taught in company with other social disciplines. (7) The subject
matter rather than the subject title is what concerns us.

Second, a point about the changing nature of schools implicit
throughout this paper which is worthy of stress; I am thinking
particularly in terms of mixed ability groups in comprehensive
schools pursuing a common curriculum, at least until the age of
fourteen. The substantive generalisations to be appreciated are to
be the same for all. No longer will we have courses for horses.
What must differ is the degree of difficulty of the learning materials used.

I must now turn to curriculum structure, curriculum change, and
the secondary school's management of change. For the purposes of
this paper, I shall consider an 11-18 secondary school, taking the
full ability range. Much of what is said can be transferred to
schools taking in a different age and/or ability range. The curriculum can be seen to have both a vertical and a horizontal dimension. The vertical dimension is the age range, the horizontal
dimension is sub-divided into the subject, or curriculum area, dimension, and the ability range. Thus economics in the vertical
curriculum refers to how the subject matter of economics is presented to young people at different stages in their development. In the
horizontal dimension, we see how economics is accommodated in the
curriculum, and across what spread of the ability distribution. The
reorganisation of secondary education has given a dynamic by way of
curriculum change that was frequently missing before. It is not for
this paper to judge whether change is good or bad; the important
point is that a dynamic curriculum situation, where schools are
asking themselves questions about what should be taught, in what
combination, to whom, and in what groups, provides great opportunities for economics teachers wishing to see economics more broadly
established in the curriculum.

In the English education system, it is inevitable that the
management of curriculum change will vary greatly from school to
school. The involvement of the local education authority, through
its advisory services, also varies, as do other extraneous influences including curriculum development projects. We can assume here
no outside influence, other than contact with other local economics
teachers, and a management structure which is increasingly demo-
cratic in nature. Thus we can imagine a headmaster delegating many
responsibilities, but with explicit views of his own, and a decisive

influence in the final decision;   a deputy head responsible for curriculum and its implementation through the timetable;   heads of department, perhaps grouped into a faculty structure;   and a head of economics who is at least a member of the heads of department meeting, and is represented at heads of faculty meetings.   Curriculum planning is at two levels;   the broad plan looking forward over several years, perhaps emanating from a staff conference;   and yearly planning, looking, say, nine months ahead to the making of the timetable for the following school year.

The general task of the head of economics who recognises this broader contribution for his subject to the secondary curriculum is to develop among colleagues generally a sympathy for his aims, and to avoid any feeling that a subject for subject challenge is taking place.   This takes time, and yet opportunities must not be missed, for those who have been involved with curriculum changes will confirm that often a new position is produced which in turn ossifies.   A note on the subject to the head, deputies and heads of departments can usefully place one's views and potential plans in a clear context so that rumour emanating from informal discussion can be checked.   Informal discussion should aim to develop friends, to reassure those who feel threatened by suggestions of a take-over bid, and to soften the opposition of traditionalists.   This is an informative exercise, and the academic respectability of the substantive generalisations needs establishing.   My experience is that scepticism does not prevent an interest being shown in some of the ideas and material of economics that might reasonably be included in the secondary school curriculum.   All of this needs to be achieved without one's zeal placing one in the role of the staffroom bore.

In placing economics in the context of a broad plan to be implemented over, say, three years, the head of economics needs to take a realistic view of the vertical curriculum, and current trends in curriculum change.   In summarising trends, the vertical curriculum tends to break down into three areas - years 1-3, years 4 and 5, and years 6 and 7.   In years 1-3, the middle school influence has been increasingly strong, this being seen as a critical basis for five years of schooling without being as dominated as in the past grammar school curriculum by 16+ examination demands.   Often school examinations are postponed until 13+. (8) Teaching groups are mixed ability, a common curriculum is followed by all boys and girls, and this is organised in large curriculum areas - science, craft, humanities and so on.   It is in integrated humanities, social studies, and environmental studies courses that economics must find its curricular home in these years.   By year 3 the influence of examination-directed option schemes is felt in the desire of departments to clarify subject areas, to prepare students for the choice to come, and for diagnosis.   This is the move from pre-disciplinary to disciplinary organisation suggested by Denis Lawton. (9) Life becomes less comfortable for economics, but the changes provide opportunities, albeit divisive.   The introduction of a second language, within the capacity chiefly of only the most able, has a disruptive effect on the common curriculum, leaving the curriculum planner to find time for the second language and a viable course of study for those not taking the second language.   As history and

geography find their separate time in year 3, so can the social
sciences blocked against a second language, with those taking the
second language getting a reduced social science provision. I have
experience of just such a course in which we identify the subjects
economics, sociology and politics, and cover a wide area of material
within the full ability range. (10)

There is not a comfortable home for economics in years 4 and 5 in
the present curriculum climate. An ideal would see accommodation in
a common core curriculum, assessed at GCE and CSE Mode 3 as part of
a multi-disciplinary approach, with economics also available as an
elective for those wishing to take it for vocational or pre-advanced
course reasons. In practice, the subject occurs as an 'O' level
option, a CSE option, or as part of a non-examination provision for
those we conveniently refer to as ROSLA children. This accommodation is more in line with preparing young people for membership
of the economists' club rather than providing 'a selection of those
elements from our culture which are so important that their transmission cannot be left to chance'. (11)

All the teacher of economics can do is to recognise that extending the availability of his subject within the options procedure is
a limited exercise and hope for substantial structural change in
years 4 and 5 in the near future, perhaps as part of the introduction of a common system of examination at 16+. The more an
options pattern can be made to recognise the need for a balanced
curriculum with at least some study of man's society to a reasonably
advanced and mature level, the greater the opportunity for economics
education. And the more accepted economics education is in years
1-3, the easier progress will be in years 4 and 5. Support from a
curriculum project directed at the full range of ability 14-16 would
be a considerable encouragement to teachers.

Since this paper was first written three developments have
provided fresh hope for economics education in years 4 and 5. On
1 January 1976 the Economics Association's curriculum project on
economics for 14-16-year-olds got under way under the direction of
Brian Holley at Hull University. By the time stage two is reached,
a situation of change may well have been reached in the whole curriculum for 14-16-year-olds. This brings me to the other two developments. While economics was not subject to feasibility tests
leading to the Schools Council report on a Common System of Examining at 16+, a decision in favour of the latter in May 1976 could
result in a substantial review of curriculum and constituent syllabuses for two-year courses leading to assessment at 16+. Finally we
have Schools Council Working Paper 53 on 'The Whole Curriculum
13-16'. (12) This is not prescriptive, but offers guidelines to
schools reviewing the curricular experiences they offer to senior
secondary school pupils. If schools accept the working paper's
advice and establish broad aims within which selections for the
whole curriculum take place, a more comfortable home for economics
may be found, in the context, for example, of political and social
education.

The sixth form curriculum is in a state of change as a wide
ability range comes into the sixth form, is in a state of uncertain-
ty as various curriculum and examination proposals are being considered, (13) and is in a state of untidiness as developments con-

tinue piecemeal in the meantime. The teacher of economics needs to keep himself well briefed of these developments, and perhaps needs to guard against the ease with which he can develop pleasant 'A', 'O' and Certificate of Extended Education courses (not to mention general studies) in the sixth, so diverting energy and resources from important commitments in the lower school.

Let us now look at a course of action for a head of an economics department with his subject established within the traditional examination-oriented pattern; relationships with other departments happily developed; and a broad commitment to economics education accepted by senior management. How can he involve himself in curriculum management in years 1 and 2 so as to establish a foundation for economics education?

If individual subject areas have yet to group into integrated or associated courses, then the economist will be among those pressing for this form of curriculum organisation, approaching the head and the curricular deputy, and raising the matter at heads of department meetings. Most important of all are his relationships with related but numerically stronger departments, especially history and geography, and probably religious education and English. Humanities is generally the first area of the curriculum to integrate, and even in schools where integration has made little impact, integrated humanities schemes operate.

The next stage is for the economist to be involved in consultations drawing up the syllabus. He must make decisions about what concepts and generalisations he judges appropriate to this stage of secondary education; how including this material in the integrated courses relates to other associated subjects now, and continued economics education later; the degree of difficulty appropriate to the age group, the full ability range of children, and colleagues who are not trained as economists but may in some course organisations be called upon to cover the economics material. The professional judgment asked of the economics teacher will almost certainly be beyond that anticipated in his professional training. He must call upon his training in his subject, his existing experience of children and their education, and his growing experience of curriculum and syllabus development.

Having spelt out what he wants taught, and related this to the rest of the syllabus, the teacher of economics must now make his contribution to the teaching situation. Clearly his own personal teaching can achieve much, but it is unlikely that he can do all the teaching, and it must be remembered that besides having the full ability range, one of the main arguments for integration in the early years of secondary education is that it keeps the learning group for longer with one teacher.

Teacher resources - geographers, historians, English teachers, and some with less specific backgrounds - must be prepared and helped by what amounts to school-based in-service training. Background reading needs to be ordered, and I have found that brief teaching notes prepared for colleagues are very much welcomed. Ideally, planning meetings should be timetabled, and working lunches permit informal discussion. Economics teachers who shudder at letting foreigners peep into their exclusive club should remember the other subjects they may once have been called upon to teach.

Team teaching may well permit the economist to meet every group to lend his expertise to discussion, but I have real doubts about the effectiveness of the lead lesson to assembled masses. We advise colleagues not to lecture at class-size mixed ability groups; why does this become acceptable when the group is multiplied four- or ten-fold?

Finally there is the production of learning resources. Mixed ability grouping demands a wide stock of resources whatever the subject. The teacher of economics is not helped by the fact that more established subjects have made uneven and inadequate progress here. Little is published, and the burden falls on the school in general and subject teachers in particular. It is difficult and time consuming enough to produce adequate resources at one, say middle, range of ability. To cater both for the very able who at eleven can and therefore ought to be given the opportunity of grasping more complex examples and formulations of generalisations, and also for the well below average, places a great demand on every teacher. Resources must be built up and developed, and ideas and materials shared between schools. Eventually teachers' centres, the Economics Association, curricular projects (e.g. History, Geography, Social Studies 8-13) must help to produce material and share ideas with economics teachers. In the meantime, the economics teacher must bear the main burden of producing economics learning materials, seeking the advice of colleagues on, for example, adjustments necessary to make generalisations accessible to the least able.

The approach to extending economics in the later years of secondary education is bound to differ in some ways, but in working for this acceptance of the philosophy, in syllabus construction, the in-service training of colleagues, and preparation of materials, it is the same. I have said nothing of assessment and shall limit myself to the comment that if some assessment procedure is included from the very beginning in the vertical curriculum, we shall be testing the viability of our assumptions on the accessibility of economic understanding, the realism of the syllabus, the degree of preparation of staff, and the quality of our learning resources. We are bound to learn a good deal as a result, and so improve arrangements over time.

In conclusion, let me say that the first practical problem in extending economics education in schools is in overcoming the economics teacher's academic love of his subject. Because so many of us concentrate our teaching in the upper years to more able young people we are more than most able to enjoy the core concepts and high level debates of our subject. I would be the last to want to take away this source of job satisfaction, but, as teachers, our responsibilities must be very much wider. This paper has sought to show how this could become a reality.

REFERENCES

1   HOLLEY, B.J., The Place of Economics in the Secondary School Curriculum, p.88 in WHITEHEAD, D. (ed.), 'Curriculum Development in Economics', Heinemann, London, 1974.

2   LAWTON, D., Economics in Relation to Other Subjects within the

Curriculum, p.85 in LEE, N. (ed.), 'Teaching Economics', 2nd
edn, Heinemann, London, 1975.
3   HOLLEY, B.J., op.cit., p.85.
4   WOMACK, G.J., 'Discovering the Structure of Social Studies',
Benziger Bros, Beverly Hills, Calif.
5   DUNNING, K., To Know Economics, 'Economics', vol.9, pt 4, 1969,
40.
6   LUMSDEN, K.G. and ATTIYEH, R.E., The Core of Basic Economics,
'Economics', vol.9, pt 1, 1969, 37.
7   SUMNER, H., Economics in the Context of Social Studies (8-13 Age
Range), in LEE, N. (ed.), 'Teaching Economics', 2nd edn,
Heinemann, London, 1975.
8   See 'Education in the Middle Years', Schools Council Working
Paper 42, Evans/Methuen, London, 1972.
9   LAWTON, D., op.cit., pp.90-1.
10 'Social Studies 8-13', Lawton, Campbell and Burkett, Schools
Council Working Paper 39, Evans/Methuen, London, 1971.
11 LAWTON, D., op.cit., p.85.
12 'The Whole Curriculum 13-16', Schools Council Working Paper 53,
Evans/Methuen, London, 1975.
13 See Schools Council Working Papers 45,46,47, Evans/Methuen,
London, 1973.

DISCUSSION

Taylor made a series of interesting observations in introducing his
paper. Describing a school as 'comprehensive' gave little clue to
the nature of its curriculum. In some schools, curriculum changes
brought about by the transition from grammar school to comprehensive
school were imperceptible. In others, curriculum change had been
pervasive. In some schools, curriculum change was regarded as a
dynamic and permanent process: in others, it represented an ad hoc
response to a particular situation and, once carried out, could be
left to ossify.
    Again, the willingness of staff to participate in curriculum de-
velopment varied enormously, and yet if development was not to fall
into the hands of a self-appointed cabal, it was essential that all
members of staff should be prepared to play their part in the
various activities that democratisation of decisions implied. How
many staff appointed as Deputy Head (Curriculum) actually spent
their time on curriculum development? Not many, it seemed. Of
those who did, how many did so alone? Too many, it seemed! A major
form of development had been integration, but this required that
colleagues liked and respected each other and each other's subject
discipline, which he had found to be an infrequent occurrence. For
many new subjects the necessary resources were lacking, e.g. the
introduction of sociology to secondary schools in England. As for
economics in particular, Taylor held out little hope of its emerging
powerfully as a separate discipline in the fourth and fifth year,
nor did he see any strong reason for wishing it to do so. He reiterated his belief in the inevitability of change, and urged economics specialists not to resist this trend, but to welcome it and
to rise to its challenge.

He believed that the Economics Association had a duty to pioneer developments in curriculum materials for use in fourth and fifth year, and also in sixth year general studies, and that any projects should be directed towards all ability groups, and not just the average and the less academic. He was in no way deprecating 'the economics teacher's love of his subject', nor was he deprecating Advanced Level courses in economics, and such inferences about his paper were, in his view, perverse.

He regarded it as inevitable that lower school economics would appear, if at all, as part of a multi-disciplinary course, and that economics material might well be introduced by teachers who were not graduates in economics. He was not averse to this development. Economists did not know everything about teaching economics, and teachers trained in related disciplines could rapidly grasp the key concepts. In-service training would have an important contribution to make in that direction. In middle schools, a specialist economist was not required. Middle schools would be looking to integrate courses if only in order to reduce the number of teachers seen by a pupil in the course of one week, thereby hopefully improving the quality of teacher-pupil relationships. Integrated courses foundered if staff turnover was excessive. One way to reduce turnover was to give applicants for a post an accurate account of the ethos of the particular school prior to appointment.

The discussion group was left in no doubt as to Taylor's keen interest in personnel management, and much of what he had to say met with approval. One teacher was able to assure Taylor that at least one school was adopting the approach his paper outlined. Another teacher admitted that in some schools it was not easy to become part of the curriculum development machine, and another gave a graphic account of how to incur the hostility and resentment of staff who might otherwise, given a different approach, have been sympathetic. There was welcome testimony to the fact that schools were becoming more openly governed and that the maintenance of control by means of the withholding of information was disappearing as a key strategy in many schools. Nevertheless, one speaker was moved to suggest that some curriculum development programmes were little more than Machiavellian machinations dreamed up by illiberal headmasters in order to outflank the liberals and effectively abort the plans of the rank and file.

Attention was directed towards the implications for teacher supply should economics expand at the rate envisaged by Taylor's proposals. It was agreed that a contingency training programme would be necessary, and there were indications that the recent survey by the Economics Association into the supply of teachers of economics was having repercussions at a high level. It was also evident that teachers would need to form panels in order to produce suitable materials. There was support for Taylor's view that geographers and historians could be recruited for lower school work, as long as an economist was available in an advisory capacity.

The session ended with a douche of cold water from one of the non-economists present. What were economists hoping to do? Were they merely seeking status for their subject and, through it, status for themselves? Was this to be a new empire-building campaign? Can't any of them utter the sentiment that at some stage their subject isn't essential? Aren't there already too many subjects offered to secondary pupils by too many teachers?

The heretic was permitted to leave before the others, clutching his copy of Whitehead's paper, but it was realised that there was value in inviting to such a gathering persons who are not privy to our own persuasions and prejudices.

ECONOMICS FOR THE YOUNGER PUPIL

Chapter 5

ECONOMICS IN THE PRIMARY SCHOOL-AN EXPERIMENT WITH STUDENT TEACHERS

J. R. Hough

Within the past decade teaching in primary schools has changed out
of all recognition. Gone are attempts at rigid discipline and the
enforcing of silence, most schools have abandoned set lessons and a
prescribed timetable, and often desks, chairs and interior walls
have also disappeared, in the attempt to adapt education to suit
children aged five to eleven years. Not in all primary schools, of
course: some have scarcely changed their approach to teaching since
the 1930s, but they are a small minority. What many writers have
called the 'revolution' in primary education has left few schools
unaffected. Children are no longer seen as pots to be filled with
as much knowledge as possible in the time available, but as individuals with differing tastes, interests, and abilities. Essentially, childhood should be happy: only when the child is interested,
and is enjoying what he is doing, will he or she work profitably.
Hence, motivation of the pupil is the key role of the teacher. As
far as practicable, the child chooses what to do and when to do it,
subtly influenced by the teacher. The 'Sunday Times Colour Magazine' (1) recorded the scene thus:

> By the end of the day in Marshlands I was beginning to make sense
> of the seemingly unsuppressed noise and the seemingly undirected
> activity. The noise was not the din of undirected exuberance,
> but the purposeful hubbub and chatter of communication. Although
> there were children constantly travelling through the room,
> always children tumbling on the lawn, doing pretend washing-up in
> the Wendy house, painting, building, writing - what is going on
> at every minute of their school day is a constant receiving and
> sorting of impressions, a learning of new words, the expression
> of new ideas. In a word, work.

This revolution in teaching approach has been accompanied by an
equally great change in the primary school curriculum. Only that
subject matter most relevant to the child's own experience, and most
interesting to him, will elicit the maximum motivation. Gone are
40-minute periods labelled 'History' or 'Geography'. One child
might be doing a small project on village life, another on towns,
another on transport; hence 'Social Studies' material has a defi-
nite part to play in one guise or another and under one name or
another. Is there any place in all this for economics? The answer

to this question must take us back to the work of Professor Senesh
(2) who noted some years ago that much of what passed for social
science teaching at the primary school level was unsatisfactory,
particularly in that there was usually no attempt to include any
valid economic concepts or fundamental economic ideas.

In the intervening decade there has been little progress. Clarke
(3) noted that economics was 'non-existent at the primary stage' and
his own attempts to implement the work of Senesh and others seemed
to encounter difficulties in dealing with six-seven year olds.
There have been very few attempts by any teachers to experiment with
introducing economic concepts to children of primary school age, although Hazel Sumner (4) discussed some of the general principles
involved. For a discussion of educational theory and the introduction of economics to young children, with suitable references to
Piaget, Bruner and other writers, one still has to go back to the
seminal paper by Lee and Entwistle. (5) It is perhaps some reflection on economists that one of the most interesting attempts by
anyone in this country in recent years at experimenting with introducing economic concepts to primary children was the work done by
two sociologists, Charles and Colinette Margerison: (6) they
reported on an attempt to lead 9-10-year-old children to understand
basic sociological concepts, especially relating to the organisation
of society, but inevitable by-products of the work included division
of labour, barter, money, and value. The focus of their experiment
was on the children learning inductively rather than deductively,
although they were later criticised (7) for implicitly encouraging
convergent rather than divergent thinking (e.g. with thirty-five
people on their desert island, the children decided it was necessary
to elect four members of parliament and a prime minister).

The purpose of the present paper is to report on a limited
'experiment' involving primary school pupils and student teachers of
economics. The work is essentially ad hoc, small-scale, unscien-
tific, and is still continuing, and any conclusions arrived at must
therefore be tentative and open to debate. The justification for
giving this brief outline is the dearth of accounts of similar experiments.

In university and college departments of education there have
been changes in recent years in the types of course offered, in the
way courses are structured, and in teaching methods used. Not the
least of the changes have related to acquisition of school experience by the students. The tendency now is for visits to schools and
practice teaching sessions to be integrated with the remainder of
the students' educational studies and to be spaced over longer
periods of time, in addition to block periods of full-time teaching
practice. Thus the student may be attached to a school for, say, a
half-day each week, may visit a variety of schools, and may be as-
signed to group work, work with individual pupils, or helping with
projects, all intended to be preparatory to full class teaching.

At Loughborough University the Department of Education offers a
series of 'concurrent' degree courses on which students study education alongside their major and minor teaching subjects throughout
the four years of the course. Thus 'Education and Economic Studies'
students study education alongside economics throughout Years 1,2
and 4, Year 3 being devoted to project work in economics and to the

block period of teaching practice. In Years 1 and 2, therefore, a variety of school experience and practice teaching situations are included in the time allocated for 'economics methods' work: these include visits to schools, attachment to one or more local schools, micro-teaching sessions involving the students in giving lecturettes and watching televised play-backs, and, to the horror of some members of the university, the invasion of the university campus by children from a local primary school. In Year 1, therefore, each student spends some time (a total of about six half-days) working with primary children, both in schools and in the university. Whilst few of the students will ever teach in primary schools, our aim is that they should have some, albeit limited, experience of working with young children, first because in their eventual dealings with secondary pupils they should have some awareness of the pupils' earlier school experiences, and second because working with primary children in small groups enables students to concentrate on the essential teaching problems of motivation and of development of simple economic concepts.

Both in the school situations and when the children come in to the university, each student is allocated a small group, varying in size from about three to six children. Each student is given complete freedom to devise suitable material which is then discussed with a tutor before the sessions take place; where we disagree on the suitability or otherwise of what has been prepared, the students are often keen to adhere to their original ideas, possibly in order to avoid doing a second lot of preparation as much as for any other reason. I was unable, for instance, to dissuade one student from embarking on the Theory of Comparative Advantage. The sessions have taken place over the last three academic years, developing in form over that time, and we intend that they should continue in future years. Our local primary schools have been very willing to cooperate, both in allowing us to visit them and in permitting their children to spend half-days at the university, and we are most grateful to them for their assistance.

When our students have visited schools, they have found, as expected, that primary school pupils are generally so stimulated and interested by a visiting 'teacher' that they required very little extra motivation; when the children visited the university, their motivation was even greater, save only that they were sufficiently excited by the visit to the campus that they did not immediately want to settle down to work. The prospect of free orange juice at break-time was a useful extra stimulus.

The approaches adopted by the students varied enormously: obviously it is not possible to describe them all here and it is not easy to generalise about them. Perhaps the majority tend to commence with some straightforward piece of economics lifted directly from a first-year textbook: week 1 tends to see demand curves, lists of prices and the history of money; the ensuing post-mortem often has the students admitting that the children were of above-average IQ (Loughborough is largely a middle-class town and schools do not give us their worst pupils to practise on), highly motivated, with no discipline problems, and yet the sessions did not go too well, with the children's interest clearly tailing off badly.

Week 2 sessions are more likely to start with: 'How much pocket-

money do you have each week?', 'Where do you spend it?', 'What do
you buy with it?', 'Can you buy everything you want?', etc., i.e.
the students very soon learn that they need to delve into the
pupils' own quasi-economic experiences if the sessions are to be
really meaningful. From such beginnings some sessions still fall
flat; some, however, have developed into very meaningful discussions of why a Dinky toy costs more than an ice lolly, why some
of the apples we eat are imported whilst others are home-grown, why
sweets cost less in the large store than in the corner shop and
whether this is worth the extra walk involved, the advantages and
disadvantages of motor-cars (cars seem to arouse greater interest
than any other commercial product), and why Mary will save up for a
large doll but Michael won't. In some such sessions, interest and
motivation are of the highest order, a variety of activities takes
place, and some excellent work is produced. But are the children
learning any economics? At the end of the day, have they really
grasped a single economic concept, let alone, to quote Clarke, (8)
been 'given a new slant on life'?

A variety of teaching methods have been used. Initial questioning and discussion has often elicited a quite excellent response
from the children, at times indicating considerable, if uneven,
economic awareness. Sometimes 10 minutes of discussion is sufficient, on other occasions it was profitably extended for up to
30/40 minutes; the children have been most willing to talk, not
always on the subject, and our students have had to learn to single
out a valuable economic thread from a sometimes jumbled and inco-
herent flow of ideas. Other activities would follow: writing,
drawing, mock dramas and role-playing, making payments to each other
via blank cheque forms and the use of films. We discovered two
excellent films, both aimed at primary children and in cartoon form,
on the essential concepts of the division of labour and the replacement of barter by money. (9)

The students experienced considerable difficulty in developing
economics concepts at the appropriate level for the pupils. These
difficulties seemed to be mainly of two kinds; first, vocabulary:
economists have developed their own esoteric language which our
students are in the process of imbibing. Now they find that for
these sessions they need to discard it and revert not just to everyday speech but to the language level of the children. This is not
an easy problem: try explaining the concept of 'opportunity cost'
appropriately for a 9-year-old who has never studied economics.
Great care had, of course, to be taken to avoid specialised terminology which would have merely mystified the children. Second, in
a number of the situations that arose a basic economic concept was
at issue, and yet often the students could not quite grasp what it
was, nor express it lucidly. (For example, the marginal cost
principle arose in a number of guises in connection with varying
social problems.) This has led to the feeling that in order to be
able to explain cogently economic concepts to children of this age,
the teacher needs to be very well versed in economics. Perhaps, at
the Year 1 stage, our students are not sufficiently well grounded in
the conceptual bases of economics (as opposed to descriptive material). This is a clear possibility, although as yet no more than
that.

Our time with each group of children is short, even though we
know that further follow-up work is sometimes organised by their own
teachers. From the point of view of the children, all we can hope
to do is to try to lead them to begin to think in economic terms.
We have not attempted any formal tests to see whether there has been
any such effect, and it is doubtful if such tests would be valid
after the small number of sessions in which each child participates:
we might simply be measuring their extra motivation. However, the
sessions do seem to indicate that whilst in some respects the
children will readily take to an economic approach to certain
aspects of life, and evidence great interest in this, some at least
of the more abstract economic concepts are extremely difficult, if
not impossible, to convey to them. Whilst we were limited by time,
the problem would also seem to arise from the nature of the subject-
matter. Gagne (10) gives the following example of how a young child
may learn a concept:

> Suppose the concepts 'liquid' and 'solid' are to be taught to a
> young child. It seems likely that the learning situation would
> be something like the following:
> 1. Show the child a glass containing water and a glass contain-
>   ing a rock. Say 'This is a solid' and 'This is a liquid'.
> 2. Using a different container, show the child some powdered
>   substance in a pile in a container and some milk in another
>   container. Say 'This is a solid; this is a liquid'.
> 3. Provide still a third example of solid and liquid, using
>   different materials and containers.
> 4. Show the child a number of examples of liquids and solids
>   which he has not seen before. Ask him to distinguish the
>   liquids and the solids.

Clearly, Piaget's pre-operational stage is being emphasised before
the child passes on to the concrete operational stage. (11) How can
this be done with economics-type material? Christie (12) suggests
bringing into the classroom bits of coal, plastic men, model cars,
and paper money: he may well be right, yet, inevitably, this would
be to use proxies for economic resources, goods, etc., rather than
the real thing. Perhaps at least some economic concepts are incapa-
ble of being demonstrated physically to the satisfaction of children
of this age? Therefore it would seem that, at present, my earlier
question about whether the children have learned any economics has
to have two separate answers: Yes, for certain economic material,
part conceptual, part institutional, and also part social (e.g. What
is a bank, Why do we use money?); No, for certain of the essential
economic concepts (e.g. scarcity). This conclusion is therefore at
variance with the work of Senesh and of Wiggins, (13) both of whom
laid most emphasis on the latter.

From the point of view of the students, they generally found the
sessions the most interesting, enjoyable, and fruitful of all their
Year 1 education course. This bears out the work of Edith Cope (14)
who found that periods of school experience or working with children
were valued by student teachers more highly than any other part of
their training courses. There seems little doubt that we are justified in continuing such sessions in the future but it is likely that
the emphasis will again have to be placed on the opportunity for
students to do some practice teaching sessions rather than on a

systematic experiment into the introduction of economics material to primary school children.

Our tentative conclusions do, however, provide further evidence of the need for such experiments: if there really is a dividing line between economic concepts that primary children can, and cannot, readily assimilate, then it would be both interesting and desirable to establish exactly where the division falls and to investigate the differences, if any, between concepts on opposite sides of the line. This seems to be rather more than a simple distinction between 'concrete' and 'abstract' concepts. Any conclusions reached might have a bearing on the teaching of economic concepts at secondary level. If, alternatively, no such dividing line validly exists, it would be desirable to investigate suitable teaching approaches for those concepts which young children do not seem to assimilate readily.

REFERENCES

1   'The Sunday Times Colour Magazine', 2 September 1973. The school described was Marshlands School, Hailsham, Sussex.
2   For example, SENESH, L., Teaching Economic Concepts in the Primary Grades, in LEE, N. (ed.), 'Teaching Economics', 1st edn, Economics Association, London, 1967.
3   CLARKE, A., The Organic Curriculum, An Experiment in Primary Education, 'Economics', Autumn 1966, and Economics in the Primary School, 'Economics', Autumn 1967.
4   SUMNER, H., Integration and Sequence in Economics for 8-13 year-olds, in WHITEHEAD, D. (ed.), 'Curriculum Development in Economics', Heinemann, London, 1974.
5   LEE, N. and ENTWISTLE, H., Economics Education and Educational Theory, in LEE, N. (ed.), op.cit.
6   MARGERISON, Charles and Colinette, Build your own Society, 'New Society', 8 February 1973.
7   In the correspondence columns of 'New Society', February 1973.
8   CLARKE, A., Economics in the Primary School, op.cit.
9   'Why we use money: The Fisherman who needed a knife', and 'Why People have special jobs: The man who made spinning tops', both hired from Rank Film Library.
10 GAGNE, R.M., The Learning of Concepts, in JAROLIMEK, J. and WALSH, H., 'Readings for Social Studies in Elementary Education', 3rd edn, Macmillan, New York, 1974.
11 See LEE and ENTWISTLE, op.cit.
12 CHRISTIE, D., Economics in the Early Stages of the Secondary School, in WHITEHEAD, D. (ed.), op.cit.
13 WIGGINS, S., Economics in the Curriculum, in MORRISETT, I. and STEVENS, S. (eds), 'Social Sciences in the Schools', Holt, Rinehart & Winston, New York, 1971.
14 COPE, E., School Experience and Student Learning, in LOMAX, D. (ed.), 'The Education of Teachers in Britain', Wiley, New York, 1973.

DISCUSSION

In his introductory remarks, Hough reiterated that his students were
not engaged in a systematic, carefully controlled experiment. The
main aim of allowing first year students to teach economics to small
groups of primary school children was to give them a gentle introduction into teaching in highly favourable circumstances, viz. a
small group of well-behaved, well-motivated children in close proximity to other groups with other students, and with Hough discreetly
available in the background. Hough stated that his main interest at
this stage is still in the impact on his students, which has been
highly beneficial. For the children, coming to the university seems
a bonus in itself and is an experience they obviously enjoy. Some
pupils show real interest in the subject matter, and none, as far as
he could see, are in any way harmed by their experience.

Hough's remarks disarmed any potential criticism. There was a
general welcome for the attempt to explore economic concepts with
primary school pupils, in view of the dearth of such attempts in
this country in the past, but it was felt that it would be unwise
to attempt to draw any conclusions about the possibilities for
teaching economics to such pupils from the efforts of unqualified,
inexperienced student teachers. There was a feeling that Hough
might consider giving more firm direction to the students rather
than seek merely to dissuade them from the more obviously unpromis-
ing lines of approach that some attempt initially.

There was some doubt about Hough's surmise that older primary
children are unable to grasp key economic concepts such as scarcity
and choice and opportunity cost. The general view was that children
have already absorbed a fair amount of economic knowledge and understanding through everyday experiences by the time that they are nine
years old. It may well be that they are able to grasp some concepts
in some contexts but not in others, and some concepts may be much
more readily transferable to different contexts than are some other
concepts. What the pupils lack is the formal language of economists, and what the students lack, it was suggested, is an ability
to abandon economic terminology and to explain key concepts in
simple language. As a result, there is a communication problem
exacerbated by the students' own incomplete grasp of the subject
matter and their lack of experience in dealing with children of
this age.

Nobody wanted to see the project abandoned. Everyone considered
there to be a place for economics in primary schools, almost
certainly not as a separate discipline but as an important contribu-
tor to individual and group projects, nearly all of which have an
economic dimension. It was pointed out that under such titles as
'People Who Help Us' and 'Work', the teaching of a distorted and
misleading form of descriptive economics in primary schools has increased, is increasing and ought to be diminished. Hazel Sumner's
work was unanimously regarded as a step in the right direction.

The main message to Hough was to urge him to video-tape some of
the students' efforts in order to provide valuable material for
analysis, and also to attempt some sort of evaluation, preferably
by means of in-depth post hoc interviews.

As for the students, it was suggested that the most profitable

approach for them might well be to ask themselves 'What sort of
activity/situation can I set up which will elicit a discussion of
this particular concept through a series of questions' instead of
the more usual and, to the inexperienced teacher, the more natural
'How can I explain this to them?'

ECONOMICS IN SI AND SII—THE PILOT SCHEME OF THE SCOTTISH CENTRAL COMMITTEE ON SOCIAL SUBJECTS

John McCafferty

1 INTRODUCTION

The Working Party which developed the course described in this paper was formed in 1971 as one element in a structure devised to under-take a wide ranging enquiry into the aims, content, teaching methods and course organisation of Social Subjects education in the first two years of secondary schooling in Scotland. Its work was one of the many investigations carried out by, and on behalf of, the Scottish Central Committee on Social Subjects, a body set up in 1969 by the Scottish counterpart of the Schools Council, the Consultative Committee on the Curriculum. Since the Central Committee was given responsibility for investigating and reporting upon the teaching of Social Subjects throughout the secondary school, the Economics Pilot Scheme represents no more than a small part of the work undertaken or commissioned by the parent body in the past six years. At the same time, the very fact that such a project was mounted at all represents a very significant advance for the cause of economics education in Scotland, when one considers that its reappearance in the secondary curriculum dates back no further than session 1967-8. (1)
   In describing the nature and conduct of this particular scheme, no attempt is being made to claim that the 'Scottish Project' is breaking entirely new ground, or that the course devised for the purposes of the experiment is the only one which could have been adopted. Even before we embarked on our task there was evidence available from the USA to show that economic concepts could be presented to and absorbed by primary school pupils. (2) Many edu-cators, however, have yet to be convinced about either the possi-bility or the desirability of teaching economics to younger pupils, and any reinforcement of the evidence suggesting that the subject can be taught to pupils in the younger age groups does at least reduce the handicap faced by those wishing to reduce the level of economic illiteracy among school leavers.

2 BACKGROUND CONSIDERATIONS

There are many different views about how (or even if) the economic
dimension of secondary school courses could be enlarged, and there
have been many arguments advanced in favour of both discipline-based
and integrated programmes which could be used to achieve a higher
level of economic literacy. In a paper of this nature it would be
neither possible nor realistic to attempt to argue the pros and cons
of subject-based as opposed to integrated courses; suffice it to
state that the Economics Working Party was asked specifically to
devise one which was subject-based, leaving others to grapple with
the wider issues.

The remit given to the Working Party required it to: (a) prepare an Economics Course for pupils in SI and SII; (b) conduct a
pilot scheme based upon that course; (c) report back on its effectiveness.

The criteria which had to be borne in mind when tackling the
remit were that the study involved should be representative of the
subject, relevant to pupils' needs, and framed in conformity with
accepted learning theory. It also had to be borne in mind that many
of the pupils who would take part in the pilot scheme would receive
no further structured contact with the subject after completing the
experiment, while others might well want to continue their study of
economics into SIII and beyond. Two other factors which would
influence the final product were that the course had to cater for
classes of mixed ability pupils in a comprehensive school situation,
and it had to be based upon a time allocation of two periods per
week.

An essential and representative core of subject matter had
therefore to be devised within a framework of an agreed set of aims
for the teaching of economics. The methods of teaching proposed for
the course were chosen because members accepted that the bulk of the
teaching would have to be conducted in concrete terms relevant to
the experience and learning capacities of the pupils involved. (3)
Above all, the content of the course had to be presented in such a
way as to make pupils aware that we are all economists to the extent
that we all take economic decisions which affect others as well as
ourselves.

3 AIMS AND OBJECTIVES

With these considerations in mind, the Working Party attempted to
identify the framework of educational aims and key ideas around
which the course objectives and content could be constructed. Since
the pilot scheme was to be a new development in the Scottish
context, it was resolved that teachers should be given as much help
as possible in interpreting the views of the Working Party.
Teachers have often criticised previous syllabus guidelines on the
grounds that the vague aims and bare content provided gave less than
clear indications of what the developers wanted to achieve. When
the last SCE Higher Grade Economics syllabus was published in 1966,
for example, there was no mention of the educational aims which the
syllabus content was expected to achieve. (4) The 1973 publication

which introduced the new Ordinary Grade (5) listed three aims,
namely -
(a)   to enable pupils to see economics as a dynamic social science
      of concern to everybody;
(b)   to provide pupils with an understanding of the basic economic
      problems which will increasingly face them;
(c)   to develop in pupils a capacity for economic reasoning and for
      logical expression of economic ideas based on a study of rele-
      vant data.
   A more systemised approach using course objectives based upon a
Bloom-type taxonomy seemed at first to offer an attractive alternative. Although helpful, they were later recognised as being less
than perfect, and attempts were made to prepare course units and
objectives in response to the questions - What must we teach? What
materials and procedures will best help us teach these lessons? How
will we know when we have taught them? (6)
   The Working Party flirted for a time with the idea of using
'Working Objectives', 'Target Objectives' and 'Criterion Objectives'
as an aid to setting out its course structure in terms of pupil-
centred behaviour. (7) Although the method of preparing objectives
had attractions in developing course content and ensuring that working party members thought seriously about standards of achievement
expected at the assessment stage, it tended to underplay the role of
the teacher in encouraging pupils to achieve the desired objectives,
and the format was later discarded on the grounds that the resultant
syllabus might well have appeared more complex than teachers would
have been willing to accept.
   In the end, a set of 'Course Objectives' set out under the
headings of Knowledge, Understanding and Application was devised for
each section of the course, and these were supplemented by more specific objectives related directly to individual teaching units.
Examples of the Course Objectives (taken from the first year
sections of the course) include:
(a) Knowledge
Pupil knows that income is gained from economic activity;
Pupil knows that income is spent in an attempt to satisfy wants;
Pupil knows that spending becomes income;
Pupil knows that saving leads to delayed satisfaction of wants;
etc.
(b) Understanding
Pupil understands the difference between human, natural and man-made
resources;
Pupil understands that the household is a basic decision-taking unit
in relation to demand;
Pupil understands the effect on consumer choice of a break in the
distribution network;
Pupil understands the relationship between production, distribution
and consumption;
etc.
(c) Application
Pupil simulates areas of economic activity by use of concrete items
in 'the kit';
Pupil completes worksheets (involving diagrams and calculations)
using his knowledge and understanding of economics;

Pupil represents different 'channels of distribution' in diagrammatic form;
Given diagrams representing different areas of economic activity, pupil identifies these areas;
etc.
The following examples of unit-based objectives used to supplement the course objectives are taken from the third section of the first year course:
Pupil identifies the producers in his own household.
Pupil identifies the consumers in his own household.
Pupil knows that at any particular time all members of society consume, although all may not necessarily produce.

4   COURSE STRUCTURE AND CONTENT

The method of course construction adopted in order to achieve the objectives which were set involved the use of a spiral curriculum approach. The particular model chosen has already been illustrated in David Christie's paper on Economics in the Early Stages of the Secondary School, (8) showing six broad areas of economic activity, three of which are examined in the first year of the course, and three in the second. In each study area, concrete teaching situations were devised in order to highlight and widen pupils' experience of economic ideas.

The basic problems of choice and scarcity were featured in the opening area of study, 'Production', although the terms were not stressed. Rather the objective to be aimed at in this connection was that each pupil should know 'that the limited income of individuals forces choice upon consumers'. To ensure that the teaching situations were developed from the known to the unknown or unsuspected, the course was introduced from the standpoint of the consumer before diverting attention towards an examination of the productive process. Thus, the first unit was 'consumer-based', but turned the pupils' attention towards the work involved in creating goods for consumption and the resources employed in that work. By the end of the Production Study Area which consists of eleven 'units', the pupils were also expected to know that the various parts of an economic system are inter-dependent, that factors of production can be substitutes for one another, that the income gained from economic activity is used to satisfy wants, that spending in one direction is never achieved without sacrifice in some other direction, and that economics is, in fact, about the allocation of scarce resources between competing demands.

The message being put across in Study Area 2, 'The Distribution of Goods and Services' (generally referred to in the course materials as 'Distribution') was that tertiary industries provide a productive function, enabling consumers to achieve a higher standard of living. The benefits gained by producers and purchasers from the services provided by wholesale, transport, banking, insurance and advertising firms were shown in the same light as the work done by pupils who acted as baby-sitters, or who delivered milk or newspapers, in that a service is provided at a price which both producer and consumer are willing to pay. By a gradual process, pupils were encouraged to think of services as being like any other group of 'economic goods'. The Production Study Area had been designed to generate general acceptance of the idea that the production of economic goods generated income. From this it is only a small step to make pupils accept that the 'production of services' is just as appropriate a phrase as the 'production of goods', and to accept that production is any activity which generates income.

The first two Study Areas having been concerned with two aspects of Production, the third was directed specifically towards 'Consumption'. By the time the pupils returned to this aspect of economic activity they were expected to have a much clearer realisation that our way of life is made possible by the combined efforts of us all in attempting to make the best possible use of our available scarce resources. The work in this Study Area proceeded to examine the nature of choice, the fact that households, firms, local authorities, and national governments were all faced with the same problem of allocating expenditure among competing needs. It also attempted to deepen pupils' awareness of the fact of their dependence upon others for the resources they consume and to draw attention to the fact that wants continue to exist even after dreams of affluence have been realised. If the general aims of the first three Study Areas could be condensed into a single sentence, that sentence might read: The first year cycle of the two year course attempts to make pupils more aware of their dependence upon others for their way of life, and to make them realise that, since they are already taking part in economic activity, their economic decisions have an effect upon the economic system.

The second year cycle was again developed in three broad areas of study, namely 'Specialisation and Location of Industry', 'Money, Trade and Exchange', and 'Income and the Standard of Living'. Since a feature of the spiral curriculum is that pupils should constantly return to familiar ideas and deal with them at an ever-increasing level of complexity so that understanding is reinforced and deepened, further work was undertaken on the theme of economic interdependence in terms of specialisation, location of industry, money and trade, and living standards. Deliberate attempts were made to ensure that knowledge acquired in SI was used as the basis for this reinforcement. By a process of broadening the application of ideas previously introduced, attempts were made in the section on Specialisation and Location to show how an economic system might evolve from a simple level of economic interdependence to one in which individuals, firms, regions, and countries become dependent upon others for both resources and income.

The second Study Area in the SII cycle drew attention to the ways in which money helped overcome some of the more complicated problems of barter, thus making it easier to trade. Increased trade, improved output, greater economic interdependence, and improved living standards were treated as some of the developments which could be seen as having their roots in the work undertaken as pupils progressed along the course spiral up to the end of this Study Area. Some time was also devoted in this section to explaining the meaning and significance of such commonly used terms as visible and invisible trade, trade balances and surpluses, and international trade.

The final section, on Income and Standard of Living, attempted to

bring together much of the learning associated with the previous
Study Areas, as well as dealing specifically with questions relating
to money and real income, income disposal, and living standards.
It contained more macro-economic ideas, themes and problems than the
previous Study Areas, thereby introducing yet another dimension to
the course as a whole.

Thus the Working Party attempted to provide a course which showed
pupils what economics is about, to draw attention to the kind of
problems faced by mankind in attempting to ration out its scarce
resources, to destroy the myth that only adults can cope with economic problems, and to show that the economic problems faced by
mankind in general are in essence the same as those faced by
households and even individuals. Descriptive institutional economics would be out of place in such a course, although many of the
omissions were often forced upon the Working Party by time constraints rather than by desire.

5   TEACHING METHODS AND MATERIALS

The teaching methods envisaged assumed a practical involvement on
the part of the pupils as well as the employment of a variety of
teaching situations and aids. Emphasis was placed upon the need for
a teaching kit of tangible objects which could serve as an economist's tool box, (9) to be used in three distinct ways. The
concrete symbols of the kit could be used -
(a) for teacher demonstration of economic ideas and relationships;
(b) for pupil participation in learning situations; and
(c) for giving substance to some ideas which might otherwise have
     been too abstract for younger pupils to understand.
Thus pupils could see economic models being created with plastic men
representing 'human resources', model trees and sacks or churns containing 'natural resources', and toy cars, furniture or plastic
blocks representing 'man-made resources'. They could gain 'hands-
on' experience of creating economic models for themselves by constructing 'production-flow models' or 'three-dimensional diagrams'
in the course of their learning experiences. They could also appreciate the concept of scarcity far more easily when they came face
to face with it in the act of using the kit. For example, it was
found that there were very real advantages to be gained by storing
the various items of the kit in transparent containers. There can
be no more concrete way of appreciating the concept of scarcity than
by discovering that 'the bag is empty' when wee Jimmy's group move
into the 'market' to lay hands on some human or man-made resources.
Equally, there is no better way to illustrate the use of resources
than to draw attention to the fact that stocks sometimes tend to
diminish as the session progresses.

It was recognised, however, that any teaching aid is only as good
as the teacher makes it. Any new device for attracting attention
can only remain new for a short period of time, and the kit is no
exception. Unless its components are used in different combinations, for different purposes, and in different ways, it will fail
to retain the interest of pupils. If it were to be used to satu-
ration point in the early stages and ignored for the remainder of

the course, it would not serve its intended purpose. If it were to
be restricted to the bare minimum of components, it would be self-
defeating in that the symbols might have to represent so many
different resources or ideas that they would cease to become
concrete symbols and take on the role of abstract three-dimensional
symbols.

The task of creating variety in learning situations was not confined to changing the use made of the kit. For example, in the
eleven units of the 'Production' Study Area alone it was envisaged
that pupils should engage in devising 'recipes' for the production
of goods, role-playing, recording and enacting 'a play', constructing production flow models, demonstrating an understanding of the
nature of economic interdependence, and completing a worksheet involving an appreciation of the interacting nature of production,
income and expenditure. All this was in addition to the bread-and-
butter stuff of question and answer, discussion, and pupil-teacher
interaction. Even 'talk and chalk' was not ruled out as a further
method of providing the variety needed to keep interest and enthusiasm alive.

The teaching materials provided by the Working Party consisted of
Teacher's Notes, Pupil Instruction Sheets and Worksheets. The
general aims (Course Objectives) are listed at the start of each
Teacher's Kit, followed by more detailed teaching notes and objectives relating to the individual lessons or teaching units.
Copies of Pupil Sheets are also included in the Teacher's Kit. The
Teacher's Notes were intended as guides or hints rather than instructions, and teachers were expected to use or discard these notes
if they saw fit, when it came to the piloting of revised course
materials.

6   THE PILOT

The original intention was that the materials be tried out in one
first year class in each of ten schools, thus providing evidence of
the progress and reactions of about 300 pupils covering the course
in two 40-minute periods per week during sessions 1972-3 and 1973-4.
This did not happen.

Three schools asked for permission to try the course with the
whole of their SI intake, but two of them could allocate only one
period per week to the project. Since they were all large comprehensive schools, it was felt that this was an opportunity which
could not be missed, and consequently the original pilot numbers
increased to around 1,200. Another school agreed to co-operate, but
was unable to start until mid-October, and consequently was unable
to complete the SI cycle by June 1973. The schools operating on one
period per week found that their progress through the materials was
less than half the rate of those who had devoted the anticipated
time allocation to the work, while those who worked on two periods
per week had to struggle to reach the end of Study Area 3 by June
1973. Three schools were forced by staff shortages to abandon the
scheme at the end of the SI cycle, and consequently the numbers involved in the pilot when revised SII materials were tried out in
session 1974-5 were much nearer to the original target of 300 than
was expected when piloting began in August 1972.

7   ASSESSMENT

Assessment of the course and its accompanying materials has been
undertaken on the basis of pre- and post-tests for each of the six
Study Areas, together with detailed reports, comments and reactions
from teachers involved. Since the evaluation procedures and results
are dealt with in a separate paper, there is little point in going
into detail here; but the pre-test for each unit consists of a
true/false section, a multiple choice section, and a short answer
section. The results obtained in the pre-tests provide a starting
point for measuring subsequent improvement, for the post-tests contain the same test exercises. The post-tests also contain additional effective assessments which seek to obtain information about
pupil reaction to the course as it develops.

The information received from the assessment process enabled the
Working Party to undertake some revisions to the original course
materials before putting them out on an extended trial during
session 1974-5. Having completed an initial trial run and a pilot
of revised materials, the Central Committee has allowed the Scottish
Centre for Social Subjects to distribute the 'Mark III' version of
the course to schools which are willing to contribute to a further
monitoring process which will add still more information to the
stock already gathered about this experiment. The type of information sought at the monitoring stage concerns the use being made of
the course materials, the units which are found to be most useful,
those which have had to be supplemented, the kind of supplementary
material being used, the adaptations made by class teachers, and so
on. Five schools were using the 'post-pilot' SI materials and completing monitoring questionnaires during session 1974-5.

By June 1976 the SI/SII Economics Course will have been well and
truly assessed by a variety of techniques and processes, and analyses of the results will have been well documented. Time alone will
tell thereafter whether the work involved was an interesting experiment or an indication of the direction of future development.

8   IMPLICATIONS FOR THE FUTURE

It would be premature at this stage to predict that the pilot scheme
will transform economics education in Scotland. So far it has affected no more than about fourteen or fifteen schools. Although
analysis of feed-back is as yet incomplete, the preliminary findings
show that the subject as presented in this course is most certainly
not too difficult for pupils in the 12 to 14 age group.

It has also been noticed that there has been a tendency for the
number of pupils opting for economics in SIII to increase in the
pilot schools, and the hope is that those pupils who have followed
the pilot scheme will find little difficulty in adjusting to the
changing nature of the 'O' grade course. Certainly the SI/SII
course should prove to be a valuable preparation, not only for SCE
Economics, but for Modern Studies and Social Studies courses of
various kinds.

One implication has already become apparent. If there were to be
a big development of economics teaching in SI/SII in Scotland, there

would have to be a considerable adjustment in the accommodation available, and there would have to be an increase in the number of staff available to teach it. The position of economics in Scottish schools is a politically sensitive one, since the subject is generally taught as one of the branches of a business studies and economics department in which secretarial studies tend to predominate. There are increasing numbers of economists coming into secondary teaching, but they are seldom able to contribute fully to the teaching load of the business studies department and are often employed as teachers of modern studies or history. The solution to this problem is seen in one light by the economists who do not wish to teach secretarial studies, and in another by those who have acquired the full range of qualifications demanded by the present situation. Perhaps it would be best left to others to go more deeply into the implications of such divergent views for the future of economics in Scottish schools.

REFERENCES

1   The separate 'H' Grade Economics was introduced into Scotland in session 1967-8. For further information, see Economics Education in Scotland (T.K.Robinson in 'Teaching Economics', ed. N.Lee, Economics Association, London, 1967).
2   See Teaching Economic Concepts in the Primary Grades (L.Senesh in N.Lee (ed.), op.cit.).
3   Further references can be found in Economics in the Early Stages of the Secondary School (D.Christie in 'Curriculum Development in Economics', ed. D.Whitehead, Heinemann, London, 1974).
4   Syllabus and Specimen Question Papers, Commerce - Ordinary and Higher Grades, Scottish Certificate of Education Examination Board. A revised Higher Grade syllabus is at present under consideration and is due to be published in 1976.
5   Accounting, Economics and Economic History - Ordinary Grade, Scottish Certificate of Education Examination Board.
6   Adapted from 'Preparing Instructional Objectives', by R.F.Mager, Fearon Publishers, Belmont, Calif., 1962.
7   See Christie, op.cit.
8   Ibid.
9   Ibid.

Chapter 7

ECONOMICS IN SI AND SII-EVALUATION OF THE SCOTTISH PILOT SCHEME

Luis Maciver

1 INTRODUCTION

In view of John McCafferty's elaboration of the principles governing the development of the economics pilot scheme, it is unnecessary to give details here of the links between syllabus content, objectives, types of learning situation, and relevant assessment. It must be emphasised, however, that assessment items were constructed in relation to the general and specific objectives stated for each section of the course.

The evaluation was complex, continuous, and perhaps over-ambitious. Many facets of curriculum process, originally included modestly as aspects of curriculum development and revision, rather than as formal evaluation, in terms of conventions applying in 1971, may indeed be considered as evaluation by more modern standards, and are therefore now included in this report. This comment would apply to such features as statement and use of objectives, observation of pupil worksheets, and canvassing of teacher comments and reactions.

2 OVERALL ASSESSMENT

During initial discussion, expressed views ranged from a desire to avoid excessive formal assessment (lest pupil and teacher interest in novel modes of learning be adversely affected) to the stated need to assess curricular material in a detached statistical manner. This report includes a statistical analysis of pre-test and post-test results. Other modes of assessment were also used and are now briefly documented. For example, teachers were invited to submit detailed reports on their experience of units, including their reaction to individual worksheets. Such reports were invaluable when the Working Party in Economics proceeded to revise units for the second cycle of piloting. Teachers' views were also canvassed during several briefing meetings over the period of the pilot scheme. Beyond this, most members of the working party visited participating schools to obtain first-hand indication of teacher and pupil reactions.

3 THE PRESENT REPORT

(a) Statistical analysis

This report deals first with results obtained from pre-tests and
post-tests linked with each of the six units in the pilot scheme.
It also quotes results obtained from an overall final test, returned
by certain schools in the pilot scheme, as well as by two classes
involved neither in the pilot scheme nor in any comparable economics
scheme, but tested for purposes of comparison.
Pre-tests and post-tests for each unit were identical in the main
sections, viz. Section A consisting of 10 to 15 alternative choice
items, and Section B consisting of 5 or 6 multiple-choice items. In
the post-tests, an additional section was included, to assess perceived interest and perceived difficulty in relation to the completed unit. The overall final test consisted of 25 multiple-choice
items.

(b) On-going curriculum evaluation

The revised account goes on to indicate other aspects, indicated in
the Introduction, all of which did occur, and which add up to a much
more balanced evaluation than a purely statistical analysis, in isolation, might suggest.

4 PUPIL SAMPLE SIZE AND SAMPLE ATTRITION

In the main, sample sizes are indicated for each element of each
table in this report. In view of the fact that a combined total of
at least 2,356 pre-tests and post-tests for the Production Unit was
returned, reflecting therefore at least 1,178 pupils completing
each, it may seem surprising that samples of roughly 200 pupils are
quoted from the outset, with even lower figures by the conclusion of
the final unit in second year.
The fact of serious attrition of sample, especially in a curriculum pilot scheme covering two sessions, will be obvious to all experienced either in general or curricular research. Some of the
reasons for more or less continuous loss of sample in the present
instance may be quoted:
(a) For any unit, numbers completing either pre-test or post-test
     are rather less than total pupils involved. Numbers of indi-
     viduals completing both pre-test and post-test are often sub-
     stantially less.
(b) Perhaps the main loss of sample is due to the fact that schools
     and classes often took longer than the specified time to com-
     plete any individual unit. Reasons for delays in completing
     work on time are many. The cumulative effect of such time-lag
     on subsequent units, themselves similarly vulnerable, is pro-
     gressively serious.
     It may indeed be tentatively suggested
       (i) that curriculum developers, devising a full subject
            programme for a period extending over more than one

session might pilot different units independently, i.e.
in different schools, each piloting only a fraction of
the total.

(ii)   Whereas in the case of the Scottish Economics Project,
the offered curriculum is 'spiral' in nature, curriculum
developers may have to be much more modest in their esti-
mates of coverage per term, especially where the subject
has only two periods per week on average.

(c)   In summary, further reasons include pupils transferring from
school and class, reshuffling of pupils at the stage of
transfer to secondary, transfer of teachers, schools opting out
for a variety of reasons and, of course, misplacement or loss
of tests returned by the evaluator and others.

5   OVERALL ANALYSIS OF TEST RESULTS (TABLE 7.1)

TABLE 7.1   Mean pre-test and post-test scores

	Unit	Number in sample	Pre-test	Post-test	Possible scores	Significance
*SI	Production	204	13.0	17.7	24	0.05
	Distribution	204	14.3	17.1	22	0.05
	Consumption	204	12.5	15.8	25	0.05
**SII	Specialisation and Location	200	11.9	14.4	25	0.05
	Money, Trade and Exchange	194	9.6	11.9	20	0.05
	Income and Standard of Living	78	9.8	10.9	20	Not Sig.

*SI   - 1st Year Secondary (Age 12/13)
**SII - 2nd Year Secondary (Age 13/14)

(a)   Note on samples

For the SI cycle, in every case, the same sample completed pre-test
and post-test for each unit. Moreover, for the SI cycle, the same
sample are quoted throughout, with only one or two exceptions: that
is to say, broadly the same sample of 204 pupils covered all 3 pre-
tests and parallel post-tests. For the SII cycle, however, samples
were independently obtained for each unit, and thus, while showing
major overlap, are not identical over the three units. In all
cases, however, the sample represents a fair cross-section of the
schools involved, except in the case of 'Income and Standard of
Living', where many schools simply had not completed the unit by the
end of the second year. It should further be noted that, because of

the small sample of returns for this unit the results may well not be typical of those obtained for the major part of the evaluation.

(b)   Significance of results

Briefly, the overall cognitive evaluation, obtained by objective tests, reflects statistically significant improvement. Similarly the improvement shown in post-tests, over pre-test performance, is statistically significant for each of the first 5 units. For the final unit, Income and Standard of Living, there is an improvement, which however is not significant.

6   MEAN TEST-SECTION SCORES (TABLE 7.2)

TABLE 7.2   Mean test-section scores

	Pre-test			Post-test			Possible scores	
	Sect. A	Sect. B	Total	Sect. A	Sect. B	Total	Sect. A	Sect. B
SI								
Production	6.8	6.2	13.0	8.9	8.8	17.7	12	12
Distribution	7.5	6.8	14.3	8.6	8.5	17.1	10	12
Consumption	8.8	3.7	12.5	11.0	4.8	15.8	15	10
(n = 204)								
SII								
Specialisation and Location	9.2	2.7	11.9	10.4	4.0	14.4	15	10
(n = 200)								
Money, Trade and Exchange	6.1	3.5	9.6	7.5	4.4	11.9	10	10
(n = 194)								
*Income and Standard of Living	6.4	3.4	9.8	6.5	4.4	10.9	10	10

*Based on the 78 completed tests

Analysis of results

The results of the test-section scores again reveal statistically significant improvements in each section of each of the first five

units. Indeed the only pre-test/post-test comparison not revealing
a statistically significant improvement is that for Section A of the
'Income and Standard of Living' test. The smallness of this final
sample has already been indicated. Nevertheless the figures for
Section B of this test, which do show a highly significant improvement, suggest that the Section A test may be at fault, and
requiring amendment.

7   IMPROVEMENT IN TERMS OF GAIN RATIOS

(a) Table 7.3 represents improvements in terms of a percentage of
the pre-test scores. While no single gain ratio measure is infalli-
ble, this measure seems worthwhile and revealing.

TABLE 7.3 Mean gains as percentage of mean pre-test scores

Unit	Section A (%)	Section B (%)	Whole Test (%)
SI Production	31	29	30
Distribution	15	25	20
Consumption	25	30	26
SII Specialisation and Location	13	48	21
Money, Trade and Exchange	23	26	24
Income and Standard of Living	2	29	11
Overall	18	31	22

Comment and analysis of results

Note that gains are expressed correct to unit percentages. Whereas
overall gains seem relatively satisfactory, they are in a sense
relative to the exercise. In a project of this type, involving a
wide range of schools, classes, teachers and circumstances, modest
overall gain must rate as satisfactory.

   For the Working Party in Economics, the pattern of gain ratios
was more useful in indicating exceptions. Where possible, causes or
explanations with subsequent remedies were sought. The following
two examples, with a brief indication of subsequent action will
serve to illustrate this:
  (i) Section A of 'Income and Standard of Living' test
       Low gain paralleling acceptable gain for Section B. This led
       to scrutiny of test, with amended Section A for future issue.
  (ii) Section A of 'Distribution' test
       In this case, a mean pre-test score of 7.5 or 75 per cent
       seems to leave little head-room for improvement. The
       McGuigan's ratio, indicated below, seems more respectable.

(b) Mean gains as percentage of possible gains (McGuigan's gain ratio)
Table 7.4 indicates these gains. Again, while only of relative value, this analysis at least eliminates somewhat the variation both in pre-test means and in 'head-room' for improvement, in that gain is represented as a percentage of possible gain.

TABLE 7.4 Mean gains as percentage of possible mean gains

Unit		Section A (%)	Section B (%)	Whole test (%)
SI	Production	40	39	39
	Distribution	44	33	36
	Consumption	36	18	26
SII	Specialisation and Location	21	18	19
	Money, Trade and Exchange	36	14	22
	Income and Standard of Living	3	15	11
Overall		30	23	26

Comment and analysis of results

Note again that these gain ratios are expressed to the nearest whole percentage. The analysis reveals again that, while overall gains are moderately satisfactory for a project of this type, there is wide variation, with particular data requiring explanation and investigation. Some of the situations actually isolated and investigated as part of the on-going process of curriculum development and revision are indicated below:
  (i)   Section A of 'Distribution' test now reveals a substantial gain ratio, indicating that low ratio in Table 7.3 was due to high pre-test mean.
  (ii) McGuigan's gain ratio, i.e. the present analysis, reveals a low ratio for Section B of the 'Consumption' unit. This fact led to much heart-searching by the Working Party in Economics at an intermediate stage. The defects of the worksheets, and perhaps of the entire unit were critically assessed. The test itself was revised for future use.
  (iii) The percentage gains for the final unit, viz. 'Income and Standard of Living' remain low, especially for Section A. This had led to close scrutiny and revision of the unit and of the test, although it would seem that the incomplete and unbalanced sample returned may also furnish an explanation. It should be added that the detailed survey of results referred to for the 'Consumption' unit revealed a wide range of mean test scores for individual schools.
  (iv) Overall gain ratios for the SII units are rather disappointing when compared with those for the SI units. Tentatively,

one comments that this need not reflect on the quality of the units. The affective responses of pupils (see next main section) also reveal a drop during second year. Both of these may reflect either a growing relative boredom with a succession of similar units into second year or, even more probably, the general growing overt apathy which seems to characterise secondary pupils, after the initial novelty of secondary education has been superseded.

8   PERCEIVED DIFFICULTY AND INTEREST OF UNITS AND CAUSE

In a supplementary section, attached to each post-test, pupils were asked to rate the recently completed unit on two scales:
(a) Perceived Difficulty - (i) Too easy; (ii) Neither too easy nor too difficult; (iii) Fairly difficult; (iv) Very difficult.
(b) Perceived Interest - (i) Boring; (ii) Not very interesting; (iii) Fairly interesting; (iv) Very interesting.
These objective items or rating scales were supplemented with open-ended items asking pupils to particularise what specifically they found too easy, too difficult, very boring and very interesting. Unfortunately, lack of time made a classification of these responses impracticable. Nevertheless it is suggested that, for many curricular developments, this combination of rating scale and open-ended report on perceived difficulty and interest would yield of itself the basis of a meaningful pupil-oriented analysis.

(a) Perceived difficulty of units

Table 7.5 presents, in summary, the percentage responses accorded to each 'Difficulty' category.

TABLE 7.5 Perceived difficulty responses percentages

Unit	Too easy	Neither too easy nor difficult	Fairly difficult	Very difficult
SI Production	11	79	10	0
Distribution	14	80	6	0
Consumption	11	72	16	1
SII Specialisation and Location	9	59	29	3
Money, Trade and Exchange	11	63	23	3
Income and Standard of Living	25	54	13	8
Overall	13	68	16	3

Interpretation of results

- (i)   Overall satisfactory result for mixed-ability classes
  This must be one of the more gratifying results of this
  entire analysis. To the extent that, overall, 68 per cent
  of pupils found the units 'neither too easy nor too difficult', the planned course may be said to have succeeded in
  attaining a satisfactory level of 'difficulty' for mixed-
  ability classes. Of course, certain individual units show
  much higher figures.
- (ii) Again, overall, 16 per cent of pupils found the units fairly
  difficult, and only 3 per cent very difficult. This result,
  also, seems gratifying, although the curriculum developers
  might have to substitute extra 'simplified' materials for
  less able pupils. It is also obvious that for the first two
  SII units, a substantial minority, bordering on 30 per cent,
  experienced difficulty.
- (iii) Not unexpectedly, an overall proportion, 13 per cent of
  pupils found the units 'too easy'. In view of the fact that
  Scottish schools are liable to have 97.5 per cent of each
  complete population age range in local authority schools, it
  is fortunate that this figure, representing presumably
  'bright' or 'high-flying' pupils, is not higher. There is
  already within the units opportunity to involve such pupils
  in extra work.
- (iv) Variation in perceived difficulty
  A scrutiny of Table 7.5 will reveal a fair range over the
  units, although only sizeable differences, say of 5 per cent
  or more, should be considered. The final unit, 'Income and
  Standard of Living', for instance, reveals itself as less
  satisfactory than the others. This, as already indicated,
  may be due either to incomplete sample or to defects in the
  unit. On the other hand, part of the apparent deterioration
  belongs to a wider pattern.
- (v)   Second year compared with first year cycle
  It seems obvious that, comparing SII with SI reactions, percentages perceiving units as too easy, and too difficult, are
  higher for SII. This may well reflect less variety within
  SII units. It is tentatively suggested, however, that it
  could largely reflect also a more critical pupil reaction,
  typical as pupils mature.

(b) Perceived interest of units

Table 7.6 below presents the pupils' reactions in terms of perceived
interest.

TABLE 7.6 Pupils' perceived interest percentages for units

	Boring	Not very interesting	Fairly interesting	Very interesting
SI Production	9	11	60	20
Distribution	5	20	66	8
Consumption	19	30	44	7
SII Specialisation and Location	20	24	48	8
Money, Trade and Exchange	23	32	40	5
Income and Standard of Living	Full data not available even for incomplete sample			
Overall	15	23	52	10

Interpretation of results

 (i)   Note that rounding off to whole percentages at times yields
       a cross-total other than precisely 100 per cent.
 (ii) These results are gratifying at a realistic level. Overall,
       62 per cent of pupils found the units 'fairly or very inter-
       esting', with significantly higher percentages for certain
       units.
(iii) On the other hand, an overall 38 per cent of pupils found
       them 'boring or not very interesting'. This might mean
       either that the preparers of units have still work to do to
       improve interest, or that all teachers using the units must
       be encouraged in a variety of ways to incorporate the spirit
       as well as the letter of the declared intentions of the
       course concerning methods and approaches.
 (iv) Again it will be seen that the proportion of 'bored and not
       very interested' pupils tends towards 50+ per cent as the
       second year units are completed. This disturbing statistic
       could mean that pupils are becoming rather bored with a
       'workshop/worksheet mode' as the course progresses, a common
       criticism of generally used curriculum materials. It could
       also mean that second year pupils are becoming more generally
       bored, and critical of education generally, including a fresh
       curriculum in economics.
  (v) The Interest Data for the final unit were incomplete, and are
       not included.

9 COMPARATIVE EVALUATION OF COGNITIVE AWARENESS IN ECONOMICS IN
PUPILS AT END OF SII

At the outset it must be stressed that this is an incomplete
analysis. The Working Party in Economics went to considerable pains
to create a 25-item multiple-choice test, sampling the main objectives of the course. The intention was to sample pilot schools,
other schools doing economics in SI and SII, and pupils doing no
economics.
   In fact, for various reasons the sampling was biased. First,
only 3 pilot schools got round to an overall test, the remainder not
having completed all the units or their pre-/post-tests. Then, it
was not easy to obtain classes with parallel economics courses, and
difficult to organise testing for pupils who were doing no economics. At this late stage it must be emphasised that all members
of the Working Party in Economics did their curriculum development
in their spare time!

TABLE 7.7

	School	Number	Mean	Standard deviation
Pilot schools	A	227	13.6	3.8 (approx)
	B	49	18.3	2.8
	C	27	14.4	4.4
No economics	D	30	14.2	2.6
	E	30	11.6	3.5

Interpretation of Table 7.7

This analysis reveals various interesting features.
   (i)   School A, with 9 classes, has a lower mean score than one of
          the 2 sample schools with no economics in SI and SII. This
          is partly due to the range of class mean scores, from 9.6 to
          16.9. At this stage, explanations of this range of scores
          can only be tentative. Briefly, quality of pupils, and
          quality of teachers are variables even in a comprehensive
          school.
  (ii)   The mean scores for Schools D and E, both 'non-economics'
          schools, are significantly different. This not only renders
          the assumption of class comparability unwarranted, but illus-
          trates the dangers of making assumptions about 'mixed-
          ability classes', as if they were all broadly equivalent.
 (iii)   Pilot School B, with a mean score of 18.3, seems clearly to
          indicate one school where learning for this pilot class
          almost approached 'mastery learning', in Bloom's terms, and
          as assessed by the test. This was in fact a 'good school'.
          Furthermore the principal teacher responsible was dedicated
          both to economics and to the pilot scheme.
  (iv)   The lowest class means obtained in this test by participating

classes suggest that, for one reason or another, these particular classes gained little from the entire exercise. It
must be emphasised however that such poor class performance
was exceptional over the whole range of schools. It would
seem likely that 'poor teaching' is the explanation.

(v) This analysis is invalid for purposes of general comparison
because of limited and biased samples. It does reveal some
interesting and unexpected results nevertheless.

10   ON-GOING CURRICULUM EVALUATION

There were, as indicated earlier, several aspects of this curriculum
development which represent on-going evaluation, with a view to
amending work units, worksheets, teacher instructions, and above all
with a view to improving the economics curriculum in the classroom.

(a) Statement of objectives

From an early stage, viz. 1971, the working party stated objectives
for each study area, and work unit. This policy involved not only
rapid induction into techniques of writing objectives, but also the
writing of lists of general and specific objectives for each study
area and its constituent work units. The use of objectives helped
curriculum evaluation in at least four ways:

(i)   The use of objectives helped to clarify and improve curricular statements for the benefit of the working party and, of
course, for the teachers.

(ii) Each team preparing work for course units listed its objectives. These were revised in due course by the full
working party, with particular reference to form of expression and relevance to the aims of the course. The finally stated objectives represent a blend of basic ideas and
concepts capable of progressive presentation through a spiral
structure, with the later components depending upon, or extending, the earlier ones. While the working party makes no
extravagant claims to attaining its goals in full, the stated
objectives represent a check list of achievement targets
which relate individual work units and study areas to the
complete course structure.

(iii) Objectives, stated mainly for the benefit of pupils and
teachers were, to some extent, used to assess the suitability
of unit content or teaching approach as a means of implementing the course aims.

(iv) Objectives served as a basis for items in the pre-tests and
post-tests used for course evaluation. This has ensured that
excessive factual knowledge has been avoided in the tests,
and that understanding, evaluation, and problem-solving
abilities have also been tested.

(b) Pupil response sheets and products

The working party initially considered the possibility of limiting assessment to an evaluation of pupil assignments and completed worksheets. This particular method was rejected in favour of formal assessment of all study areas. Nevertheless, the following informal, but functional, evaluations of pupil responses were also used:

(i)   Members of the working party often brought samples of pupils' work to meetings as indices of curriculum presentation which had succeeded or failed. This process often led to substantial revision of curriculum materials.

(ii) Teachers were asked to observe pupil involvement and performance, and to submit reports not only on complete study areas, but on individual work units.

(iii) Some working party members observed parts of the course being tried in pilot schools, and obtained teachers' reactions to the materials provided.

(iv) Such observations led to a regular appraisal of course materials from an early stage in their development. For example, the final diagrammatic exercise in the 'Production' unit was shown to be successful with a wide range of pupils. Another assignment, intended to illustrate division of labour in the SII study area 'Specialisation and Location of Industry', had to be extensively modified because pupils found the first form of the exercise too difficult.

(c) Involvement of teachers

Teachers involved in the pilot schools had ample opportunity to comment on the content of the study areas/work units and on the quality of pupil involvement and response. Their contribution to the evaluation consisted of:

(i)   Completion of Teacher's Comment Sheets which circulated to every pilot school with the set of materials for each study area. These comment sheets invited teacher reaction to every component of the study area, and extra, more lengthy, comments where the teacher wished to make them.

(ii) Observations and comments at briefing meetings of participating teachers. These meetings served the dual purpose of obtaining reaction to materials already piloted, and discussing the aims and approaches of materials about to be distributed.

(iii) Making special comments and providing additional reactions to visiting working party members, especially at times when revisions of units were being contemplated.

(iv) When it became clear that both teachers and pupils wished to know how the test results turned out, the working party arranged that post-test scores were returned to the pilot schools. This was a departure from the working party's original intentions.

While teachers' comments contributed significantly to the revision of pilot materials, it must also be admitted that many teachers seemed reluctant to return Comment Sheets, especially in the latter stages of the piloting. This was perhaps due to the fact that the place of their comments in the final formal evaluation was inadequately clarified or stressed. A formal analysis of teacher reaction was not planned by the working party. Nevertheless, such an analysis might well have provided evidence as vital as that obtained from pupil responses.

CONCLUSIONS

This evaluation of the economics for SI and SII curriculum development makes no claims to being total or as thorough as it might have been. In accordance with convention, especially in Scottish educational research up to about 1970, pre-testing, post-testing and statistical analysis of results may have figured too largely in our reckoning, even to the extent of eliminating certain more illuminative evaluations, e.g. of teacher and school reaction to a specific innovation. (The continuing monitoring of units will attend to such aspects.)

What does the formal test analysis reveal? There were in most cases significant cognitive gains. Where there were exceptions, attention was paid both to unit content, and to the tests themselves with a view to revision and improvement. No undue claims are made for the assessment of pupils' perceptions of difficulty and interest. Yet, so often this aspect is not assessed at all, and our assessment did reveal some interesting patterns of results.

As far as the wider aspects of evaluation are concerned, the working party did in fact pay attention to teacher reaction, and to the 'feel' of the new materials in the classroom. Without a doubt certain features of evaluation, expected in a modern curriculum development, are more or less lacking. Two facts may serve to explain this. All members of the working party, including the evaluator, operated on a part-time or virtually spare-time basis, each having a full-time work role not directly connected with this curriculum development. In addition the piloting and evaluations were devised in 1971, i.e. before current modes of curriculum evaluation were fashionable.

DISCUSSION

McCafferty clarified a few points raised with him in earlier private discussion. First, we must accept that in Scotland any pioneering work involving children of all abilities in secondary schools is almost certainly destined to be undertaken with SI and SII, since there is no common course thereafter. Second, the detailed objectives set out in the scheme should not be regarded as inhibiting. They were included as an aid to teachers who might otherwise have felt short of sufficient specific guidance. McCafferty believed that the scheme had achieved limited success in very difficult circumstances.

Maciver explained that the pilot scheme had been operated and overseen by members of the working party in their spare time. No

staff had been especially employed, and very limited resources had
been available. It was inevitable that the statistics would reflect
this. Moreover, the working party had wanted to keept the statistical demands on teachers to a reasonable level in terms of quantity
and complexity. Samples were frequently smaller than desired, and
returns were occasionally incomplete. Nevertheless the statistics
had served a purpose for the working party by showing when all was
not well, and he maintained that a reasonable measurement is better
than none at all. He felt that some of the most valuable information gathered was on pupils' reaction to the course. The evaluation was bedevilled by frequent changes of staff in schools, and
by wide discrepancies in the circumstances in which children in the
pilot schools were taught.

Discussion concentrated largely, perhaps overmuch, on Maciver's
paper. Three main criticisms were made. First, information on some
vital matters was lacking, e.g. Were the multiple-choice items
validated? How many distracters were used? What constituted a
significant score? How did those pupils who professed boredom perform compared with those who professed interest? Were pupils in
School A (Table 7.7) streamed? Was intelligence partialled out of
the results?

Second, some of the methods appeared an indifferent means of
achieving their implied purpose, e.g. Table 7.5 is highly subjective. Why not test for 'degree of ease' by setting specific
tasks and applying a time limit? Again, in Table 7.6, do we know
what children mean when they use the words 'boring' and 'interesting'? Do they find their leisure pursuits 'boring' too? Was it the
teacher who was boring rather than the materials? Would not a
better idea have been to discover on which parts of the syllabus and
on which types of activity the pupils would have been happy to spend
more time?

Third, Maciver's interpretation of the results was regarded as
questionable in places, e.g. Tables 7.1 to 7.4: How can we be sure
that the results do not simply indicate that pupils tried harder in
the post-test than the pre-test? Table 7.5: Is there not a built-
in bias here? By omitting a column headed 'Fairly Easy' are not
pupils pushed towards the 'Neither too easy nor difficult' response,
thereby producing 'one of the more gratifying results'? Table 7.7:
'The mean score of 18.3 out of a possible 23 means that for these
pupils (School B) the course succeeded.' Does it? How well did
they perform in the pre-test? What proportion of these pupils found
the course 'too easy' and 'not very interesting' or 'boring' as a
result?

Maciver referred his critics to other remarks in his paper,
notably 'This analysis is invalid for purposes of general comparison
because of limited and biased samples. It does reveal some interesting and unexpected results nevertheless.' The statistics were
better than nothing at all. Proper evaluation would have required
a full-time researcher. Many of the paper's omissions stemmed from
a desire to keep it to a reasonable length and to make it digestible
by persons with minimal knowledge of statistics (its circulation was
not confined to those who attended this seminar). With so many
variables (size of class, ability and interest of teacher, continuity of teacher, use and misuse of course materials, etc.) highly

sophisticated statistical techniques might well have yielded
precious little additional valid information at a far greater cost
in time and money, and would have been unjustifiable in his view.

The course material aroused considerable interest. Some thought
they detected a male bias in some units, another regretted the
absence of a Scottish dimension in the material, but in general the
units appeared to be received with approval. In answer to
questions, McCafferty stated that the use made of the kit had varied
enormously. Some teachers had abandoned it fairly rapidly, others
had used it successfully with much older pupils too. Not all pupils
had managed to go beyond the point of referring to 'bits of Lego and
plastic men' but some had made highly imaginative use of the pieces
as 'productive resources'. Particular references to Scotland in the
material had been omitted deliberately. No teachers had complained
about this, and the working party hoped that teachers would add
local colour for themselves.

One speaker wanted to know why it was that Scotland appeared to
provide conditions much more conducive to innovatory experiment than
did the rest of the United Kingdom. Several speakers made contributions towards a possible answer, viz. the Scottish educational
system is much more of a unit; over 97 per cent of all pupils are
in local authority schools, the very great majority of which are co-
educational and comprehensive; secondary schools work almost exclusively towards the examinations of only one examination board;
the personnel involved in curriculum development are generally well
known throughout Scotland and well known to each other; there is
greater scope for prescriptive measures when it comes to implementation; and, like England, the decisions on acceptance of new
courses are taken finally by individual schools, many of which are
in close geographical proximity to each other.

The piloting of the project is now complete and the material can
now be used in other schools, where monitoring will take place.
Many of the variables influencing its success or otherwise will be
scrutinised. There are several obstacles currently preventing the
course being offered in England.

Chapter 8

ECONOMICS AND THE HUMANITIES IN THE LOWER SCHOOL

R. T. Winsor

It is often argued that economics has no place in the curriculum of the lower school. Indeed some feel that it should not be taught below 'A' level or even university level. This paper is intended to show that there is indeed a place for economics in the lower school, as defined by years I,II and III of the secondary school.

I do accept part of the anti-lower-school argument which states that economics as a self-contained subject may not be all that relevant. Many children in the 12-14 age group are quite simply not interested in economic matters, and little that can be done in the classroom will alter their views.

However, I feel that economics should not be taught as an isolated subject, especially in the lower school. The sixth former can see the links and appreciate the overlapping of subjects. The younger pupil tends to regard each subject as an entity in itself. One of the major objectives of the teacher should be to break down this belief, and the teacher of economics is one of the best placed in the profession to do this. How then are we to link economics to the other humanities and present a relevant course to the 12-14-year-old pupils?

We should be preparing for the pupil a basis for his future understanding of the world we live in. After all, when a child looks at the reasons why we inhabit particular places he will see the interweaving of historical, geographical and economic reasons. Thus, I think we should aim in the lower school at providing a combined course in economics, geography and history. At this point I must apologise for omitting such studies as sociology and anthropology, but they are not a part of the curriculum in my own school.

The first problem encountered by the economist is simply to convince the geographers and historians that there is a need for the combination of the three subjects, and then there is also the timetabling problem. In my own school the 13-14-year-old begins his combined economics, geography and history education in the third form. Economics is a relatively new subject in the school and has now only been running as a third form subject for one year. Little linkage was achieved between departments during the year and thus what I am putting forward in this paper is what I am attempting to work towards.

For the purpose of these three subjects the pupils are divided
into three sets each having two periods per week of each of the
three subjects. The periods are timetabled as closely as possible
together so that each group will be having either economics, geography or history at the same time. Thus group talks and lectures on
overlapping subjects can easily be organised. Of course, it is a
tremendous help if one teaches more than one of the three subjects
as this encourages closer links.

Assuming that such problems as timetabling are overcome, and we
are about to embark on a combined economics, geography and history
course in the lower school, then what is to be our programme for the
next session?

In the economics periods I set out to follow loosely D.Baron's
'Economics - An Introductory Course', when not linking directly with
the geographers and historians. I find this book simple, well
illustrated and, most important, thought-provoking for the younger
pupil. The second step is to take up certain points that arise from
this study and attempt then to link up with the other two departments. The third step is simply to take up any economic issues
that arise during the year that are either relevant or important to
the students. For example, ROSLA and unemployment, cup final
tickets and prices.

Hopefully, the most rewarding and perhaps the most relevant of
these steps will be the combination of the three subjects. What I
hope to begin with this year is a local study of industry. This
will be a natural follow-up to a few weeks' classroom work talking
about business in its various aspects. As already mentioned we have
three groups and what I find one of the best methods of undertaking
this study is to label each group as either economists, geographers
or historians. Then having chosen certain industries the groups
will be asked to go out and examine why the industries are sited in
particular areas from an historical, economic or geographical point
of view depending on the label of the group. The groups will com-
pile their information in project form and then combined lessons can
take place where each group puts forward its views. From a small-
scale attempt at such a study last year the results of these discussions were most interesting, and heated exchanges often took
place as to just what is an economic, historical or geographical
factor. For example, government intervention in location of industry may be strongly argued to be an historical factor in that it was
originally brought about by an Act of Parliament, whereas the ge-
ographer may say that it is a geographical factor as the government
were concerned with particular areas of the country. And, of
course, the economist will argue that, if it is concerned with unemployment, declining industries and growth, government intervention
is therefore an economic factor. The end result is that the pupils
appreciate that the study is an interwoven one and that subjects
cannot be given their particular labels and pursued without some
overlapping with other subjects.

I shall also be using this study to introduce to pupils an
awareness of the employment situation which faces them in this area.
For this it will be necessary to obtain information from the local
Employment Exchange and from the firms themselves about what is
available in the area. I feel that this is an important part of the

study, as the pupils find that they live in a town which has an unemployment rate above the national average and also that as it is a small town the type of available employment is limited. Thus I am trying to introduce some element of careers awareness before the pupils choose the 'O' level courses they wish to follow.

Having undertaken a study such as the one mentioned above then one may find it difficult to persuade the geographers and historians to depart further from their syllabus for the year. However, it is still possible to incorporate all three aspects into the economics lessons or, if one teaches some history and geography, to involve all three subjects in those lessons. For example, James I sold monopolies in order to raise money for the government. What is a monopoly, why were they sold and of what use were they to those who bought them? Henry VIII brought about an effective devaluation of sterling by introducing base metal into silver coinage. The effects of this devaluation were historically most important to England's trading position in the following years and the effect on the balance of payments was quite severe. Thus through important historical events one can hopefully bring about a keener understanding of Britain's present economic problems and the realisation that these difficulties are not unique to the twentieth century.

In the geography lessons, one can easily relate the growing of particular crops to both economic and historical factors - for example, location of industry in the tea-growing areas of India and China, economies of large-scale production on the wheat fields of the Canadian prairies, the historical and economic significance of the imported labour on the American cotton-fields. One can go on adding to the list and the teacher should find, as long as he does not have a tight work schedule to follow, that the geography lesson may lead into discussion in the economics lesson, the history lesson into the geography lesson and so on. We are, in effect, cross-referencing three subjects and providing an interesting approach to the topics for both teacher and pupil.

Besides the project mentioned earlier concerning the location of industry, I hope to introduce two further projects into the course. The first will be a continuous piece of work throughout the year but with the major work-load coming at the end. In essence, it will take the form of calculating a simple Retail Price Index. In order to add more weight to the study, as I have found from experience that younger pupils soon get bored with collecting prices week after week, the shops to be used for the study will be especially selected. Basically there will be three; a small corner shop, a supermarket in the centre of town and, if possible, a large out-of-town hyper-market. This presents problems in small communities but is more of a practical possibility in large towns and cities. In approaching the study in this way we are not only able to compare prices over time but also between different establishments. The more detailed piece of work following the price study will be in a project form and will be related to the three types of establishment. Historically, how did the shop as a unit develop and how has it changed in recent years? Geographically, what pattern is shown in the location of these establishments, i.e. originally many small shops scattered all over the town, then central supermarkets and later still out-of-town hyper-markets? Economically, why have the

locations changed and why have the units grown progressively larger?
It is hoped that such a study will introduce the younger pupil to
some of the basic economic concepts such as the theory of price via
supply and demand, markets, economies of large scale and the point
of optimum location. This is all being done without the use of
diagrams and graphs, something for which I believe the younger pupil
is not yet ready and might also find rather boring.

The third project that I intend to use will be undertaken during
the second term of the session. Having looked at business and work
and introduced the concept of prices during the first term, we will
go on to examine the role of money. The project involved will be an
obvious and well-used topic, namely banking. The project will not
be one concerned with the creation of credit, money supply, etc.,
but more with the historical development of banking and the services
offered today by the banks. I justify such a project on two
grounds. First, I am constantly aware of the repetition of basic
economic knowledge in 'O' and 'A' level courses. If the project
were to include the creation of credit, distribution of assets,
etc., then we would be extending this repetition further down the
school. Second, a project on these lines is one which provides an
easy source of information for pupils. Booklets and leaflets are
readily obtainable from the banks and thus pupils can produce more
colourful and interesting finished projects.

One need mention this project no more as it is one commonly used
in economics teaching. However, it completes the scheme of economics for the third form pupil. The plan for the year is therefore
as shown in Table 8.1.

TABLE 8.1

Continuing investigation of the Retail Price Index	Work Business Local study project Wages	Term 1
	Money Banking project Spending Budget	Term 2
	Shopping/prices project Exams Current economic issues	Term 3

We are therefore presenting a broad base for study, which introduces
the subject of economics as being one which is necessarily linked
with other subjects, and one which is concerned with the real world
in which the pupils live.

What I am attempting to produce in my own school is a pyramidal
structure in the teaching of economics, the third term course being
a broad social science base followed by an 'O' level course in economics and public affairs of the Cambridge Board Syndicate in the
fourth and fifth years and then on to a straight economics 'A' level

in the sixth form. In this way we begin by providing a general approach for the younger pupil free from facts, figures, detailed
analysis and diagrams; the 'O' level course then narrows the area
of study down a little but is still not a pure economics course as
it involves the public affairs paper; and then in the sixth form
we come to the apex where economics is studied as a single subject,
not always related to the real world.

By introducing economics at an early age we can attempt to develop in the pupils habits of enquiry necessary for study at a more
advanced stage. The most obvious example is the reading of
newspapers. It is quite a simple task to begin scrap-books on
topics studied throughout the year. Scrap-books can be kept by
different groups according to the papers read by their families and
every so often the groups can present articles from their papers and
discuss the differing approaches and the different views expressed.

We can also begin to create a critical mind in the pupils such
that, for example, they begin to question why particular economic
decisions are taken by the government. If we can make these habits
natural assets of the pupil then we are preparing the way for better
study in later years.

To conclude, not only is it possible to teach a relevant economics course to the younger pupil but it is something that we ought
to be doing, whether it is as a combined course or whether as a
basic introductory course for future study. Economics creates good
academic habits, is relevant to the world we live in and is a most
useful study for the early school leaver. The earlier we introduce
the subject into the curriculum, the better.

DISCUSSION

Winsor revealed a situation in his school that must surely be
without parallel: the Head, the Deputy Head and the Head of Sixth
Form Studies are all qualified to teach economics, and this in a
school of 450 pupils and 23 full-time staff. Opinion was divided on
whether this state of affairs should be considered conducive to the
development of economics!

Some speakers found his course too descriptive, and his description of it too general. Not everyone could support his claims
for the benefits accruing from teaching economics to younger pupils.
One speaker wondered where all the resources to sustain the projects
were going to come from, and another expressed doubts as to the
likelihood of achieving a satisfactory long-term liaison with a
history department. The parametal structure was welcomed, since it
was felt that all too often the descent of economics into the middle
school sentenced pupils to excessive repetition of content if they
went on to take economics at Advanced level or Scottish Higher
grade. One speaker suggested taking 'Change' as a theme, and developing it by asking pupils to discover the occupations and the
domiciles of their forebears. Not only would this highlight occupational and geographical mobility, but it would also permit an
identification of the forces underlying the changes that had taken
place.

Chapter 9

VISITS AND FIELD STUDIES– NON–CLASSROOM TEACHING METHODS FOR THE YOUNGER SECONDARY PUPIL

Dorothy Davidson and Brian Robinson

1 PURPOSE OF NON-CLASSROOM TEACHING METHODS FOR 11-16-YEAR-OLDS

Much of the alleged difficulty of teaching basic economic concepts to the younger secondary pupil (11-16-year-old) is due not to any inherent 'difficulty' of the subject but to an initial over-concentration on abstract classroom-based work. Such work is regularly used and very appropriate for 16-19-year-olds, but, as the Scottish Project for the 12-14-year-old pupil has demonstrated, practical work (in this case via materials in the classroom) can provide a valid introduction to the abstract nature of economic concepts. The use of visits and field studies by 11-16-year-old pupils gives them first-hand experience of the economic facts and events upon which these concepts are based, and difficulties related to teaching abstract concepts can be solved by direct acquaintance with the real world, with all the generation of pupil interest which work outside the classroom brings.

Piaget implies and Bruner strongly argues that learning for all age groups requires plenty of experience of concrete operations (e.g. through practical work) in order to come to grips with the facts and events of life upon which concepts and theories are based. Senesh, moreover, maintains the hypothesis that 'children on every grade level with proper motivation can become excited about the abstract ideas underlying their experiences, and these ideas can be presented in such a way as to reflect the basic structure of economics'. (1) But, as Senesh would agree, younger pupils require very much more experience of concrete operations than older students before they can grasp the abstract concepts, and such experience is vital in providing them with the 'proper motivation'.

There are two further uses for visits and field studies for the younger pupil - the provision of real world facilities to apply concepts already learnt, and the reinforcement of understanding of basic theory after it has been learnt. (See sections 4 and 5, especially, for examples of this.) We are not seeking here the development of skill in applying theory, which is a formal operations technique usually only possible with older students, but a deeper, more realistic analysis of a basic theory; that is a strengthening of pupil understanding of the theory. The application of concepts

and reinforcement of theory can, of course, be done very well by
practical classroom-based methods such as case studies, business
games, simulation and role-playing. The characteristic strength of
non-classroom methods is direct experience of economic situations,
and new skills are developed through the observation, collection and
analysis of data from primary sources. We need to examine in some
depth the objectives and organisation of business visits and field
studies before making a necessarily briefer study of the other less
frequently used, non-classroom teaching techniques.

2   OBJECTIVES OF BUSINESS VISITS FOR THE 11-16s

These are usually thought of as factory visits, but they could
equally involve any type of business enterprise - a supermarket, a
farm, a bus undertaking. The main theme of the visit may be to
supply younger pupils with particular concrete experiences as a
means of introducing them to certain basic economic concepts - e.g.
'capital', 'labour', 'industrial location'. Alternatively it could
be to apply concepts already learnt such as 'scarcity' and 'choice'.
Illustrations of possible specific objectives of this first kind of
visit are given below.
  (a) Capital: What examples of machinery and raw materials can
be seen at the firm? What is the date of manufacture of some of the
machinery? What new machinery has been introduced into the firm in
the last ten years, and what effect has this had on the firm's
profit? How is money acquired to buy new machinery for the firm?
  (b) Labour: How many workers are there for each machine? What
training do workers in the factory have? What are the main unions
in the factory, and the causes of and time lost by strikes? Is
output of goods increased more by new training of workers or by
putting in new machines?
  (c) Industrial location: Where do the firm's raw materials come
from? What is the firm's main finished product, and to where does
it go? Why was the firm built on this particular site? Did government grants help the firm to decide on its site, or would a government grant cause the firm to build its next new factory at a different place?
  (d) Scarcity and prices: What price, approximately, are the raw
materials and what proportion, roughly, are they of the final
selling price? What has been the increase (actual and percentage)
in the price of raw materials in the last three years? Has their
price gone up because they are difficult to obtain? Is it difficult
to obtain skilled labour for the firm and by how much has a skilled
worker's wage gone up in the last three years?

3   ORGANISATION OF BUSINESS VISITS

(a) Pupil preparation

To focus attention on the specific economic objectives of the visit,
the pupils can effectively use a questionnaire which has been drawn
up by means of prior class discussion and edited by the teacher.

The questionnaire would have items related to the tour of the
technical process and the talk/discussion session with a management
representative at the firm. In class work prior to the visit some
explanation of the main features of the technical process is necessary, including, e.g. a duplicated diagram for each pupil, as well
as discussion on specific economic facts and events concerning the
visit.

(b) Preliminary arrangements

It is not always practicable for the teacher to visit the firm prior
to the class visit, but a letter giving long notice of the visit
(4-5 weeks), and outlining in detail the type of visit requested is
essential. The letter would suggest arrangements concerning
(i) major importance of a talk/discussion on the economic problems
of the firm and industry with a financial director or other manager,
(ii) a visit to the technical process, (iii) forwarding of information about the firm for preliminary work in class, (iv) timings
for different parts of the visit, (v) opportunities, if possible,
to put questions to some employees.

(c) Group size

The size will vary with the firm's requirements, but most large
firms will accept the full secondary class of 30 pupils for a visit.
Sub-groups on any visit should ideally be no larger than 6-7, in
order to hear clearly what the guide says.

(d) The visit

   (i) Introductory talk   When the party arrives at the firm, a
very brief talk to explain the technical process by a manager would
reinforce the teacher's explanation and discussion of this in class
prior to the visit. It is essential with younger pupils that
teacher and manager explain the same basic points.

   (ii) Visit to technical process   This tour enables the pupils, by
means of the questionnaire, to observe and note economic facts and
events (e.g. age of machines, number of workers per machine, final
products), which can be discussed with a manager later. Technical
apprentices would normally accompany the pupil sub-groups, but they
can usually cope with younger pupils' questions, based on the
questionnaire. However, the teacher should emphasise to the apprentices that they give the minimum of technical information so
that pupils may not be confused.

(iii) Talk/discussion session   This section of the visit is the
most important part in terms of economic knowledge and understanding
gained, and questionnaires and pupil notebooks can be used. It is
essential, therefore, to have a manager to talk briefly and simply
about the economics of the firm and industry, and to answer pupils'

questions. With younger pupils it is helpful if the teacher chairs the session, so that he can make sure that questions cover all the specific objectives of the visit and do not over-concentrate on some to the exclusion of others.

(e) Follow-up work

Once the visit is completed the information has to be analysed and the economic lessons to be learned from it have to be drawn. This will involve, no doubt, class discussion and use of the questionnaire information. The final product by the pupil will depend of course on age and ability, and may range from an essay with a 15-16 high ability range, to a series of drawings and brief notes by an 11-12-year low ability group. It could also involve taped reports or pupil answers to a second, different questionnaire.

The follow-up work derives directly from the visit's objectives, which may be of a general economic nature, or, as in the Understanding Industrial Society Project for 14-16-year-olds, of a more specific nature. The advantages of the business visit are that it can be easily adapted to meet particular needs, e.g. to reinforce elementary theory (pricing, industrial location) with 14-16-year-olds, or to gain experience of basic concepts (capital, labour) with still younger pupils.

4   OBJECTIVES OF FIELD STUDIES FOR THE 11-16s

Lee states in an article on teaching economics to the younger average and below-average ability child, 'The level of economic understanding of the Newsom child is therefore to be measured in terms of the economic concepts he has understood, level of sophistication in his understanding and range in which he can meaningfully apply the concepts'. (2) The field study provides many opportunities for the pupil to acquire this economic understanding, since it enables him to learn and apply concepts, and reinforce basic theory in real world conditions over a period of time, and can embrace most aspects of the subject content in the process (for practical examples see later in this section and in section 5). To follow through Lee's criteria, the field study permits the pupil facilities to comprehend basic concepts (e.g. income distribution, industrial location), and, especially, a range of real world situations in which he can meaningfully apply them (e.g. by visiting several firms and discovering factors causing industrial location). The level of sophistication in his understanding of these concepts can be further developed by discussions with management (which of itself interests him) at firms in development areas, which will show the influence of government grants on why a motor or chemical firm was located there. As Holley points out, it is the acquisition of skills, rather than knowledge, which benefits the pupil in the long term, and the skill of applying concepts is being developed in an on-going real world situation. (3) An intensive development of these skills is produced in a continuous one-week field study course, because each day's experience is built upon the cumulative experience of the previous days.

A full field course for younger pupils could be organised around the comprehension and application of the four core concepts of economics, described by Lumsden and Attiyeh (4) and could be sited in any major industrial area. For example:

(A)   Scarcity and choice: scarcity of land and housing can be examined by mapping the land available for development and recording of house price changes (from newspapers). A study of prices in a local retail market or of prices in shops over a week, would illustrate price change in relation to scarcity and choice.

(B)   Economic efficiency: during many steelworks visits, pupils can see steel-making plants which have replaced old capital, and thus increased efficiency by altering the capital/labour ratio. A visit/talk at an employment exchange could be used to show how labour resources in a town are being utilised.

(C)   Income distribution: in talks with management and trade unions, pupils can discover proportions of firms' incomes going to payments of wages, rent, interest and profit. During a visit to a firm such as ICI, management can be questioned on the effects of its one-firm wage-negotiating structure, and of its profit-sharing scheme on income distribution.

(D)   Aggregate output and income: the mapping of new manufacturing industries, the discovery of recent earnings changes by factory visits, and the mapping of and visits to new tertiary industries can be valuable in experiencing the factual basis of links between changes in aggregate output and income.

On such a course, a knowledge of basic theory for 15-year-olds would be reinforced by a deeper, more realistic analysis of theory. In relation to (A) above, and demand and supply theory, pupils could do further work in which they could analyse the land shortage and land/ house price rises from newspapers and visual observation, and discuss with estate agents and solicitors the causation and trends. The pupil would be asked to relate theory, not to an imaginary situation, nor to a once-removed practical situation (as in case studies), but to the actuality itself with all the abundance of data, impetus to learn and reality that this situation possesses.

5   ORGANISATION OF A FIELD STUDY COURSE

Several differences arise when a field course is planned for younger rather than senior pupils. The first considerations are usually theme, time and venue. The theme must be worded in such a way that the pupils will understand the terminology, in the first place, and also the reasons for the work they will be asked to do. The question of time may be rather easier than for senior pupils as the demands of outside examinations are less pressing. The venue depends on the theme, and several suggestions are offered. If the school is situated in an area of particular economic interest, e.g. a New Town, an area with full development status, or a highly industrial area, it may be advisable to have a field course in the home area. This means there are no problems about accommodation and the school and all its facilities (e.g. projectors, rooms, tape recorder, etc.) are readily available. On the other hand, a certain

impetus is lacking if things are too familiar. Another possibility
is to go to an area not too far from the school and possibly study a
smaller community. The advantage of this is that the whole area can
be clearly observed. Job opportunities, industrial inducements
(e.g. industrial estates, advance factor factories, special housing)
can be seen, and local co-operation is usually very enthusiastic as
officials and managers are not receiving dozens of similar appli-
cations throughout the year. The status of speaker in a factory
visit in this case is often higher than one could hope to expect in
a city. (An example of this course is given later in the section.)
  If the field course is to be held away from home it is important
to find the right kind of accommodation. Youth hostels with field
study facilities are very good and many local authorities provide
accommodation for outdoor education. If a course in London is decided on, several firms deal with school visits to London and can
provide good accommodation. They will also amend the tours they
offer (e.g. sightseeing tours) to fit in with a different programme.
Hotel and guest house accommodation is usually either too expensive
or unsuitable for younger pupils. Accommodation usually has to be
booked several months ahead, and with local authority hostels often
much earlier.
  Transport can be by public buses, school minibuses or it may be
advisable to hire local transport in the area. Bus companies will
provide quotations for a hired bus and party travel can be cheaper
by British Rail. The most flexible situation is to have the use of
minibus/es with two members of staff on the course who can drive.
  The main visits should be chosen first. Firms are often helpful
if the party comes from a distances and will do their best to give
the time requested. Other visits can be fitted in when these have
been arranged, taking into account travel time and meal times.

Example of an actual course for 14-15-year-old pupils (at Leith
Academy, Edinburgh)

The beginning of Certificate Economics in the third year in 1973
meant that for the first time economics was given an important place
on the school timetable. In the first term Economic Behaviour was
studied by means of projects and activities to induce interest in
the subject, and to introduce basic concepts. They studied the producer in the second term, why he produces, how much he produces and
the effect of his production on consumers. The Field Course took
place at the end of that term and was based on the East Lothian
County Council Field Study Centre at Innerwick, near Dunbar. Its
main academic aim was to enable pupils to practically apply the work
they had been learning for the previous seven months.
  Programme:
  Day 1: (a) Visit to local farm and discussion with farmer.
          (b) Visit to Dunbar Grammar School. Slide talk by
              Geography teacher.
  Day 2: (a) Visit to local pottery and Town House.
          (b) Visit to International Golf Holdings and discussion
              with Manager. Commercial and social survey of
              Dunbar.

Day 3:   (a) Visit to Lifeboat Station.
         (b) Workbook session. Visit to North Berwick.
The most valuable sessions were those at the golf club factory and
the farm, where good discussion took place. The pupils were able to
apply readily some basic concepts, especially industrial location,
markets and production. They discovered for themselves the importance of the cement works in employing local labour; the new
market for farm produce in the frozen food trade; the use of industrial estates and the necessity for offering housing where jobs
are to be provided; the dependence of the people of Dunbar on the
tourist trade.

6 OTHER NON-CLASSROOM TEACHING METHODS

There are two main types of local area study which can be used for
younger pupils.

(a) Economic planning study of an urban area

The aim is to study in some depth industrial change in an urban area
in a full day's work (related to the concepts of aggregate output
and aggregate income but without specific reference to Keynesian
employment theory, which would be used with older pupils). In a
town in a Development Area the pupils in groups could map new manufacturing industries and new tertiary industries, including new
shopping areas. In later discussion work, the simple links between
growth of output and income in the new manufacturing industries, and
growth of spending in the area and consequent increase in tertiary
industry and retail stores output could be established. In an area
of rapid industrial growth similar work could be done on links
between aggregate output and income in new manufacturing and new
tertiary industries, and pupils could also map land and housing and
do traffic counts to discover the deficiencies in the social infra-
structure for attracting new industries to the area. In each case,
they would be reinforcing knowledge of basic theory of industrial
location.

(b) Study of prices and demand in local markets

As a means of developing understanding of the concepts used in the
theory of prices, price behaviour in a variety of local markets can
be analysed, e.g. in retail outlets in a town, a town retail market,
the market for houses in the district around the school, or the
market for transport in the local area. Pupils can observe varying
prices for standard products in retail outlets, analyse the reasons
for this variation and subsequently analyse price changes through
the year in a single retail outlet. They may also study the demand
for transport in the local area and by sample interviews assess the
influence of price and quality of service on transport use.

7 EVALUATION AND CONCLUSIONS

Evaluation on visits and field courses has been of pupil performance
rather than of the success of teaching method in inducing economic
understanding. Therefore our evaluation of the method is im-
pressionistic, but from experience of many business visits and a few
field courses with under-16s we think that pupil interest is stimulated not only in the material studied on the visit/course but is
extended to other areas of the subject. Allied to increased interest is a fuller understanding of the material studied, and this is
particularly apparent amongst average and below average ability
pupils. There is scope for the Curriculum Project of the Economics
Association to assess more scientifically these claims, but they are
particularly substantiated by Senesh in his experiments (see section
1).

Non-classroom teaching methods aim to provide opportunity to
learn and apply concepts and to reinforce knowledge of theory in the
real world. They also indirectly assist in early learning of theory
since application of concepts provides a practical foundation for
theory learning; e.g. in a study of prices and markets concepts of
scarcity and choice are applied to retail markets, and upon this can
be based early study of supply and demand theories of pricing.

Many economics teachers recognise that there is a problem of
subject structure in any attempt to teach in the classroom elementary economics to the under-16s, and it is a problem only too readily
seized upon by those headteachers, who believe that the social
sciences are 'too difficult' for pre-sixth-form education. Non-
classroom teaching methods are important means of solving these
problems by providing younger pupils with real world laboratories
in which they can experiment with concepts, and even theories, basic
to the subject.

REFERENCES

1 SENESH, L., The Organic Curriculum, 'The Councillor', 1960.
2 LEE, N., Economics Education for the Newsom Child, 'Economics',
   Spring 1969.
3 HOLLEY, B.J., The Place of Economics in the Secondary Curriculum,
   in Whitehead, D.J. (ed.), 'Curriculum Development in Economics',
   Heinemann, London, 1973.
4 LUMSDEN, K.G. and ATTIYEH, R., The Core of Economics,
   'Economics', Summer 1971.

DISCUSSION

Brian Robinson argued that visits had a crucial role to play in any
economics course for younger pupils in the creation of learning
experiences, and that visits were, if anything, more important for
younger pupils than for older ones. In his experience, too, it was
often the less academic child who derived most from a successful
visit, and, by the same token, derived least from an unsuccessful
one. He recommended that teachers consider the possibility of

highly specific visits. For example, half a day spent in reinforcing the concept of capital could be very worthwhile. For this
sort of visit to work properly, meticulous planning was essential
and a prior visit by the teacher virtually obligatory.

There was general agreement that visits were highly useful, but
not everybody felt able to support all of Robinson's claims as to
their merits. Some speakers wondered whether some of the experiences derived from visits could not be simulated in a classroom at
great saving in time, money and effort. For example, the film 'Hard
Times' contained a scene which both illustrated and commented on
modern techniques of mass production, and most schools owned ampli-
fiers and loudspeakers which were fully capable of simulating
typical factory floor noises and noise levels. One speaker cited
examples of schools where this sort of thing was being done.

Robinson was unimpressed by these observations. Certainly such
ventures had something to offer, but were a poor substitute. Their
great disadvantage was that they still took place in a classroom and
constituted classroom experiences. What children needed was experience of the real thing, which is outside the classroom. If economics pupils were to emulate the discovery work done by pupils in,
for example, the natural sciences, then the only worthwhile labora-
tory was the real world, which nobody could truthfully describe as
being inaccessible to teachers.

Nevertheless, arguments were put in favour of bringing the
outside world into the classroom, and these were based on the
premise that the alternative suggested by Robinson was impracticable
in certain instances. In schools where visits were strictly ration-
ed, visiting speakers, films, and tape/slide programmes might well
have an important role to play. Had he managed to persuade firms to
allow his school parties to be addressed on the firm's premises by a
shop-steward or other union official? Had his pupils ever been
taken on a conducted tour solely by such a person? He confirmed
that such events were rare. The solution was, he suggested, to
invite such persons to speak in the school subsequent to the visit.
This remark prompted one speaker to urge that teachers should involve firms in follow-up work as a matter of course. This might
mean sending them a copy of a completed project or, as in the case
he had in mind, inviting representatives of the firm to a showing of
a tape/slide programme produced as a result of the visit. This sug-
gestion was very well received, and seemed to transform the session;
participants turned from airing doubts about worth to discussing
ways and means of overcoming practical difficulties.

It was generally agreed that the hardest task was to arrange a
visit to a firm which was used to receiving visitors. Such firms
normally provided a 'package tour' in which the only deference to
the existence of differentiable groups of people was the variable
standard of the valedictory refreshments and of the souvenir
leaflet. The problem was to persuade such firms to offer something
pertinent to economics classes, and in some cases the problem was
insuperable, the insuperability tending to be in direct relation to
the size of the organisation concerned. In very large vertically
integrated industries the best solution was often to seek access to
the smaller ancillary firms.

Nobody had an answer for the participant who wanted to know how

one persuaded a firm to release key personnel to talk to pupils
below the rank of sixth form Advanced level, but Robinson gave
useful hints on how to gain the confidence of managers who were
reluctant to divulge information about wage-rates, product developments, pricing policies, etc. His main technique was to convince
the manager that the pupils in his charge were well under his direct
personal control, and that all written material would be vetted by
him personally and would be confined to the school. The question of
using cameras and tape-recorders during a visit was clearly a matter
that needed to be settled well in advance of the visit. Tape-
recorders might well prove counter-productive. Shorthand allied to
a good memory were attributes that teachers might well develop to
their advantage on factory visits.

Cautionary tales were legion, and appropriate morals were drawn.
Herewith a selection. Be extra tactful if you intend taking women
into industrial situations which are traditionally men's domain and
declare your intention at the commencement of negotiations for a
visit. Ascertain who has the obligation to provide adequate pro-
tective clothing. Prepare your classes so that they know what to
expect and dissuade them from staring at workers as if they were
inanimate curios. (As one speaker pointed out, in close-knit communities the worker may well be some other pupil's Mum or Dad.) Try
to discover what experiences the firm has had with recent school
parties, and how these experiences might have affected the firm's
attitude. Give serious consideration to visiting small firms, where
speakers are normally well-informed. However disastrous the visit,
try to depart on terms that enable a return visit to be arranged
sometime, because, you never know, things may change for the better!
Give serious consideration to visiting a firm more than once with
classes on two-year courses - the contrast between the firm's activities on each occasion can be truly enlightening with regard to
the teaching of 'change - the reaction to market forces'.

There was a final word of comfort for those teachers for whom
visits remain an impossible dream. One speaker mooted that there
was evidence to suggest that intellectual conceptualising may occur
at a time and place removed from any particular relevant experience.
There were things that fifteen- and sixteen-year-olds could learn
and understand without recourse to materials. He doubted whether
visits were essential to the formation of concepts, and many years
of observation had led him to place great faith in what an imaginative teacher could achieve in a classroom with pupils who were
also prepared to exercise their own imagination. He was not arguing
against visits. He was in favour of them, but he could not accept
the inference that the child who was deprived of them was as severely disadvantaged as Robinson's views appeared to suggest.

Part three

ECONOMICS FOR LESS ACADEMIC PUPILS

Chapter 10

CSE ECONOMICS
Pamela M. Morrison

For the past seven years economics has been offered at Townfield School as one of the two-year courses leading to CSE or 'O' level. What is perhaps unusual is that the 'O' level course has developed from the CSE course rather than the other way round, and it is still the CSE work which dominates the activities of the department. Before going into a more detailed study of the economics course, it will be useful briefly to describe the school and the general developments at CSE level.

Townfield School is a large comprehensive (1,500 students) set in the middle of a 1920s council housing estate, in an industrial area on the fringe of London. It was formed in 1972 from the amalgamation of two secondary modern schools, which were fortunately on the same site. During the five years before amalgamation there had been considerable curriculum innovation at the girls' school, which was therefore willing to introduce new courses in the hope that these would be as successful as the ones already introduced; there were comparable developments in the boys' school at the same time. The introduction of Mode 3 CSE linked studies had been the main development, where each student followed a central theme 'The seven ages of man' through a variety of subjects, each subject maintaining its own independence. This involved the students in a variety of project work and independent study, and this often overflowed into subjects not directly concerned with this scheme. This meant that the students were not only prepared to tackle new subjects, but were also able to use the methods they were using in their linked studies in every subject. It was this situation that the CSE economics fitted into easily and happily.

AIMS AND OBJECTIVES OF A CSE ECONOMICS COURSE

The economics that is taught is intended to give students an understanding of how they are affected by economic decisions made by other people, how to make decisions of their own, and how their decisions may affect other people. Most of them will be young school leavers, and so one of the priorities is to give them a broad coverage of as many topics as possible rather than to delve deeply into any one aspect of economics.

Most of those students who do remain at school for the full two years will enter the Middlesex CSE Elements of Economics; however, I would emphasise that the course is not constructed so that its sole aim is that each student passes the CSE with as high a grade as possible. For many of our students this type of goal is too long-term and too abstract; what we try to do is to maintain their interest from week to week and develop the topics so that they see the links between the different aspects themselves, then at the end of the course they sit the paper regarding it as an extension of their work rather than as its culmination. This is partly because of the influence of the linked studies course, which is continuously assessed, but more importantly because of the nature of the 'Elements of Economics' examination. This examination has been de-scribed in detail in Economics for the Sixteen-Year-Old School Leaver (1) and in Terminal Economics: the Experience of CSE. (2) Thus, broadly speaking, the educational objectives of the course we teach are those specified in 'Terminal Economics'.

THE CONTENT OF THE COURSE

The work is based on half-term units. Each unit is divided into approximately five topics, a week being spent on most topics although some may take considerably longer. It is divided in the following way:
Year One: Money
            Financial Institutions
            Buying and Selling
            Production
            The British Economy
Year Two: Population
            Social Services
            International Trade (divided into Trade and Develop-
            ment).
From the division between the two years, it is possible to see how in the first year much of what is learnt is of a factual nature, whereas in the second year each student is asked to consider topics which can be said to involve some moral considerations, and the lessons are generally designed to provoke more discussion and to encourage the students to make value judgments based on evidence.
    The start of the course is almost totally descriptive, the students actually handle money, both British and foreign, and gradu-ally the concepts of exchange, and measure of value are understood. As the year progresses, some topics are examined rather more closely, and gradually a little economic theory is introduced, but at all times the emphasis is on working from the students' experi-ence rather than from any abstract concept. This means that eco-nomic analysis is not an intrinsic part of the course. It would be more correct to say that it is the economic aspects of their everyday lives that form the basis of what is taught.
    By the end of the first year topics such as trade unions are studied and lively discussions are often provoked by studying a current industrial dispute. It is at this stage that normative con-siderations enter into the course, and the students are encouraged

to discuss the issues involved and if possible reach some conclusions of their own. The content of the second part of the course
goes on to extend this decision-making process over a range of
topics. It calls upon the students to use some of the factual
knowledge contained in the first part of the course and to apply it
to the broader issues studied during the second year.

THE METHODS USED IN TEACHING CSE ECONOMICS

The young school leaver needs a very different type of approach from
that used with a conventional '0' level group. The raising of the
school leaving age made this difference even more apparent, although
it existed before. As Hugh Cunningham says of these students, 'The
"early leavers" will now be staying on for a further year. In many
cases they will be the "average and below average" pupils mentioned
in the Newsom Report's terms of reference ...' (3) He goes on to
say that there is 'a conflict between the aims of teachers and those
of their pupils' and that those pupils 'value those objectives in
their education which can be seen to be useful - in other words they
want the bits of knowledge and the kinds of skills that will help
them to get decent jobs'.
  In a school such as ours, where this type of student predomi-
nates, any course that is to be successful needs to concentrate on
this and to work from it. As Jackson and Marsden (4) pointed out,
the working-class student has short-term aims, and is only able to
retain short-term concrete goals. During the fourth and fifth years
for most students the most important aim is to obtain employment, so
that they become wage-earners and their status within the family
group rises. Although economics is not directly vocational, most
students do feel that it is very relevant to their working lives and
are quite able to see how it can be useful to them in the future.
Also, the course is made as directly relevant to the local economy
as possible, in order that the work is based directly on the
students' experience.
  For example, when price changes are studied, it is the task of
one or two of the group to monitor price changes over a few weeks;
this is done at one of the local supermarkets, chosen by the
students. This links the Retail Price Index with their own local
shops, and helps them to see what the RPI indicates. For most of
the students with whom we are concerned, the technique of weighting
is far beyond their capabilities, although they are quite able to
understand its importance.
  The study of wholesaling and retailing is almost always based on
the local shopping centres, involving a good deal of local discussion and argument on the relative merits of the small corner shop
and the department store.
  When population is studied the starting point is usually the
origins of each member of the class. In a multi-racial class in a
London school, this usually provides enough work to last at least
half a term, and ranges from population drift in the 1930s from the
depressed areas, to indigenous Londoners moving from Shepherds Bush,
and of course the number of immigrants from developing countries.
It is a policy of the department that we do not brush questions that

cause tension under the carpet, but rather that we explore them as
far as possible in the classroom and try to deduce why tension
exists and how it might be reduced.

The problems that are posed in teaching this type of course are
very different from those met with a more able group. There is a
much wider ability range than in an 'O' level group; it varies from
those who will obtain a 'Grade One' CSE, which is the equivalent of
an 'O' level pass, to those who have learning difficulties. It is
impossible to treat this type of group as a single unit, and as far
as written work is concerned it would be unfair to ask them all to
do the same amount of work in the same time. This is tackled by
giving as much individual work as possible once a certain amount of
core work is finished. The least able very rarely do more than this
initial amount, which is teacher-directed and usually very simple.
The more able amplify their work by note-taking and more detailed
explanation, while the most able will quite frequently do a good
deal of reading and more original work in their own time. This is
perhaps one of the most rewarding aspects of the informal atmosphere
created by this approach; many of the more able students do produce
excellent pieces of work and are often more independent than the
more able student not required to mix with the 'young school
leaver'.

The difficulties of dealing with apathetic students of below
average or average ability must not be underestimated, and while
they are sometimes prepared to make quite lively contributions to
discussions, and will listen to somebody talking, to get them to
work on paper at all is almost impossible and can result in some
very trying periods. However, it is a consolation to find that this
happens in most if not all subjects at some time or another and is
no reflection on economics itself.

Because such an emphasis is laid on individual work, an important
part of the course is the presentation of studies or projects.
These range from very small pieces of work on individual topics done
at the beginning of the course over a relatively short time span, to
the full-blown CSE project which many of our students present at the
end of their course. The school is very orientated towards this
type of work and so there is a base on which to build. Most
students are accustomed to presenting their work in this way, and
know how to tackle a subject. What is more difficult is to show
them how to be selective in the material they use so that the work
they do is relevant to the topic they are studying and is basically
economic in nature. The quality of the work that many of the
students produce is not outstanding, but it is often as good if not
better than the work that would be done in a conventional lesson in
a more accepted discipline.

EVALUATION

With such a range of ability, we find it difficult to evaluate the
work on the usual scale, because certain students will always receive low marks and will rapidly become discouraged. Thus within
the term's work, there is very little formal marking; instead,
students are encouraged to keep their work up-to-date with no more

than the teacher reading the books, rectifying errors, and commend-
ing good pieces of work. However, there are school examinations and
students are required to sit a paper at least once a year. This we
base on the final CSE examination which they will sit at the end of
the second year, but only covering work that they have done. This
does have the effect of encouraging many of them to sit the CSE
paper when they were previously very unwilling to sit any public
examinations. However, strong emphasis is not laid on these examinations and they take place within normal lesson time.

CONCLUSION

In the approach used, a direct appeal is made to the students'
interests, via their short-term goal of entry into the working
world. All the topics are studied from their direct experience
rather than from abstract economic ideas. Furthermore, a student-
centred approach is used, so that each student is extended as far as
possible, but so that the below average student is not put into a
threatening situation. Economics does lend itself to this on the
basis of the spiral approach to the curriculum advocated by Bruner.
Finally each student is encouraged to produce individual work, done
mainly out of the classroom in the form of projects.

Although economics has been taught to the full ability range for
seven years, as in many other subjects there are one or two students
who are unable to cope with this type of course, because they are
either so anti-school that they will not respond even to a heavily
student-centred course, or they are unable to cope with even the
simple levels of core work. For these students we have devised a
course with a much broader base within the social sciences, but with
a great deal of practical work involved and with little or no theory
at all. Economics will be introduced but at a much simpler level
than in the CSE course. However this is necessary only for about
10 per cent of the year group. For the rest of the ability range
the CSE economics course that we provide is very successful and it
is proving to be increasingly popular as time goes on. At the same
time we are aware of the need for a more academic approach with the
most able students as they come up through the school.

In this way, we feel that we have shown that the fears of
teachers (and others) that economics cannot be usefully taught at
this level are groundless.

REFERENCES

1 ROBINSON, T.K., Economics for the Sixteen-Year-Old School Leaver,
   in 'Teaching Economics', 2nd edn, LEE, N. (ed.), Heinemann,
   London, 1975.
2 SMITH, F.S., Terminal Economics: the Experience of CSE, in
   'Curriculum Developments in Economics', WHITEHEAD, D. (ed.),
   Heinemann, London, 1974.
3 CUNNINGHAM, H., The Young School Leaver, in 'ROSLA and After',
   Book 1, BBC Publications, London, 1971.
4 JACKSON, B. and MARSDEN, D., 'Education and the Working Class',
   Penguin, Harmondsworth, 1969.

Chapter 11

CSE SOCIAL ECONOMICS
Jennifer H. Wales

The aim of the CSE social economics course is to provide the student
with knowledge of areas of economics likely to be of importance to
him in future. Hence the course concentrates on economic problems
related to the individual as a wage-earner, tax-payer and consumer.
It is aimed at providing the student with both the economic information and a suitable mode of conceptual analysis to enable him to
deal with issues of this type.

It is also aimed at giving the student an insight into the
workings of the mixed economy in which he is growing up and into his
own position in the economic structure of society. The interdependent nature of economic relationships in modern society and of
separate national economies within the world economy are particularly important in developing a mature outlook in economic thinking.

An integral part of the course is to attempt to enable the
student to form a discriminating opinion on the main sources of economic information available to him, those provided by broadcasting
and the newspapers. By concentrating on current issues and attempting to analyse them, as popularly presented, in the light of the
basic concepts of Western economics, it is aimed to give the student
the critical apparatus with which to evaluate them usefully.

The content of the East Anglia CSE Social Economics Course is as
follows:

Introduction
A simple explanation of the scope of economics, i.e. the problems
facing people who go to work, earn their incomes and satisfy
their daily wants.

Division of Labour
The reasons for specialisation. Variety of occupations.

Money
The barter system. The uses of money. The changing value of
money.

Earnings
How wages and salaries are determined - professional, skilled and
unskilled; day and piece rates, simple bonus systems.

Trade Unions
Types, aims and organisation. Union methods, e.g. collective bargaining.

Methods of Buying and Selling
(a)   By description and grade, sample, auction, direct dealing (inspection of goods, comparison of prices).
(b)   Sales techniques such as hire purchase, credit sales, trading stamps, gift schemes.
(c)   Protection of the consumer, e.g. by Consumer Advisory Councils, British Standards Institution, Consumers' Association ('Which?'), Citizens' Advice Bureaux to deal with consumers' complaint at local level. Protection by Acts of Parliament.
(d)   Price fixing.

Advertising
Methods, costs, advantages and dangers.

Bank Services
Deposits and current accounts. The cheque system. Credit transfers. The Clearing House system (including local clearings). Overdrafts and loans; travellers' cheques; other services of banks. Functions of the Bank of England. All the foregoing should be treated simply.

Post Office
(a)   Monetary services - postal order, money order, telegraphic money order, cash on delivery, Giro.
(b)   As agents for government departments - licences, pensions, etc.

Savings and Investment
(a)   Post Office, trustee savings banks, building societies, unit trusts.
(b)   House purchase.

Insurance
(a)   Principles of insurance. Personal risks, business risks. How insurance works.
(b)   Life and endowment assurance (link with savings above).
(c)   National Insurance.

Rates and Taxes
(a)   Central Government income and expenditure. The Budget, chief items.
(b)   Income Tax and PAYE (calculations not necessary).
(c)   Local Government income and expenditure.

Forms of Business Ownership
Their management, provision of capital, disposal of profits.
(a)   Private enterprise - sole trader, partnership, private and public limited companies, co-operative societies.
(b)   Public enterprise - Local Government trading. Central Government - nationalised industries. Public corporations.

Buying and Selling
(a)   Retail trade - the different forms of retail unit, including small shopkeepers, department and multiple stores, self-service stores, mobile shops, travelling salesmen, retail market, mail order business.
(b)   Wholesale trade - the different ways of marketing goods in bulk between producers, manufacturers and retailers, including manufactured goods, perishable foodstuffs, non-perishable foodstuffs and raw materials, home produce. The Co-operative Wholesale Society.
(c)   Cash and trade discounts.

Overseas Trade
(a)   Necessity for imports and exports.
(b)   Visible and invisible trade, balance of trade, balance of payments (simple treatment only).
(c)   Tariffs. Trading areas, e.g. European Economic Community, European Free Trade Association.

Location of Industry
(a)   Reasons for distribution of major industries.
(b)   The changing pattern. Central and local government measures.

Transport and Communications
(a)   Advantages and disadvantages of road, rail, sea, canal and air transport. Considerations in choosing form of transport, including cost, convenience and speed.
(b)   Communication services of the Post Office - letters, parcels, post cards, printed papers, telecommunications.

The examination is divided into two sections - a written paper of two hours' duration and a teacher's assessment of the work done in the previous two years. The written paper is divided into two sections. In the first part there are 20 short answer questions worth 20 marks. The second section is composed of short essay-type questions of which 5 must be selected. The essay questions carry 60 marks.

INTRODUCTION TO THE COURSE

It is always necessary to start the course with a general introduction because the majority of students come to the subject with no previous knowledge of it. This introduction is a simple explanation of the scope of economics. A useful way to begin is to look at it in terms of the problems which face people who work, earn their livings and satisfy their daily wants. A diagram can be built up through questions and answers to show these problems. Each question added to the diagram leads to a brief discussion on a section of the syllabus. The topics can be linked together and related to the individual through the discussion. (See Figure 11.1.)
   Although many students have no direct knowledge of the subject, they will have experienced many aspects of the course already in

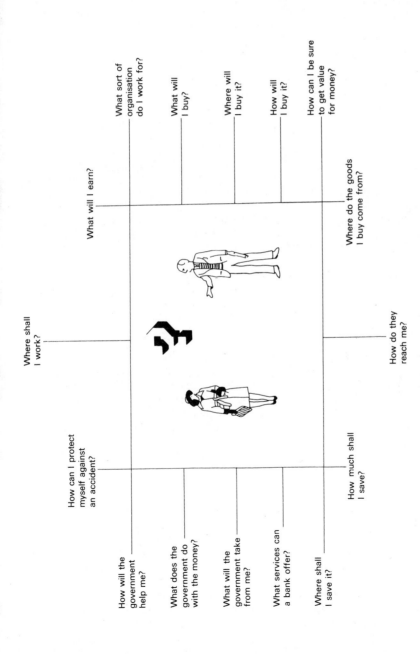

Where shall
I work?

How can I protect
myself against
an accident?

How will the
government
help me?

What does the
government do
with the money?

What will the
government take
from me?

What services can
a bank offer?

Where shall
I save it?

How much shall
I save?

How do they
reach me?

Where do the goods
I buy come from?

What will I earn?

What sort of
organisation
do I work for?

What will
I buy?

Where will
I buy it?

How will
I buy it?

How can I be sure
to get value
for money?

FIGURE 11.1   A build-up diagram for the opening lesson

their everyday lives. If the first topic is chosen carefully it can
be used to give the group confidence in dealing with the course.
Shopping is a good example of a first topic for a group of girls as
they feel that they know something about it and can therefore contribute. A great deal of field work can be done on this topic, so
students start to develop a method of investigation and thought
which will be of use to them throughout the course.

From the discussion of shopping simple elements of price theory
can be developed. Demand schedules can be drawn up by simple
questioning. Price changes can be followed in local shops and compared with the national price index.

TEACHING TECHNIQUES

In any group of students taking this course almost inevitably some
are passing the time until they leave school. In order to maintain
the interest of these students it is necessary to employ a very
varied range of techniques both in and out of the classroom.

The basic written work can usually be done through worksheets
after some discussion of the topic. A great deal of basic information can be put into charts and diagrams. Building up diagrams
appeals particularly to girls and helps the logical development of
the topic. They also provide material that is easy to learn for
revision purposes.

It is important to use the varied abilities of the students.
Those who enjoy writing will happily make up short plays and develop
role-playing situations. Consumer protection and trade union negotiations adapt well to this treatment. Some students enjoy demonstrating their artistic talents and can show such situations in
strip cartoons. Both these methods give the students the satisfaction of seeing their own work displayed to others.

Simple games can be developed to show, for example, how share
prices fluctuate. When doing this, interest is always aroused among
the girls when they discover that the 'Financial Times' is pink!

Throughout the course there is plenty of scope for a great
variety of work outside the classroom. Group visits to local shops
and factories are easily organised, especially if the lessons are
timetabled into an available block of time, such as an afternoon.

Field work is generally most successful and less time consuming
when individuals or groups investigate different parts of a project
which is then correlated in the classroom. Charts and other displays can be made by the groups so that the whole topic can be shown
to the class.

Projects from field work provide interesting material and aid the
understanding of many concepts. The selection of subjects for the
projects must be guided carefully in order to produce work of a
genuinely economic nature. There is considerable scope for subjects
on local industry and commerce. The project often has a dual
purpose in that students often select a field to study that they are
considering entering on leaving school. The two topics that are
often chosen for this reason are banking and the retail trade.
Those who have jobs on Saturdays or during the holidays also have a
good source of material, as they have some insight into their chosen
subject before they begin.

A variety of topics can be looked at usefully through the medium
of a project, especially those of current interest as the media form
a useful source of material. Using newspapers and television
reporting also helps to develop a discriminating attitude to such
sources. Many students merely accept the things they see around
them and much can be learnt by looking more carefully. Parents are
often a useful source of information and can help to expand on a
practical level subjects covered in school. Interesting details can
be obtained on, for example, trade unions and shopping habits
through questionnaires filled in for homework.

RESOURCES FOR THE COURSE

There is a great deal of information available for use in the
classroom as many bodies provide large quantities of information
about themselves and associated topics. The financial institutions
and government bodies are particularly willing to provide material.
They also often have a variety of films and speakers available.
Visits to such institutions are of varying value as they do not
always give a great deal of insight into the functions of the institution. A visit to the Bank of England, for example, is of little
use to students of this age and ability as they would see very
little activity. On the other hand, a visit to the Stock Exchange
can be very beneficial as it brings to life material already covered
in the classroom.
    There is still plenty of scope for books and other material, es-
pecially for the less able. 'Economics - An Introductory Course' by
Donnan Baron and 'Social Economics' by Jack Nobbs are both useful
textbooks, but both cater for 'O' level and the top end of the CSE
ability range. A half set of a book like 'Business World' by
Winston Barber is a valuable addition to a basic text as it forms a
simple introduction to many topics in the course and provides good
material for the less able child. There are some games and simu-
lations on the market at present and there are many areas of the
syllabus that are good subjects for such treatment; for example,
Transport and Communications and Business Ownership are likely
candidates. This method of teaching is particularly useful for
aspects of the course that are not easy to see functioning outside.
As yet there has been no series of television programmes catering
for this age group and ability range taking a course in social economics. This would be a valuable development, as students taking
this course usually respond well to the medium of television.

CONCLUSION

The social economics course is more descriptive than CSE economics
as it concentrates on the institutions and influences that affect
the individual in the economic aspects of his life. It is necessary
therefore to teach the subject with emphasis on personal experience
and involvement, which requires that field work becomes an integral
part of the course. The basic economic ideas are extracted as far
as possible from field work, which gives the student a practical

grasp of them. For these students, this is preferable to evolving economic concepts purely theoretically. In the classroom it is always necessary to work at a practical level.

Several parts of the syllabus provide scope for looking at the local area. The project is the most notable example of this. A Mode 3 examination could, however, permit a more thorough study of the economic structure of the area in the context of the national economy. The syllabus can be treated in a reasonably flexible manner, as some topics are dealt with most effectively when they are of general interest. The Budget is an excellent example of such a topic. The referendum on the European Economic Community provided a convenient time to deal with international trade and trading groups.

The most important aspect of a social economics course is the relationship of topics chosen to personal experience and the student's future life. It also provides valuable opportunities for the teacher of economics to work closely with colleagues in other departments, especially when dealing with such themes as Advertising and the Consumer. The course is useful both to the student leaving at sixteen, as it should increase his ability to cope with economic problems and decisions, and to the student taking up further studies in the commercial field.

Chapter 12

SCHOOLS' 'UNDERSTANDING INDUSTRIAL SOCIETY' PROJECT-ASSESSMENT

D. Lyne

THE PROJECT

This is a Mode 3 course in social economics, designed to be taught in four or five periods per week in the fourth and fifth years at secondary school, and leading to an examination at CSE or 'O' level. Further details of the course are provided in an Appendix to this paper. It is not intended as a vocational course for those preparing to enter industry and commerce, but rather as an element in the general education of pupils. The stated aims of the course are as follows:

1 To enable pupils to appreciate (a) the motivation of people as they play different roles, e.g. owner, manager, worker, consumer and citizen, (b) the possible conflicts of interest between these roles.
2 To enable pupils to discern for themselves the pattern of relationships in economic and social structures so that in later life they are able to assess both constructively and critically the information and opinions which are fed to them through the media.
3 As a result of the above, to enable pupils to appreciate, and participate actively in, the choices which are open to them as individuals and as a community, both nationally and globally.

CERTIFICATION

Certification for the 'O' level examination is by the Associated Examining Board, and for the CSE examination has so far been by the West Midlands Examinations Board, since the original participating schools were from Warwickshire, Coventry and Staffordshire. Originally, the possibility of some form of single examination for both CSE and 'O' level was investigated. Suggestions considered included the possibility of a common Paper 1 (possibly of objective questions) for all candidates, with alternative second papers for CSE and 'O' level candidates. Where there was any doubt about which examination was suitable for a particular candidate, the examination might have been arranged so that it was possible for such a candidate to attempt all three papers, and to be awarded a CSE or 'O' level grade according to his performance. However, there were profound differences in the requirements of the GCE and CSE examination boards, and it proved impossible to reach agreement on a single examination. It now seems unlikely that there will be any development in this direction in the near future, although in the long term much will obviously depend on the general pattern of examinations at 16+.

A single examination for all candidates would have obvious merits. However, there would be considerable difficulties in devising an examination paper which would be capable of stretching the more able candidates, while avoiding the situation in which the performance of the less able candidates was such as to leave them totally dispirited by the examination paper, and to make any worthwhile assessment of their relative achievements impossible.

ASSESSMENT

It is clearly essential that the assessment procedure should be so designed as to comply with the basic underlying aims of the course, and consequently it needs to test:
1 Knowledge and understanding of the subject matter.
2 The ability to use and apply this knowledge, to familiar and to new situations, and to appreciate the conflicting interests of different groups in society, and the often conflicting aims of economic policies.
3 The ability to analyse and to comment critically upon information presented in a variety of different ways, and to communicate to others (both orally and in writing) arguments, opinions and assessments of situations.

GCE 'O' level

The allocation of marks is:
Course work (including an individual project on a topic of restricted scope)   40%
Written examination   60%
(A) Course work
The items to be assessed are: Relative weightings
                                                     within the 40%
1 A study of either a small or a medium
   sized manufacturing firm   20
2 An individual study on a topic of
   restricted scope   20
Any four of the following: Each item 15
3 Planning a market research survey
4 A study of a department store
5 A study of the negotiating machinery
   in a local industry
6 Role play exercise and a case study
   of a worker
7 An advertising campaign

8   A study of either a small or a medium
    sized manufacturing firm (whichever
    is not done as No.1)

It is recommended that all pupils should attempt all pieces of
work. The choice of pieces for assessment allows for the practical
difficulties which may arise (e.g. with visits) and for absences.
Each item is marked out of 100 by the teacher, and the course work
is then moderated on the basis of sample scripts which the external
moderator requests schools to send to him, and finally the moderated
mark is multiplied by the scale factor to give the scaled mark.

The following guide to the writing and marking of course work is
given:
1   Study of a small or medium sized manufacturing firm
    A fairly substantial piece of work is required (about 1,500
    words) and should be based on the information which pupils have
    themselves collected on their visit to and study of a firm.
2   Individual study on a topic of restricted scope
    A piece of work of about 2,000 words is required, and the topic
    chosen should arise directly out of the work of the course, and
    should show evidence of the kind of insights obtained from doing
    the course.
3   Planning a market research survey
    Pupils write out instructions to the interviewer and a
    questionnaire. The main credit is given for the clarity of the
    instructions and the skill in making the questions appropriate
    to the product.
4   A study of a department store
    A piece of work based on information collected by pupils on a
    visit to such a store.
5   Description of negotiating machinery
    This piece of work is intended as a test of the ability to render
    a clear account derived from listening and questioning, and is
    based on a talk by a local trade unionist about the wage negoti-
    ating machinery in his industry.
6   Role play exercise and a case study of a worker
    This is based equally on three exercises:
    (a) The teacher's assessment of participation in role play.
    (b) Written work on a case study given in the project materials.
    (c) Case study of a worker.
    Items (a) and (b) are intended to test the pupil's ability to put
    himself in another person's position and to put that point of
    view clearly in group discussion. Item (c) is based on infor-
    mation gathered on questionnaires during works visits, and pupils
    are asked to put themselves imaginatively into the position of a
    particular worker.
7   An advertising campaign
    Each pupil individually should formulate a fairly detailed adver-
    tising campaign for the product which the class had originally
    decided upon in the early part of the course.
8   Study of a small or medium sized manufacturing firm
    A similar (though less substantial) piece of work to that in
    Item 1.
(B) Examination
This consists of two papers of $1\frac{1}{2}$ hours duration each, both taken in

the same session. Paper 1 consists of five structured questions, all questions to be attempted. Paper 2 gives a choice of three out of seven 'essay-type' questions, though again the questions, while requiring more continuous writing, are structured to some extent.

The possibility of the use of objective questions in some part of the examination has been considered, but the examining boards' requirements concerning the setting and pre-testing of such questions would make their use very difficult for this type of examination.

Both Paper 1 and Paper 2 are designed to test not only knowledge, but also comprehension and application in terms of the aims of the project. Paper 2 does allow for more lengthy and detailed analysis, comment and reasoned argument.

The examination scripts are marked by an external examiner, who also prepares a draft examination paper for discussion and amendment by the participating teachers before it is finally sent to the board's moderator for approval.

CSE

From 1976 onwards the allocation of marks will be the same as for '0' level, i.e.
Course work (including an individual project)   40%
Written examination   60%
(A) Course work
Further, from 1976 the West Midlands Examinations Board has agreed that course work requirements and arrangements for CSE should be the same as for '0' level, except that for CSE the work will continue to be moderated by the teachers.
(B) Written examination
There is one paper in which the candidates have a choice of five out of eight structured questions, each question containing sections of varying lengths and degrees of difficulty.

The time allocation for the examination is:
Reading time: 15 minutes
Working time: 2 hours
Extra time if required: 30 minutes

Teachers mark the scripts for their own candidates and these, together with lists showing marks for all the components of the assessment, are sent to the Board's Assessor who then makes his recommendations for grade divisions.

FUTURE DEVELOPMENT

As the number of schools involved increases and spreads over a wider area, it will become increasingly difficult to continue to operate the '0' level examination on a Mode 3 basis. A Mode 1 examination would necessarily imply some loss of teacher control of the project, but may become necessary because of organisational difficulties. (This will be introduced in 1978.)

The WMEB CSE assessment, as mentioned above, has now been brought more into line with the '0' level procedure, which has the advantages of making it less cumbersome, and of allowing the decision of whether a candidate should be entered for 'O' level or CSE to be made at a later date than was previously possible.

However, because of the structure of examination boards, an expansion of schools undertaking the project at CSE level would necessitate schools (individually or in groups) submitting the project to their own local CSE Examinations Boards for approval. Such Regional Boards would apply their own requirements, and make their separate judgments on the syllabus, assessment, etc. and might require some modifications to the pattern accepted by the WMEB (the East Midlands Examinations Board has already accepted the project for examination). This might result in a radical departure between the CSE and the 'O' level examination.

APPENDIX: SCHOOLS' 'UNDERSTANDING INDUSTRIAL SOCIETY' PROJECT

The summary below is taken from a paper prepared by the co-directors of the project, P.A.Birch and A.P.Sanday, for the Annual Conference of the Economics Association at Oxford in April 1974. The teaching and learning materials of the project have been published under the title 'British Industrial Society' by Hodder & Stoughton in April 1976.

1   Introduction

About six years ago the Government Social Survey carried out on behalf of the Schools Council an enquiry into attitudes towards school, and their report was published as Schools Council Enquiry No.1 (HMSO). Exploratory interviews were held with large numbers of parents, pupils and teachers at which they were encouraged to talk freely about how they saw the role of the school, and it emerged from this that the functions they regard as the most important are those concerned with self-development and careers.

However, teachers are well aware that little of what is done as part of the traditional secondary school curriculum contributes directly towards these aims, and therefore in at least one local authority in the Midlands discussions took place in Curriculum Development Groups as to how courses might be devised which make a more direct contribution.

The way in which self-development takes place during adolescence by a process of social experiment has been ably explored by Peter McPhail and others (see, for example, 'Moral Education in the Secondary School' published by Longman, especially Chapter 3). Basically, what adolescents do is try themselves out in a variety of different roles until they find the ones which fit in the sense of allowing them to fulfil their needs in a socially acceptable manner. What schools can do to help them through the curriculum is to enable them to gain insights into a variety of roles such as those of worker, consumer and citizen.

Self-development and career structures are intricately interwoven and both require fundamental choices to be made. In order that these choices shall be meaningful, people need to be able to work out the probable consequences of their choices and, therefore, need some appreciation of the patterns of relationships in economic and social structures. Another reason why they need this scaffolding of theory is that in adult life they will be dependent largely on information and opinions fed to them through the media, and they should be able to assess these both critically and constructively.

Self-development does not take place in isolation but in relationship to other people. The crisis of self-development is how far one has to adapt to society and how far one is able to adapt society to oneself. Both as an individual and as a member of a group there will be conflicts of interest, and part of our education is learning how these conflicts can be contained or resolved.

Our analysis therefore leads us to appreciate the need for a curriculum course whose objectives can be defined as follows:

(a) To enable pupils to appreciate (i) the motivation of people as they play different economic roles, e.g. owner, manager, worker, consumer, citizen, (ii) the possible conflicts of interest between these roles, and ways in which these conflicts might be resolved.

(b) To enable pupils to discern for themselves the pattern of relationships in economic and social structures, so that as adults they will be able to assess both critically and constructively the information and opinions which are fed to them through the media.

(c) As a result of the above, to enable pupils to appreciate, and participate actively in, the choices which are open to us as individuals and as a community, both nationally and globally.

2   The structure of the course

It was decided that secondary schools would wish to teach a course of this nature in the fourth and fifth years, with a time allocation of four periods per week. Another requirement was that it should be used by a wide range of pupils of average and above average ability, and it was therefore decided to construct the course as a series of pupils' activities which could be interpreted at a variety of levels according to the ability of individual pupils.

The material therefore consists of 'pupils' books', 'pupils' activities' and a teachers' guide. Although the comprehension level in the pupils' activities is for pupils of average and above average ability, teachers have found that the same activities can be used also with pupils of well below average ability. These activities are effective in increasing the pupils' awareness, although the conceptual level of their interpretation will be less sophisticated.

Pupils start the course by simulating the setting up of a small manufacturing firm. Having decided upon a business opportunity they market-research their product, discuss pricing policy, and find out how to raise initial finance. In these activities they may be helped by outside speakers from local firms and banks. They study the organisation of a small firm, first from documentary evidence, then at first hand by visiting, and finally by listening to taped interviews with a variety of employers. They discuss how they might organise their own firm, having regard to a variety of economic and social factors including 'job satisfaction'. This is followed by a study of retail organisation so that they can decide how to market their product, and the first part of the course ends with some simple management games.

Having established a small firm, pupils think about how they might expand. They 'go public' in order to raise more capital, and they make a careful study of where to locate their much larger mass-production factory, perhaps considering not only Britain but the whole of Europe as a market for their goods. This leads to some understanding of the changing location pattern of industry and the reasons for regional unemployment. There follows a detailed study of a mass-production firm from documents and from first-hand, which raises some interesting comparisons with the smaller firm with respect to aspects such as job opportunity.

Pupils are asked to simulate the roles of managers and owners, because these may be less familiar roles, and they are not the ones they would play immediately on leaving school (or college) and it is important that they should understand the motivation of these roles. But they are then asked to change roles and think of themselves as the employees who wish to share the increased profits. They consider ways in which they might organise themselves; they engage in a number of role-play exercises on industrial relations problems, and a study of job satisfaction based on films and material collected earlier in the course provides some fruitful insights.

After they have simulated the establishment of a mass-production firm, pupils become aware of the economic and social pressures to keep the production line going. They consider some of the marketing techniques which firms might employ, and they question whether the consumer may require more adequate protection. They begin to focus on problems which can be caused by the impact of business activities on the environment.

The third part of the course begins with sample studies on the change in demand for various products and the way in which supply adjusts itself. This elucidates the way in which prices and profits act as a mechanism for the allocation of resources, and the question is raised whether this might be done in other ways. Pupils see how the changing pattern of demand and technological changes in the means of supply may result in unemployment, and become aware of a possible clash of interest between the role of a worker demanding stability of employment and the role of a consumer requiring response of supply to demand.

Pupils are led on to consider how resources are allocated in the public sector, and to question whether the private and public sectors between them provide an adequate mechanism for resource allocation. This leads to a consideration of how the government tries to manage the economy to achieve aims such as full employment, stable prices, balance of payments and economic growth, and the complex inter-relationships of these.

Having considered the distribution of resources, pupils look at the other side of the coin, which is the distribution of personal incomes and wealth. They examine a variety of personal case histories, and these raise questions of whether income and wealth are distributed as we would wish, and if not, how they might be redistributed by means of taxation and benefits.

The course then takes up again questions raised earlier about the effects of business activities and considers ecological disturbance, conservation of resources, waste disposal and the wealth gap between developed and undeveloped countries. The effect of increasing population in exacerbating these problems is also considered. This part of the course gives an excellent opportunity to draw together a number of threads in the curriculum from both science and the humanities.

Finally, pupils look at how decisions are made on these problems at a national level through the way in which ministerial departments consult pressure groups of various kinds, and they can consider also the decision-making structure of the EEC and how this might develop to meet changing needs.

A number of features of this structure require further comment. First, the course seeks to avoid the excessive preoccupation with factual material of a transitory nature which is a feature of some social studies courses. The patterns of experience which it seeks to explore are of a fundamental nature, and although they can be appreciated at some significant level even by pupils of well below average ability, if explored in depth they can extend the ablest minds.

Second, the course was designed to meet certain objectives of a general educational nature. It was not designed to be an integrated course preparing pupils for further courses in economics, sociology, business studies, etc. Nevertheless, because the relationships which are explored form parts of these disciplines, the course may in practice fulfil this function for suitable pupils.

Although the framework of the course is tightly structured and even teachers relatively inexperienced with respect to this area of the curriculum find ample guidance in the teachers' books, there is sufficient flexibility within this framework for teachers to develop their own initiatives and adapt part of the course to local circumstances.

DISCUSSION

Mrs Morrison, in summarising her paper, indicated that she was giving serious consideration to planning a course which involved no note-taking and little extended written work on the part of students. She also intimated that if really able students came along she might well want to see them given an entirely separate course. Mrs Wales emphasised the importance in her course of contact with the town and local community in which a great deal of enquiry was undertaken. She also stressed that time was found to give attention to current affairs throughout the course. Mr Lyne spoke warmly of the merits of the 'Understanding Industrial Society' project, but hinted that it was perhaps over-structured and restrictive in operation for teachers.

Opinions on the worth of the three schemes were highly diverse. One speaker had serious doubts about the quality of work being done by students on these and similar CSE courses. As an examiner, he considered the standard of the typical examination script to be very low indeed, with little grasp of fundamental economic principles.

Another speaker wondered whether teachers were giving up trying to
stretch students and were aiming merely at keeping their interest.
Another questioned whether the sort of material being offered ought
to be examined at all. One speaker wanted to know to what extent
Mrs Morrison and Mrs Wales thought they succeeded in giving their
students an insight into the causes of unemployment, the causes of
inflation and the economic policies of the EEC, because if they were
being successful then in his view this was indeed progress. How
would their students cope with television news bulletins, newspaper
leading articles on the economy, and the recent government-sponsored
economic homilies sent to every household? In short, are these
courses increasing economic literacy, or are they so piecemeal and
descriptive that students collect a welter of superficially related
facts about a plethora of half-understood institutions?

Not everybody was sceptical. The 'Understanding Industrial
Society' project was commended for being eminently teachable to a
wide ability range, though one speaker wanted to see the syllabus
extended to cover an outline of the United Kingdom social structure,
too. Several speakers expressed admiration of the degree to which
Mrs Morrison and Mrs Wales displayed, both in their papers and in
their comments, a striking empathy with their students, and others
remarked favourably on the extremely low levels of absenteeism among
their classes.

Neither teacher saw any need to apologise for putting relevance
to students, intrinsic interest, and social usefulness high on the
list of the essential characteristics of any material being considered for inclusion in their courses. Both insisted that they
developed each topic to a depth that was reasonable in terms of the
abilities of their students. The teachers' philosophy was that they
were determined to cover material which they believed to be relevant
to the needs of their students, material which the students accepted
as relevant and which the students found rewarding to study. What,
they asked, is the alternative? The children have forced these
courses on to schools by their total rejection of the more traditional offerings of the secondary school. The teachers work
within a syllabus, but neither specifically towards an examination
nor because of the examination. The examination is there for those
who wish to take it, and marketable pieces of paper can be earned if
desired. The students enjoy the lessons, don't stay away from
school on those days and enjoy a good rapport with their teachers,
generally.

In this section, the cause of 'Erudite Economics for Everyman'
made little headway. It was even suggested that the teaching of
economics is too important to be left wholly to economists, and
indeed 'Understanding Industrial Society' was devised by two non-
economists. Finally, one speaker thought that the session had
succeeded in demonstrating that curriculum developers who think
entirely in terms of the promotion of subject disciplines by subject
specialists ignore at their peril the contribution to be made by
practising teachers with flexible and philosophical minds.

Chapter 13

ECONOMICS LINKED WITH COMMERCE-CSE AND CEE LEVELS

H. A. Ramsay

A TEACHING STRATEGY FOR THE LESS ACADEMIC STUDENT

More and more these days teachers are being asked to devise their own courses and take responsibility for assessment, including the terminal examination. For example, the new Certificate of Extended Education, to be offered in 1976, is expected to be 'particularly fruitful of Mode 3 submissions'. In the first decade of CSE a great deal has been learned about the role of the teacher as examiner in a system of school-based assessment and few today would question the legitimacy of Mode 3. With this question out of the way attention should perhaps now be directed towards devising new teaching strategies appropriate to school-based assessment. Two aspects of the situation hint at the need for a fresh look. Courses have to be more firmly based on the locality of the school, and teachers have to do their own research because textbooks designed for external examinations are not a great deal of help where curriculum control is devolved in this way. Instead teachers have more need of guidelines, i.e. hints on relating the fundamentals of their subject to the environment in which they operate, and it is in this light, as a description of one possible approach to teaching economics to the less academic student, that this paper is intended.

In terms of economics as a school subject, there is also room for experiment, particularly as there is now an area of agreement on what should be taught in courses for the less academic. The problem facing the classroom teacher is often the translation of basic concepts into examples (and language) meaningful to students, and the objectives of a trial of materials carried out at a West London comprehensive in June 1974 reflect this concern for effective communication. These were as follows:

Objectives

1 to harness the students' considerable knowledge of professional football to the business of teaching elementary economics and commerce;
2 to put over concepts in an uncompromising student-centred context

beginning and staying with the interest and experience of the
class;
3   to take advantage of the liberating variation offered by the
Mode 3 option by devising a course as localised as possible.

CONTENT

The idea behind this project was to draw on and adapt for classroom
use some of the vast volume of written material on soccer, most of
it ephemeral but some, like the offerings of Davies, (1) Douglas (2)
and Chester, (3) ranking as serious analyses of one of the more re-
silient branches of the entertainments industry. This approach has
been ably pioneered by Savidge in 'Your Soccer Team and its Management', (4) a small volume intended for students in commerce, but it
is not thought that this method, or the materials, are appropriate
to every part of an economics or commerce syllabus (Savidge seems to
stretch things a bit by including a chapter on Soccer and the
Balance of Payments!). A list of elementary concepts amenable to
this kind of treatment would include specialisation, opportunity
cost, supply and demand relationships in a market, and there is a
certain value in retaining a common theme for as long a period as
possible.
    Economics courses for the less academic benefit from the study of
service activity, too often regarded as the poor relation of manufacturing. A glamorous service industry like football almost
certainly has more appeal, especially for boys, than those hoary
favourites of teachers, the motor car and shipbuilding industries.
    Against this background the content of the four trial units was
as follows:
Unit 1 - Football as a business.
Unit 2 - The demand for football.
Unit 3 - Selling football.
Unit 4 - Where a club's money comes from and how it is spent.
Had there been time for further teaching sessions subsequent units
would have been (5) What you pay to watch football (i.e. ideas of
pricing and opportunity cost) and (6) Footballers' wages.

METHODOLOGY

A variety of methods was employed in trying out these materials,
including the following:
1   Multiple-choice question sheets, which were used in Unit 1,
    'Football as a business', and where general knowledge questions
    and 'serious' questions were intermingled to arouse pupil
    interest (see examples in Appendix 1).
2   Formal exposition, used in teaching Unit 2, 'The demand for
    football' (see the teaching notes for this unit, Appendix 2).
3   Passages for comprehension, with questions, as in Unit 3 with the
    article by T.Lyons (5) as the basis. Appendix 3 gives examples
    of the kind of questions set on advertising and on club origins.
    Savidge employs this technique with good effect.
4   Worksheets for students to complete at their own pace, e.g. the
    material on transport, Appendix 4.

5 Problem-solving exercises, used to advantage in Unit 4,
   Appendix 5.
In this type of teaching it is important that the objectives of each
unit are detailed, at least in terms of the kind of questions
students should be able to answer at the end of the course. Examples of such questions are given in Appendix 6.

EVALUATION AND ASSESSMENT

As only a trial of some of the materials and not of a full-blooded
course was possible attempts at evaluation must be tentative. The
project was helped by the prevailing euphoria of the World Cup 1974
and at the same time hampered by non-co-operation by the local club
(a visit to a ground and discussions with the manager, for example,
would have complemented the work done in the classroom).

In summary, one might essay the following conclusions about this
approach and materials based on soccer -
1 Not surprisingly, the football enthusiasts in the class benefited
  most and showed sustained interest; included in this number were
  students with learning problems. The class was far from homo-
  geneous, however; perhaps a quarter were not particularly interested in football and there is no doubt that the experiment was
  rather lost on them.
2 Among the latter group, which included some of the brightest
  students, a similar approach based on the motor cycle or sound
  system industries might have evoked a good response, and as
  manufacturing activities, these might make useful complementary
  studies to football.
3 The approach recommended in this paper requires an enthusiastic
  and knowledgeable teacher willing to spend time and money (considerable expense may be involved in amassing newspaper cuttings,
  club programmes, etc.) to convert commonplace materials into
  equipment for classroom use. Even if it is regarded only as a
  starting point before moving on to apply economic concepts to
  more traditional examples likely to occur in examination papers,
  the exercise of researching his own teaching material is invaluable for the economics teacher.

APPENDIX 13.1

UNIT 1 - FOOTBALL AS A BUSINESS

1 Match clubs to ground capacity
    (a) QPR   (a) over 60,000
    (b) Arsenal   (b) 50,000
    (c) Southampton   (c) 30,000
    (d) Milwall   (d) 40,000
    (e) Leeds United   (e) 35,000

2   Match club with population of town or city
 (a) Leicester   (a) 280,000
 (b) Burnley   (b) 160,000
 (c) Wrexham   (c) 120,000
 (d) Norwich   (d) 75,000
 (e) Luton   (e) 10,000

3   Match average home gate to London club
 (a) 31,000   (a) West Ham
 (b) 26,000   (b) Fulham
 (c) 20,000   (c) Arsenal
 (d) 10,000   (d) Crystal Palace
 (e) 6,000   (e) Brentford

4   Match proportion of ground under cover to club
 (a) Spurs   (a) 40%
 (b) Brentford   (b) 100%
 (c) Luton Town   (c) 90%
 (d) Everton   (d) 50%
 (e) Crystal Palace (e) 70%

5   Match season to minimum admission charge
 (a) 1937-8   (a) 20p
 (b) 1955-6   (b) 45p
 (c) 1969-70   (c) 10p
 (d) 1971-2   (d) 25p
 (e) 1973-4   (e) 30p

6   Match Football League attendances to season
 (a) 48-9   (a) 26 mill.
 (b) 67-8   (b) 30 mill.
 (c) 72-3   (c) 41 mill.
 (d) 74-5   (d) 25 mill.

7   How many spectators on average attend Saturday League games?
 (a) 1,000,000
 (b) 800,000
 (c) 500,000
 (d) 350,000

8   How many viewers watch televised soccer each Saturday?
 (a) 25 mill.
 (b) 10 mill.
 (c) 2 mill.
 (d) ½ mill.

9   Match competition to sponsor
 (a) Manager of the Month (a) Texaco
 (b) A Scottish Cup competition (b) Watneys
 (c) A British Clubs' competition (c) Bells
 (d) A pre-season competition (d) Dryboroughs
 (e) An amateur league   (e) Rothmans

10   Match directors to clubs
    (a)   D.Hill-Wood   (a)   Millwall
    (b)   S.Longson   (b)   Burnley
    (c)   J.Dunnett M.P.   (c)   Arsenal
    (d)   M.Purser   (d)   Fulham
    (e)   J.Mears   (e)   Notts County
    (f)   T.Trinder   (f)   Derby County
    (g)   D.Robbins   (g)   Coventry City
    (h)   R.Lord   (h)   Chelsea
(Example of general knowledge/interest question.)

APPENDIX 13.2

UNIT 2 - THE DEMAND FOR FOOTBALL: TEACHER'S NOTES

If people WANT to go to see football and they are able to pay the
price of admission there is a DEMAND for football.
    The actual amount of football that fans want to see (or the
numbers that turn up) depends on two things -
A   The PRICE of admission
B   The size of their wages, the price of doing something else, and
    their fickleness.
    Clubs are always concerned to keep up attendances at home games
but it is often difficult to predict the demand for any particular
match in advance. Let us see if we can give the clubs any help in
predicting what their gates will be. Are there, for example, any
rules which apply?
A. First on PRICE. It is generally true that when the price of
    anything is high the demand for it is usually low (and when the
    price is low demand is usually high). You don't believe this?
    Well, let us look at the price of admission to football matches
    and see if we can demonstrate that this is so.
        In September 1973, Glasgow Rangers played Arsenal in a
    friendly game to celebrate the club's centenary. Admission was
    5p (the charge in 1873!) and the game drew a capacity crowd of
    60,000.
        On the previous Saturday Rangers had played a top league
    match. The lowest price was 35p and the attendance was only
    20,000.
        If we put this information on a diagram we can see at once
    that admission price has an important effect on attendances. We
    measure the price of admission in an upward direction and the
    size of crowd from left to right (Figure 13.1).

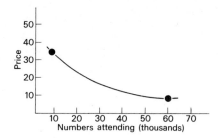

FIGURE 13.1

   Question: What would be the likely attendance if the price of
               admission was 20p?
   N.B.   Changes in demand resulting from a change in PRICE are
   called CONTRACTIONS or EXPANSIONS of demand.   So as the price
   falls to 5p the demand to see the game (which Arsenal won 2-1)
   expands to 60,000 spectators.
B.   Second on WAGES and TASTES.   Here it is generally true that
   larger pay packets mean higher attendances - an INCREASE in
   demand.   The same thing will happen if it suddenly becomes
   fashionable to be seen at a football match on a Saturday afternoon.   More people will want to attend at the same prices and
   it will show on the diagram as the demand curve SHIFTING to the
   RIGHT (Figure 13.2).

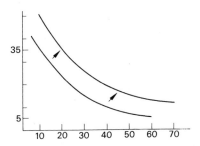

FIGURE 13.2

   Question: Find out from the diagram how many will attend after
               an increase in popularity of the game, at price 35p.

       In the same way smaller wages or bad publicity will mean
   smaller attendances - a DECREASE in demand.   Fewer people will
   attend at the same prices and this shows on the diagram as the
   demand curve shifting to the LEFT (Figure 13.3).

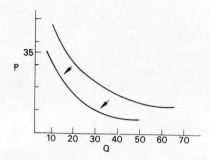

FIGURE 13.3

    Question: Find out from the diagram how many will attend after
              a three-day working week comes into force, thereby
              cutting the amount of take-home pay. (Price 35p.)
    So if we are to advise clubs on how to attract more spectators
    we must make a list of the likely outcomes of changes in prices
    and tastes. These are shown in Figure 13.4.

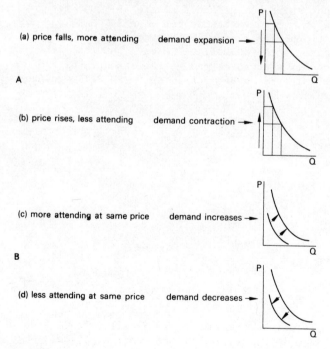

FIGURE 13.4

    Exercise: Each of the following events will have an effect on
              the demand to see a football match. Decide which of
              the four effects shown above applies to each event
              and hence try to predict how the diagram will change.

To make things simpler, let us assume that to begin with, there is just one price of admission, 45p, and the game is due to take place at 3.00 p.m. this coming Saturday.

1 Power cuts bring forward KO to 1.00 p.m.
2 The Derby horse race is live on TV at 3.00 p.m.
3 The only game being played in London.
4 A derby game with a neighbouring club.
5 The opposing team brings 10,000 fans with them.
6 The game is on pre-Christmas Saturday.
7 A dog track is built obstructing the view.
8 Entrance is free at half-time.
9 The game is switched to Sunday afternoon KO.
10 Referee's inspection in the morning - snow.
11 A new heated stand is opened.
12 Overcrowding and discomfort on the terracing.
13 The game is a friendly.
14 Hooliganism is expected.
15 A special attraction is arranged at half-time.
16 People know beforehand the match is being televised.
17 Mid-week KO.
18 Injuries.
19 VAT increased.
20 Redundancy in the area.
21 Rain - terracing uncovered.
22 New members' club completed.
23 Increase in bus and tube fares.
24 New covered enclosure, no price increase.
25 England out of World Cup last week.
26 Star player sold.
27 Home side challenging league leaders.

APPENDIX 13.3

UNIT 3 - SELLING FOOTBALL

Advertising

1 Give two reasons why a football club might use advertising.
2 Make up an advert for your club which is purely informative.
3 Design an advert which is persuasive as well as informative.
4 What difference is there between advertising and publicity?
5 Why don't newspapers charge clubs for the publicity they get on the sports page?
6 Unlike most companies football clubs make money from advertising. How do they manage this?
7 What are the media and how do they help football? Give examples of three different forms of the media.
8 What is the IBA? Give the names of three commercial TV companies and three commercial radio stations.
9 Both the Football League and the Scottish League claim copyright over their fixture lists. What does this mean?
10 What kinds of things are advertised at football grounds?
11 Make a list of all the ads you can see at your next visit to a football match.

12 Do the same for the next televised match you watch.
13 What differences would you expect in the adverts at a non-televised 3rd Division game and at the Cup Final?
14 What are branded goods and why do manufacturers use trade marks on their products?
15 What does it mean to sponsor a match or cup competition?
16 Wills, Gillette, Bell's and Texaco all sponsor sporting events. What products do these companies sell?
17 Some clubs employ P.R.Os who issue press releases. What are they?
18 How can an advertising agent outside the game benefit players?
19 Both FA Cup Final teams operate 'perks' pools. What are these?
20 Why do England players have the name 'Admiral' on their track suits?

Club origins

Many of the leading English and Scottish League clubs were formed a century or more ago, usually by groups of workers. For example Arsenal was formed by northerners working at the Royal Arsenal in Woolwich; Stoke City by railwaymen and Third Lanark (now defunct) from the Third Lanark (Rifle Volunteers) Battalion. Even teachers got into the act, Hamilton Academicals owing its origin to masters at the local school!
Question: Can you guess at the origins of the following football clubs?
           Hibernian, Sheffield Wednesday, Dynamo Kiev, Distillery, Carl Zeiss Jena, Ferranti Thistle (now Meadowbank Thistle), Lokomotiv Leipzig?
    In the beginning clubs were run by volunteers in their spare time (like your local youth club or school side) but today 91 of the 92 English League Clubs are organised as limited liability companies.
Question: What is meant by a limited liability company?
    Many clubs have moved to a more favourable site while keeping their own name.
Questions: Which league clubs, formed in other places, now play in these areas?
            London; Croydon - Shepherds Bush - Highbury.
            Glasgow; Maryhill.
            Suggest two possible reasons for their decision to move to the areas shown.

APPENDIX 13.4

Transport

1 There are two sides of transport, passenger and freight. As a football supporter which is the more important to you?
2 Why do most league sides travel to away games by coach?
3 You are the manager of QPR planning next season's travel. Which places on the list would you want to travel to by rail instead of by coach?

      Birmingham
      Carlisle
      Charlton
      Edinburgh

4 Would air travel be the best way of getting to any of these places?

      Munich
      Bristol
      Rotterdam
      Crewe

5 Imagine there is a British League of the following clubs – Leeds, Cardiff, Celtic, Liverpool, Derby, Linfield and Arsenal. Which clubs would have the greatest transport problems?

6 Which way of travelling (sea, rail, road or air) is the best for away sides in the following matches?

      Torquay v Carlisle
      Burnley v Blackpool
      Shamrock Rovers v Liverpool
      Chelsea v Fulham
      QPR v AC Milan

7 QPR are playing Manchester City at Maine Road. Leaving home on Saturday morning, what is the best way to get there?

Coach	£2.35	4½ hours
Rail	£5.15	2½ hours
Air	£10.00	1 hour
Canal	£7.00	3 days
Private car	£3.00	4 hours

Which is the best way (a) if money is no object?
                   (b) if you can't leave until 1.00 p.m.?
                   (c) if you want a comfortable journey, with no changing?

8 Match destination to railway station to time taken for the journey.

Norwich	Victoria	55 mins
Cardiff	Euston	1.55 hours
Brighton	Paddington	2.43 hours
Newcastle	Liverpool Street	2.11 hours
Preston	King's Cross	3.30 hours

Travelling by 'Rangers Rocket' special charter train, which station for Derby?

Is the fare lower or higher than the ordinary day return?

APPENDIX 13.5

UNIT 4 - WHERE A CLUB'S MONEY COMES FROM AND HOW IT IS SPENT

Money is raised by selling share certificates and if the sale is advertised to the general public the club becomes a public company. If they are sold privately (to relatives or friends) the club is a private company. Most football clubs are private companies and because they are not required to publish an annual balance sheet only the small group of shareholders may know the financial position at any time.

Profit or loss?

All companies have to send copies of their accounts to the Government's Registrar of Companies where they can be inspected by anybody.

The revenue account gives information about the club's receipts and its expenditure during the year.

If the receipts are greater than the expenditure a profit has been made. If the receipts are less than the expenditure a loss is the result.

If the club makes a profit the Government takes more than a third of it in Corporation Tax so this encourages the rich clubs to spend money on buying players, thereby reducing their profits and their tax liability.

If the club makes a profit the balance of money left after tax may be distributed to shareholders as dividends or used to increase the reserve fund.

Table 13.1 shows the income and expenditure account of a Scottish Premier League club for 1974-5.

Questions on income and expenditure account

1 How much loss did this Premier League club make in 1974-5?
2 How did this compare with the profit or loss position two seasons ago?
3 What happened to gate receipts over the two seasons?
4 The fight to make the 'Top Ten' Premier League in 1974-5 forced up costs. Which items under expenditure were affected?
5 Which items under expenditure show the effects of the rise in fuel prices?
6 In your opinion, which of these would turn the club's loss into a profit?
   Staging pop concerts in the summer
   Allowing a large company to sponsor home games in return for exclusive advertising rights
   Arranging half-time displays, e.g. by the Women's League of Health and Beauty

General questions

1 Complete the following, using the words listed below -
  The high _____ of a few clubs are based not just on admission fees but also on _____ fees. Receipts of lesser importance, in comparison with match _____ and transfer fees, are those for advertising on _____ in the stadium, and _____ contracts with businesses that sell their goods inside the stadium.
     'takings' 'concessionary' 'profits' 'transfer' 'hoardings'
2 Why is there usually a rush of transfers of footballers before the deadline in mid-March?
3 What would be the effect on the income and expenditure of a club of the following?

TABLE 13.1

EXPENDITURE	1972-3	1974-5
Transfer and signing-on fees	£10,025	£24,135
Wages and National Insurance	48,997	55,879
Secretary and treasurer's salary and expenses	300	397
Visiting team's shares	18,523	18,987
Match expenses	8,024	10,080
Playing and training expenses	2,699	2,003
Team travelling expenses	3,636	4,673
General charges	3,215	4,382
Rates and insurances	2,464	3,139
Audit fee	70	90
Legal and accountancy expenses	90	147
Overseas tours	674	–
Work on ground and general repairs	2,104	1,196
Depreciation	5,537	5,444
Surplus carried to profit and loss account	25,486	–
	£131,844	£130,552

INCOME	1972-3		1974-5	
Gate receipts		£72,969		£61,611
Season tickets		8,146		9,341
Transfer fees		30,000		–
Donations – Texaco	1,000		£2,660	
– Supporters' Association	600		800	
– Sundry			15	3,475
Ayrshire Football Pools remittances		6,000		4,000
Advertising receipts		1,065		1,729
Scottish Football League Pools allocation		7,120		13,110
Scottish Football Association World Cup distribution		–		2,000
Match draws		318		721
International youth match		140		–
Radio and television fees		825		2,890
Ground rents		70		–
Profit on sale of programmes		–		455
Gain on sale of car		185		–
Interest received – Deposit receipts	931		£812	
– Clydesdale Bank Ltd	–		–	
Deposits		2,475		7,372
Deficit carried to profit and loss account		–		8,184
				23,036
		£131,844		£130,552

Source: 'Ayrshire Post', 12 August 1975.

Discontinuing the running of a reserve side
Increase of VAT to 20%
Installing a new floodlighting system
Reduction in rates
Signing a top-class player for £200,000

APPENDIX 13.6

Final questions

(The kind of questions students ought to be able to tackle at the end of this kind of course.)

1   The boys' gate has been abolished because boys have been running on to the pitch at the end of games. It now costs you 45p entrance instead of 25p. What effect will this have on your spending?

2   Your club raised the price of stand tickets for the visit of the League champions. Why did they do this? Was it justified, do you think?

3   Why is it a good thing for a club to have a lot of supporters holding season tickets?

4   What is meant by saying that most football grounds are wasted assets?

5   The minimum prices of admission are fixed by the Football League and are standardised (that is, the price is the same at Leeds as at Darlington). Is this unfair to clubs in the lower divisions?

6   On Saturdays between 12.30 and 1.00 p.m. there is a monopoly of football on television. What does this mean?

7   League soccer fixture lists are the copyright of the Football League and the Scottish League. What advantage does this bring?

8   If your club was to be taken over by the town or city where you live, what difference might it make to
        (i) the manager
       (ii) the use of the stadium
      (iii) the price of admission
       (iv) control over the affairs of the club?

9   Say you are appointed commercial manager of your football club. How would you go about raising extra money for the club?

10 Do you think that Supporters' Associations should donate money to their clubs if they have no control over their expenditure policies?

11 Your club is a public company and you are dissatisfied with the way it's being run (sale of star players, gates falling, relegation threatening). What would you have to do to gain control and change its policies?

12 How can a club boost its advertising revenue when a home game is televised?

13 Is it true that professional footballers are overpaid for their services?

14 You are given the chance of 'signing forms' with a First Division Club at sixteen. What would you have to think about before deciding?

15 Why is there sometimes conflict between the manager and the board of directors of a football club?

16   Which activities compete with football spectating on a Saturday
     afternoon?

REFERENCES

Some source materials used in the soccer project

Referred to in the text

1   DAVIES, H., 'The Glory Game', Sphere, London, 1971.
    In-depth study of Spurs, the richest club in Britain, which
    brings out the differences between soccer clubs and other
    businesses.
2   DOUGLAS, P., 'The Football Industry', Allen Unwin, London, 1973.
    A good source of information on soccer and the media - written
    by a Club Public Relations Officer.
3   'The Chester Report', HMSO, London, 1968.
    Outline of the structure of the industry and penetrating analysis
    of the game's problems.
4   SAVIDGE, L., 'Your Soccer Team and its Management', Pitman,
    London, 1973.
    CSE Commerce textbook - descriptive in approach but chapters and
    exercises easily adapted to local situations.
5   LYONS, T., Why Soccer Depends on TV, 'Sunday Telegraph', 28 April
    1974.

Other references

'Rothmans Football Year Book 1973-4', Queen Anne Press, London.
Immensely detailed, up-to-date and particularly informative on Board
membership, ground facilities and transfers.
'Book of Football', A Marshall Cavendish Encyclopedia (75 weekly
parts), 1972.
Only a few articles useful to the teacher but highly popular reading
for the less able pupils.
VINNAI, G., 'Football Mania', Orbach & Chalmers, London, 1973.
Contains one good critical chapter on football economics.
WILLIAMS, G. and VENABLES, T., 'They Used to Play on Grass',
Mayflower, London, 1971.
Soccer technology! A novel, set in the future and part-authored by
a leading light in the game.
YOUNG, P.M., 'History of British Football', Arrow, London, 1973.
McLEOD, R., '100 Years of the Scottish Football Association',
Scottish TV Ltd, 1973.
FORBES, A., Football is Their Business, 'Business Scotland', June
1974.

DISCUSSION

Ramsay stated that his trial programme was a reaction to the over-
serious, under-relevant nature of much that passed for economics in

secondary schools. In his view, there was in society a great deal of discussion of economics which was not reflected in what schools do. Soccer, including the economics of soccer, was a matter frequently discussed by all and sundry. As a topic for use in schools, it had obvious limitations in that it tended to appeal more to one sex than the other, but it should not be difficult to find other topics equally appealing to girls, and some topics appealing to boys and girls alike. The major limiting factor with any project was the availability of relevant and suitably presented information.

His paper provoked spirited comment. Everybody liked the exercise designed to bring out twenty-seven factors that might influence demand in some way, and saw it as eminently transferable to other topics, but some considered that the teacher's notes on Demand which preceded it were erroneous, misleading and in need of drastic revision. It was generally agreed that football offered a great deal to an economics teacher, but some speakers wondered how one ensured that one dealt with the economics of football without allowing activities to degenerate into a discussion of football trivia; which some of the exercises appeared to do.

Nobody, including Ramsay, saw the topic approach as a basis for a two-year course, but some saw an important place for the development of work cards on a variety of topics using a similar approach. It was generally agreed that success was much more likely where the chosen topic was of interest not only to the students but also to the teacher, since topic work demanded hard work, detailed knowledge and sustained enthusiasm on the part of the teacher. Finding topics of mutual interest became harder, it was suggested, as the age difference between teacher and students increased. Soccer was a good choice from this aspect, as it appealed to all age groups. Non-examination courses would give individual teachers greater freedom of action, but Ramsay believed that it was perhaps unrealistic to expect teacher training colleges to turn out young teachers versatile enough to perform well both as innovators of internal courses and as efficient mentors to students on traditional courses leading to external examinations.

Chapter 14

THE ECONOMICS OF LIVING
F. S. Smith

I am concerned in this paper with putting together a course of study
for those in their last year at school who are taking economics for
the first time. The objectives of the paper are
1 To take a look at who it is we are teaching: that is, the
   characteristics of the school leaver.
2 To look at what we believe our students ought to learn.
3 To examine the question, how is this to be learned.
   At the same time I wish to introduce two themes: (a) the importance of the needs of the learner of economics - as against the
requirements of the subject; (b) an examination of the case for a
return to the teaching of political economy. The main question
which I shall be asking, I suppose, is 'Should we be doing something
different from what we are doing now, and if so, what?'
   I want to look first at the characteristics of the early school
leaver, the boys and girls themselves. We are dealing with 15-16-
year-olds who are not going on to university or other forms of
higher education. Some of them will of course be going on to some
kind of further education, either full-time or part-time, either day
or block release, as a result of the job that they take up on
leaving school.
   Thus the course we have in mind must have something for these
whether for CSE or CEE, or else for the examinations of the many
professional bodies such as the Institute of Bankers, which now have
compulsory examination papers in elementary economics. We also have
to consider the interests of the school leaver who will have no
instrumental purpose in taking economics and who will probably be
going to jobs which have no requirement of attainment in economics.
   What have these various groups got in common? Well, one thing is
that soon all of them will become 'fully fledged' citizens, they
will soon have the vote, may participate in the political life of
the country, earn money and so on. The first question the course-
builder must ask himself therefore is: 'As economists how can we
help them to realise this participation?'
   As citizens, I would suppose, they ought to have an awareness of
those factors which affect their economic livelihood. This might
therefore be taken as a statement of the general aim of an economics
course. The trouble is that we as economists, when formulating a

course in economics, tend to fall back on our own training, gathered at either university or college, and then to suppose that something like this is what these children should have. This is what I would call subject-orientated teaching: the content and method of the course being determined by the requirements of the subject. This is an academic kind of learning, setting up elegant models and theories; the sort of teaching that clever sixth formers might appreciate. I believe that the children we are talking about will turn their backs on this 'sort' of economics as being of little relevance to their immediate need to make sense of the society in which they will soon expect to play an adult role.

Having summarily rejected the traditional 'principles of economics' course, the question arises: What do we put in its place? I wish, at this point, to go back to the general aim stated above, 'an awareness of those factors which affect our economic livelihood', and partially to define what I mean by this. (I say 'partially' here because later on I wish to place the suggestions which follow within the rather wider context of political economy.)

I believe that pupils should

1 Appreciate the functions of the more important economic institutions such as banks, stock exchange and so on.
2 Recognise the inter-dependence and inter-relation of the different parts of an economy.
3 Acquire skills enabling them to find economic information; to evaluate and interpret this information.
4 Be able to read or listen to with understanding and interest, newspaper articles, news broadcasts, etc. which have an economics content.

Now it may be that none of these aims appears to be exceptional and one might ask how all this throws light upon the construction of an economics course. What do we put in place of a subject-centred course? It seems to me that what the school leaver is interested in, almost by definition, is living, and thus what we ought to be teaching is 'the economics of living', i.e. the contribution that economics can make to (better) living. What are the insights, what are the perspectives that economics can give? Given the constraints that we face in the classroom - and here the biggest constraint will be that we have less than one year in which to complete the course, in all probability with pupils who lack the background of a systematic, sequential social science training - what kind of course and what sort of methods ought we to adopt? I believe that teaching methods and course content are inextricably bound together.

Teaching method is obviously a function of many variables - the age, ability and family background of pupils; the teaching environment, including the teaching and learning materials available; and of course, the personality of the teacher. Not all pupils progress at the same rate, though in class-teaching it often appears to be assumed that they do; some may need to dwell at the 'concrete operational' stage longer than others and will require special treatment. An example from 'wage determination' will illustrate what I mean here. The subject-centred approach would generally consist of an exposition by the teacher of how the forces of demand and supply determine the wage that is paid, possibly accompanied by demonstrations of supply, demand curves, marginal productivity and so on. The approach that I am advocating will still get you to the same conclusions, but by a rather different route, and one which has, I suggest, greater immediacy and interest for these children. The teacher begins by posing a question such as 'Why do doctors generally earn more than bus conductors?' This is a realistic, interesting question, and questions similar to it will in all probability have passed through the mind of a sixteen-year-old. The answers will come: long training, anyone can be a bus conductor, the doctor has a lot of skill, not many people are prepared to train for five years, only a few have the brains, etc. So we get our major economic factors - scarcity, supply, demand and so on. The principle I wish to establish is well known: begin at the concrete operational stage, use simple examples, until you establish the formal concepts and principles which can help the child to make generalisations.

I said earlier that not all pupils progress at the same rate. I believe also that children will be motivated at different levels: some at a personal level - their interest is in their immediate future, in the jobs they might take up, the taxes they will have to pay and so on. Others respond at a domestic level, or a local one, or even a national level. Such a situation calls for a structuring of learning around what may be called 'circles of interest', for example 'shopping', 'markets', 'factories'. Again an example will illustrate the point. I remember one particularly difficult pupil who came alive only when it was discovered that her father was a shop-steward in a local factory, and we got her to develop a study of trade unions. This was a piece of work which she was later able to present to the rest of the class, and which was richly illuminated by the experiences of her parent.

Similarly, the pupil who is trying to understand the concept of inflation may achieve a far clearer and more vivid understanding when he works on a chart showing his family's weekly expenditure in relation to rapidly changing prices in the shops. He is able to 'see' inflation at work, and the process of collecting and interpreting information helps to arouse and maintain his interest, without formal teaching, and greatly enriches his understanding of the subject.

Such a course structure may perhaps be criticised on the grounds that though it has advantages in suggesting relevance and generating interest, it lacks the intellectual rigour of providing a systematic framework for the study of economics. We must, however, think very carefully about what the school leaver is to get out of his course. Is it to be a set of neatly arranged concepts and principles, called 'division of labour', 'marginal productivity', 'perfect competition'? Do these help him to make sense of the realities of the world into which he is shortly to be pitched? Does the elaborate array of assumptions underlying each of our economic models help in his understanding of things as they actually are?

I wish now to turn to my second theme: the question of whether or not there should be a return to 'political economy' in our courses. Two considerations prompt me to raise this issue, one philosophical and one practical. A person's understanding is a function of his being aware that there are a number of ways of looking at a particular institution, and that one's understanding is more or less profound according to the number of perspectives one can actually bring to bear. In a practical sense, given that we are more concerned with a child's education rather than just his knowledge of subjects, we must face the problem of how he is to become aware of the different ways of looking at economic institutions. We tend in the school to chop up knowledge into neat 35-minute periods labelled sociology, British Constitution or economics, expecting our pupils at the sound of a bell to switch off from one of these subjects and on to another. The result of much current teaching is I believe to make it extremely difficult for children to relate, to make links and associations between, the different subjects that they take. Those with examiner-experience will know this problem as it exists within a subject, let alone between subjects. Furthermore, we tend in our lessons to break off at what are often the most interesting points in a discussion with a statement such as, 'Well, let's not pursue that, it's not economics'. It will almost certainly be the case that to pursue the matter will involve some political or moral (or value) judgments, or questions of what 'ought to' or 'should' be done. In our everyday lives, problems do not arrive on our doorsteps neatly packaged and labelled 'economic problem' or 'political problem': rather they are human problems.

As far as the teaching of economics is concerned, I think that there are two factors which may have led to the difficulties I have mentioned. First there has been a decline in normative as opposed to positive economics, and secondly there is the absence, from syllabuses, of comparative studies of the various economic systems, capitalist, socialist and so on. In spite of all this, we pretend to give children a complete course on economic principles, or the economic institutions of the UK. One has only to glance at the elementary economics textbooks currently in use in schools to realise how misleading this pretence can be.

Let us take as an example a textbook (D.Baron, 'Economics: An Introductory Course', Heinemann, London, 1973) chosen at random to illustrate this point. The preface sets out the aims of the book: 'to concentrate on the British economy as it is today' and 'the book provides a year's course which is complete in itself'.

Opening the pages at random, one finds that Chapter 2, for example, deals with wage determination, using elementary supply and demand analysis, and describes in these terms the parts played by government, trade unions, employers' federations, and even introduces the notion of marginal productivity. But nowhere is the notion of power introduced, power as political strength, power as shown by the miners in their recent confrontation with government. Accepting the importance of the influence of supply and demand, we have surely to examine the process of decision-making, the question of who can force whom to do what, and the whole social background to wage bargaining.

Taking a second example from the book, Chapter 8 deals with the size of firms. It gives the advantages and disadvantages of large-scale manufacture and the motives for expansion. But again we find nothing about power, the power to expand, the power exercised in taking over other firms, the need to gain sufficient strength to avoid being taken over oneself, and, again, above all, the pursuit

of power as a political advantage which often constitutes an over-
riding consideration as far as the businessman is concerned.

It seems to me that our pupils can thus either accept our economics course as a complete explanation of the economy as it is
today, thus achieving an imperfect understanding, or else reject it
out of hand as bearing little relationship to what is actually going
on - to the actual problems of living. In order to give them a more
complete picture we must, I contend, include in our courses a more
searching examination of the moral and political determinants of the
characteristics of our economic institutions. There will undoubted-
ly be problems in pursuing such a course, not the least of which is
the difficulty of deciding how far and how often we 'stray' from the
traditional content of economics into the realms of the political
and moral implications of the issues that will arise; nevertheless
I think that it is a difficulty that we ought to grapple with. If
you were to ask, 'Why should we as economists do this?' my reply
would be, 'Who else is going to do it?'

DISCUSSION

Smith introduced his paper by stating that his proposals were really
rather modest, based on two unexceptional propositions, viz. pupils
learn best through doing things rather than through listening to
other people, and pupils show most interest in material which they
readily accept as being relevant to their own needs.

By and large the paper was well received, but some speakers did
criticise Smith's proposals as lacking in intellectual rigour, as he
anticipated in his paper. Several participants would not accept his
claim that his approach to teaching inflation 'greatly enriches a
pupil's understanding of the subject' and, whilst conceding that his
method provided an interesting introduction, they claimed that it
offered little scope for developing insight. Other speakers queried
the absence of any reference to learning about the social structure
of the United Kingdom and about the determinants of political and
economic power in the United Kingdom, which struck them as odd in
view of Smith's concentration on these themes later in his paper.

Some speakers wanted to know how he proposed to encourage pupils
to want to talk about economics, and one offered hints on how to
create an environment conducive to relaxed conversation. Smith
warned his audience against reading too much into his paper with
regard to its implications for teaching methodology.

Most time was devoted to the question of the role of the teacher
in Smith's plans, and particularly to the teacher's role in the
excursions into politics, sociology and moral philosophy advocated
in the paper. Clearly, Smith's ideas remained 'teacher-centred' in
the sense that the teacher continued to control what took place, but
how far should the teacher relinquish his claim to be 'an authority'
and be content to be 'in authority' when it came to discussing 'the
moral and political determinants of the characteristics of our economic institutions'? Some speakers invoked the legendary two-armed
economist as neutral chairman, others urged teachers to recognise
their prejudices prior to any discussion, and yet another group appeared extremely reluctant to venture into such mine-ridden terri-

tory at any price. Nobody volunteered an answer to Smith's rhetori-
cal 'Who else is going to do it?' At least one person saw no
dangers worth worrying about. It may be true that there is contention over the exact point at which teaching ends and indoctrination begins, but Smith was confident that the amount of seditious
material necessary to jeopardise the stability of a school was way
beyond the capabilities of even the most zealous purveyor disguised
as an economics teacher.

The greatest risk run by teachers who carried their views into
the classroom was, in the opinion of one speaker, an infringement of
the laws relating to slander, and, in the opinion of another, a
breach of the code of professional conduct. Finally, one speaker
stated his conviction that so-called positive economics was itself
value-loaded, and many statements that one might wish to make, for
example, about 'power' were no less positive and no more normative
than some utterances with regard to national income, for example.
So perhaps, he concluded, Smith was not asking economists to enter
deeper water than they were already in, however unwittingly.

Chapter 15

A NON-CERTIFICATE COURSE IN ECONOMICS
Leslie W. Orton

BACKGROUND

The Economics Department at Dunfermline High School has offered a non-certificate course in Economics to pupils of SIII and SIV (age range 14-16) since 1972. This course, timetabled as business economics, is now open to both boys and girls. (In previous sessions it was effectively open to boys only as girls went to retail distribution classes organised by the Business Studies Department.) The course operates in four periods of a seven period per week option - the other three periods are for arithmetic. Thus in this timetable option pupils select arithmetic and business economics rather than, inter alia, arithmetic and certificate mathematics. Pupils who take business economics are studying for no, or very few, 'O' grade examinations, and some pupils have spent their first two secondary years in the Remedial Department. The ability level of the pupils taking this course is not high in absolute terms but it covers a relatively wide range. (For last session's pupils the distribution of IQ, measured by a Moray House test, had the median in the upper-eighties and the upper and lower quartiles in the mid-nineties and mid-seventies respectively.) Our aims and objectives have, therefore, to take this into account. The non-certificate course in economics extends over two years and two teachers are involved in each year, each with a class of between twenty and thirty pupils. If this can be timetabled a class has the same teacher in both years of the course so that continuity of approach is achieved and personal relationships strengthened.

AIMS AND OBJECTIVES

Given the abilities and backgrounds of the pupils taking non-certificate economics, our aims and objectives are wider, and perhaps less clearly formed, than for a certificate course, and they encompass as primary rather than secondary aims many objectives in the affective domain. Our aims and objectives are as follows.

    1 To stimulate the pupils' interest. Most of the pupils taking the course would have been eligible to leave school at the end of

SIII but for the raising of the school leaving age, so that it is
one of our major aims to maintain enthusiasm and interest. Since
the second year's work is an integral part of a two-year course
rather than a separate 'ROSLA course' there is no discontinuity in
the work and, more importantly, in the pupils' perception of both
the course and their teachers' attitude to them as individuals.

2 To help pupils to make the most of their resources and talents
and to help to prepare them for their future life as producers and
citizens. Our aim here is to give pupils an understanding of the
need for production before there can be any consumption, to show
them the nature and importance of the major economic institutions
and organisations and the hard economic facts that will influence
their lives once they have left school and which have already influenced their lives to date. We want them to be more able to pass
informed judgments on the past and likely future economic decisions
of others - notably administrators and politicians.

B.S.Bloom has written,

it is very clear that in the middle of the twentieth century we
find ourselves in a rapidly changing and unpredictable culture...
Under these conditions much emphasis must be placed in schools on
the development of generalised ways of attacking problems and on
knowledge which can be applied to a wide range of new situations.
(1)

We tend to the view that economics has a distinctive role to play in
pupils' education since it concerns itself inter alia with some of
the things that are changing most rapidly - industrial organisation,
the pattern of industry, the replacement of human labour by
machines, state intervention in the lives of individuals and so on.
We hope that pupils will come to relaise that economic change is
important for their welfare and that it is not something to be
feared but something with which they have to come to terms.

In this, as in other areas of economics, we want pupils to take a
broader view than the self-centred view that they have probably held
and to see how all the economic pieces fit together to form a
(usually) coherent whole, in which they have a vital part to play
and from which they have much to gain.

3 To develop the pupils' thought processes. We want the pupils
to develop a much greater degree of 'economic literacy' than exists
at present and to develop the 'economic way of thinking', as summa-
rised, for example, by Richard Szreter. (2)

4 To give pupils a chance to exercise and improve their basic
language and number skills.

5 To give pupils a chance to exercise and improve their motor
skills and co-ordination.

6 To encourage in pupils positive attitudes to school and work.
It could be objected here that 'positive attitudes' are different
things to different people and that this aim could lead to a charge
of indoctrination. However, as R.M.Hare has argued, this is not the
case 'provided that our aim is that the children should in the end
come to appraise these principles for themselves'. (3)

7 To broaden pupils' experience of teaching methods.

8 To develop pupils' personalities and sociability.

9 To make the pupils want to come back for more!

SYLLABUS

The syllabus is geared largely to the pupils' post-school life and can thus be used as a first approximation to a scheme of work. It would seem most useful to indicate the extent of the syllabus in the form in which we use it. It is the basic element in the course but individual teachers are encouraged to digress when the media or local events throw up suitable pegs on which to hang items of economic understanding, and when their own or their pupils' particular interests provide a suitable teaching medium.

Economics Department: economics in SIII and SIV - basic syllabus

1 Leaving school and finding a job
(a) Why we need to work:
Limitless wants, scarce resources.
Barter and money economies.
(b) Economics - study of man in the ordinary business of life: keeping health and strength to use limited skills and resources to satisfy as many desires as possible.
Idea of standard of living.
(c) Finding a job: what to consider - own interest and abilities, and job's pay, conditions and prospects. Not all jobs are open to us.
Role of education and training.
Where to get information and help - parents, careers staff, friends, newspapers. Practical hints on interviews - first day at work and first pay packet.
2 At work
(a) Production of goods and services.
Local industries and occupations.
Interdependence of people at work - few can work in isolation, most rely on the services and products of others in order to do their own job. Our efficiency is largely dependent on that of others and is influenced by specialisation, division of labour, automation, forms of business organisation, and so on.
Review of Britain's major industries and occupations.
Location of industry, geographical and occupational distributions of population, concept of working population, the transport and service industries.
(b) Conditions
Factory legislation, industrial safety.
Trade union activities, strikes.
Need for responsible behaviour by all.
3 Personal income and expenditure
(a) Wages
Methods of payment, structures, amounts, fringe benefits.
Why are there differences?
Need to raise productivity to get higher incomes.
Taxation, graduated insurance, family allowances, other benefits and allowances, trade union subscriptions.
(b) Budgeting
Prices - what are they? how are they determined?

Priorities in spending - practical tests.
Sensible use of income - primary and secondary poverty.
Cost of HP, car, marriage.
Need to save and insure.
(c)   Savings
SAYE, commercial and savings banks, building societies, hoarding.
4 Local income and expenditure
Central government grants, rates, borrowing.
Expenditure on e.g. education, housing, police.
5 National income and expenditure
(a)   Income - taxes, borrowing, National Debt.
(b)   Spending - e.g. social services, defence, education, local
authorities.
(c)   Government policy:
The Budget
Prices and Incomes Policy
Employment and money
The Bank of England
Balance of payments and international trade.
6 The place of the individual in the life of the nation
The political parties.
Elections.
The work of MP's.
Parliament.
The Monarchy.
7 Changing jobs
(a)   Why?   - causes of unemployment and redundancy.
(b)   Where? - industrial re-training, new towns.
(c)   Ease? - economic conditions, age, family commitments.
8 Leisure and retirement
Need to determine proper use of leisure before retirement in order
to enjoy retirement when it comes.

METHODOLOGY

Purists among music-lovers would argue that each performance should
be a fresh experience so that one ought not to listen to a recording
more than once. Similar claims have been made about teaching
methods, particularly those for non-certificate pupils, but I am
happy to say that we do not achieve a state of grace in this matter!
We try to vary our approach as much as possible but our repertoire
revolves around the following approaches.
(a)   Topics based on the idea of 'Me and ...' (e.g. 'Me and the
      school', 'me and the trade unions') which is bad grammar but
      seems to produce good learning.
(b)   Work in jotters - notes, diagrams, sketches, maps, graphs, and
      so on. We have experimented with a loose-leaf system but have
      found that this rapidly becomes untidy and disorganised.
(c)   The use of worksheets devised for non-certificate courses in
      social subjects by national working parties in Scotland, or,
      more usually, made up within the Department.
(d)   Work with a tape recorder. Pupils have in the past been en-
      couraged to express their opinions verbally and to conduct

formalised debates. Radio programmes are 'produced', for example, on the effect of a strike in an important local industry. We hope that next session pupils will make their own
slide-tape sets on local industries.

(e)   Work in groups or as individuals. Pupils are encouraged to
work harmoniously as part of a group and to work on individual
assignments.

(f)   Model making. Pupils have in the past produced balsa wood and
cardboard models of such things as a coal mine, an oil rig, a
steel works, and fishing boats. Meccano is now available and
one group built an 'inflation machine' to show the effects on
prices of changes in demand and supply. Another group is producing a relief model of the local area to show the locations
of important local industries and routeways.

(g)   Game-playing and simulation exercises. As introductions to
topics pupils have played 'Monopoly' and attempted to play
'Speculate'. They have also simulated the House of Commons at
work, and held mock trade union meetings.

(h)   Films and television programmes. Suitable films are shown as
and when available. In SIV a television series, 'Going to
Work', is shown - one episode per week. This series of job
descriptions and job situations stimulates a certain amount of
discussion, and accompanying workbooks sometimes, though not
often, offer useful follow-up work for our purposes - in other
contexts the workbooks would be more useful.

(i)   Visits and speakers. At the end of SIII pupils visit the Royal
Highland Show at Ingliston, and, if it can be arranged, they
visit a coal mine at the end of SIV. Ideally, we would like to
be able to arrange more visits and excursions but the commitments of teachers to other classes, and of the pupils to
other departments, make this difficult.
    'Outside speakers' is an area which we have not fully ex-
plored as yet. It ought to be an area that would yield
important results. The difficulty has been that of finding
speakers who are both (i) available at the time the classes
meet and (ii) likely to be able to pitch their remarks at the
right level. Our search continues.

(j)   Practical tests and experiments. Pupils have carried out experiments on division of labour and the location of industry,
and been given a chance to try their hand at budgeting for a
family of five, reading and checking pay slips and so on. One
teacher even brought in his dog for a period to illustrate the
economic aspects of dog ownership.

   Whichever approach is adopted, the basic requirement is that it
is an attempt to get across one or more basic economic ideas in a
form that is obviously going to be relevant in later life if it is
not already relevant. We appeal unashamedly to the pupils' vocational impulses wherever possible, and we encourage pupils to ask
questions not only about what they are studying but also about any
aspect of life after school. We lay ourselves open to the charge
that we are involving ourselves in a form of Civics but we believe
that for these pupils it is a necessary part of their economics education.
   A word should perhaps be said about discipline. We try to keep

these classes on as informal a footing as possible consistent with good classroom behaviour and consideration for others. Occasionally pupils take advantage of this but by and large they give the impression that they appreciate the informality and some even admit to looking forward to the next period!

EVALUATION AND ASSESSMENT

Assessment of the content of the two-year course is made in November of each year and in May of SIII by examination. At other times pupils are given opportunities to use their acquired knowledge more informally.

Pupils seem to increase in 'economic literacy' but still find the 'economic way of thinking' rather difficult. To what extent this reflects their home environment, and general educational attainment, and to what extent it is a reflection on our teaching it is difficult, at close quarters, to be certain. They do not improve noticeably in their language and number skills but pupils who claim not to be good with their hands have eventually produced some excellent models and wall charts.

It is very difficult for us to assess our achievements in the affective domain. Most pupils give the impression that they are interested for much of the time. Their personalities visibly develop and most become more sociable. To what extent we achieve our objective in encouraging positive attitudes to school and work is again very difficult to judge given the interaction of behavioural effects from different subjects and teachers, and from the non-school environment. One of the big problems facing anyone who teaches these groups is absenteeism. Continuity is difficult when attendance is irregular and the personnel present at one period may bear little resemblance to that of the previous period. The effect of this on our ability to offer a sustained piece of work over more than a single period can readily be imagined, as can the frustration of those who attend regularly but whose work is subject to periodic delay and interruption while absentees 'catch up'. The teacher then faces a problem. Should he abandon the attempt at sustained work and thus yield to pressures from those regularly absent? Should he ignore these interruptions to the work of the regular attenders (and perhaps force them to become absentees) on the grounds that the absentees are more in need of his teaching? Should he abandon the absentees 'to their own wickedness'? Should he abandon any attempt to establish a class identity and a class or group commitment to a piece of work and make each pupil's work an individual undertaking, pursued at his own speed, without involving any other pupil at all?

The course is now entering its fifth year and six groups have now completed the two-year course. Our impression is that pupils quite like the course - the consumer seems reasonably satisfied - but we must possibly make our approach even more concrete and locally-oriented, and move the emphasis further towards a less literate and less numerate methodology.

In this paper I have attempted to show the nuts and bolts of a non-certificate course in economics as we run one. Justifications for such courses are contained in a number of publications and I

have not thought it necessary to outline them here. Besides myself,
three teachers have been involved in teaching this course (Alan
Blyth, Derek Gibson, and Ian Baxter), and I should like to pay
tribute here to their hard work. Any successes we have had stem in
large measure from their efforts. Any defects in the course remain
my responsibility, as Head of Department, and I should welcome
comments that might lead to an improved course.

REFERENCES

1 BLOOM, B.S. and KRATHWOHL, D.R. (eds), 'Taxonomy of Educational
   Objectives - Handbook I - The Cognitive Domain', D.McKay, New
   York, 1956, p.40.
2 SZRETER, R., Economics Education in Schools, in LEE, N. (ed.),
   'Teaching Economics', 2nd edn, Heinemann, London, 1975.
3 HARE, R.M., Adolescents into Adults, in HOLLINS, T.H.B. (ed.),
   'Aims in Education', Manchester University Press, 1964.

DISCUSSION

There was no discussion of this paper because Mr Orton was unable to
be present at the seminar.

Part four

ECONOMICS AT SCHOOL AND FURTHER EDUCATION LEVELS

Chapter 16

LINK COURSES IN ECONOMICS?
Pat Noble

1 LINK COURSES: ORIGINS AND AIMS

Courses linking the work of secondary schools with that of colleges
of further education or technical colleges have recently become a
growth sector in the education of pupils of 14-18 years; most of
this growth has occurred since 1969-70. In 1968, the study conference at the Further Education Staff College framed a definition of
link courses: 'a properly planned and co-ordinated course, jointly
organised by school and college, for pupils in full-time secondary
education, usually in their fourth or fifth year.' To some extent
this definition gives a way of evaluating the administration of such
courses - it does not suggest the role or scope for any one subject
specialism.

The 1944 Act identified further education as the sector offering
full- and part-time education for those over compulsory school
leaving age; fourteen-year-olds have none the less been able to
enjoy part-time day release from school to the local college. In
some cases, the reason has simply been that a particular educational
resource has not been available or viable in the secondary school;
the link course has offered a subject specialist or possibly
equipment for practical work in computer appreciation. Viewing
education authority resources as an entity, this integration seems
an excellent compromise where time and space permit. Some of the
courses have been fostered to offer pupils a chance to work with
older people still studying while in employment - the homogeneity of
school learning groups is at variance with experience later in life;
such opportunities usually arise where pupils join classes already
organised in the college where they will be taught as young adults.
There can be a positive motivational effect in such part-time day
release. Attendance at a college may offer an exciting opportunity
to meet staff both qualified and experienced in industry, commerce
and the public services; qualified caterers, engineers and marketing men are rare in the secondary schools.

The 1968 Schools Council Enquiry 'Young School Leavers' (1) sur-
veyed the attitudes of school leavers, their parents and their
teachers to the aims of education and found a firm expectation from
both pupils and parents that secondary schools should inform them

about different sorts of jobs and provide knowledge of direct use in qualifying for and adjusting to work. However, Tyrell Burgess (2) reported that

> when asked what new elements teachers hoped to introduce into their teaching when the school leaving age was raised, the largest group of answers concerned things to widen the pupils' interests, to develop their aesthetic appreciation, to make them self-sufficient and generally to enrich their lives. In other words, the teachers hoped to use the longer secondary school course to offer the pupils more of what the pupils considered unimportant.

It is perhaps reassuring that planning for ROSLA should have included the growth of courses linked to FE colleges - courses that are patently offering a chance to sample vocationally-oriented study and perhaps provide some influence towards the choice of further study by full- or part-time routes.

Some doubts about this approach to vocational preparation have been expressed. Careers Officers (3) sound somewhat sceptical about how far the experience of a link course really affects choice or subsequent job satisfaction. They seem equally sceptical about courses attempting to offer information about different sorts of jobs, when the range of courses reflects more the existing departments of a college than the known employment patterns of school leavers, especially girls. They are equally concerned that link courses aiming to ease the transition from school should not be confined to the least able groups.

Stuart Maclure (4) recently wrote pleading for diversity of provision from 14+: 'how can you provide a rich diversified choice which really has meaning and links up with the world of work as well as the world of continued education?' He suggested that school need not be the continuing focus of attention but that link courses, pre-industrial experience and social service activity could give a possibility of other kinds of success and other kinds of experience.

Other agencies are emphasising the links with further education. The Manpower Services Commission plans to subsidise one-year craft and technician courses in conjunction with the Industrial Training Boards. The Training Opportunities Scheme is being expanded from 68,000 to 80,000 places to offer some full-time educational alternative to unemployment amongst school leavers.

In 1969, about 12,000 pupils were attending colleges on this link course basis; by 1970, 15,000.

2   THE TYPES OF COURSES OFFERED

The types of courses offered are as diverse as the aims discussed above. There are externally examined courses run by college staff in the college - economics, sociology, politics, business studies and law are taught in this way, especially at 'A' level. Similarly commerce is offered at CSE, RSA and 'O' levels and can cover considerable parts of an introductory course in economics. Alternatively the college staff may attend the school to teach pupils. This may merely reflect a shortage of specialists rather than any jointly planned curriculum development.

A wholly different approach is the 'taster' courses, where pupils make a visit for a short course in a subject that interests them probably in order to discover as much about the college as about the course. 'Linked courses are a valuable addition to the means whereby post-school education is brought to the attention of the young school leaver.' (5) 'Sampler' courses may be laid on for pupils who try out a range of subjects but there may be problems of motivation where pupils are already fairly sure where their future lies.

'Bridge' courses are devised to help in the process of transfer. The Training Services Agency has put forward the idea of 'Gateway' courses (6) of three months, 'end-on' to secondary school, with students attending colleges of further education, skill centres and workplaces. The indication is that transitional preparation for young workers is still inadequate.

It is in this last group of courses that some of the most imaginative work is found in CSE Mode 3 or as non-examined options; teachers in further education have here made a real contribution to curriculum development, but it is in this type of course that, as yet, economics seems to figure least often. Most of the courses are organised within college departments and this may limit the possible role of economics.

3   POTENTIAL FOR ECONOMICS IN LINK COURSES

In the surveys reported by Regional Advisory Councils and in the many summaries published by the large LEAs, economics is usually listed with other 'A'/'O' link courses available. It could be that in some of the published summaries, economics is subsumed under other headings in the commerce field. It could reflect the problem posed by the Schools Council (7) in 1965: 'Everyone these days needs some contact with the language and ideas of elementary economics; what we do not know is how far they can be pursued with pupils aged 15-16 of widely differing abilities.' Significance would seem to attach both to the idea of immaturity and to that of mixed ability groupings. In 1975, we have a much richer knowledge of what is possible - enough perhaps to try to evaluate the possible contribution of a local college to the subject area. In particular, we might examine the 'applied' contexts where the expertise of the local college staff would have a special motivational contribution to make. On higher technological courses, economists and sociologists often provide 'servicing' courses; might there be a similar role in link courses for those pupils who are mainly exploring practical subjects? What has the subject to offer the many girls who will go on to work in the retail trade? The Training Services Agency have certainly identified some areas of social economics that they regret to find lacking in the preparation for work of school leavers in general, especially the social and economic aspects of industry. (8)

4 ORGANISATIONAL CONSTRAINTS

These can indeed be set out for consideration but most have been coped with where both schools and colleges want to make possible a jointly planned course. Attitudes of staff are apparently undocumented; no survey seems to have been published reporting interviews with staff in colleges or schools. Retrospective interviews with students have been reported in at least one local study.

Timetabling and transport have posed problems; pastoral care during the day-release period has in some cases been covered by the appointment of a senior tutor in the local college. Examination entries have usually responded to clear liaison with the appropriate examining board. Liaison and communication between school and college has been more of a problem. In some cases a course is run for a specific school; in others, over ten schools may be sending pupils into just one course at the college which may be providing for over a thousand link course attenders. Liaison can be set up for matters of administration but may become more difficult at the level of course planning and assessment. Schools may want some measure of continuous assessment - or even of self-assessment - built into courses designed to aid self-awareness and the process of vocational choice.

5 ISSUES FOR DISCUSSION

1 In the absence of an economics specialist in the school, where does the responsibility lie for curriculum planning in Mode 3 and non-examination courses?

The absence of an economics specialist in a school may itself reflect a curriculum choice. Pupils will none the less be meeting the subject matter of economics as presented in English, current affairs, RE commentaries and perhaps general studies courses offered by historians and geographers. The school may delegate the selection of course content to subject specialists in the colleges - but the college staff may have different objectives, different attitudes to student learning and to assessment - all questions of curriculum planning.

2 How far is the opportunity to study economics likely to be affected by link course facilities?

It seems that FE colleges are providing examination courses in economics when these are not available in the secondary school. There is little evidence that the economic literacy of the majority of school leavers is being met by provision through link courses except in so far as commerce includes aspects of economics.

3 Is the quality of the economics studied likely to be affected by this type of course and its varied aims?

The effect on the quality of economic understanding achieved depends on how far economists in further education are able to contribute. Where they fulfil only a servicing role outside the Business Studies Department, their professional involvement will be limited; lower ability students on link courses will rarely meet them.

4 On what grounds would one select students to follow a course

including economics at a local college? Who should make the selection?

In practice, release to study economics on an FE link course is available to able students from 16-18 years old. Selection is largely by the schools, the students themselves and parents. This provides the college with students similar to those enrolled on its own full-time and part-time courses. The Business Education Council has announced that its first level award will involve students in reaching a level 'at least equivalent to the pass level of the present Certificate of Office Studies'. (9) Should link courses include an ability range wider than that currently accepted for commercial courses, the schools will be posing serious problems for their economics colleagues in further education.

5 What would be the professional and curricular implications of inviting FE lecturers to teach economics courses in the schools?

The implications would seem to be inherent in the different conditions of service and the different background of lecturers in further education. The FE teacher may not be certificated; industrial and commercial experience and professional qualifications may be more significant in the colleges where teacher training is still not a priority. Apart from examinable courses, the work in secondary schools would be expected to be of a lower grade than that likely to be available in the college; this might prove a stumbling block to much expansion of link courses in economics.

ACKNOWLEDGMENT

I should like to express my appreciation for discussion and access to much unpublished material held by R.Brown (Garnett College) who has made a special study of this field.

REFERENCES

1 The Schools Council Enquiry - 1, 'Young School Leavers', HMSO, London, 1968.
2 BURGESS, T., The Further Education Option, in TIBBLE, J.W. (ed.), 'The Extra Year', Routledge & Kegan Paul, London, 1970, pp.77-8.
3 HARROWER, N.D., 'Linked Courses and School Leavers', The Institute of Careers Officers, London, 1973.
4 MACLURE, S., On Trying to have our Cake and Eat it, 'Times Educational Supplement', 4 July 1975, p.2.
5 DES, Reports on Education No.72, September 1971.
6 'Vocational Preparation for Young People', Training Services Agency, London, 1975.
7 Schools Council Working Paper No.2, 'Raising the School Leaving Age', HMSO, London, 1965.
8 Business Education Council, First Policy Statement, March 1976.
9 Ibid.

DISCUSSION

Mrs Noble spoke with qualified enthusiasm about the educational
possibilities of link courses, and made five specific appeals:
1 Let us respond positively to pupils' and parents' desire for
   vocational training without asking schools to provide vocational
   courses.
2 Let us acclimatise pupils to day-release whilst they are still
   full-time pupils.
3 Let us play a positive part in launching young people into a
   pattern of life-long education.
4 Let us regard link courses as a real chance within curriculum
   development to increase educational opportunities for all young
   people.
5 Let us, as economics teachers, use link courses to help solve the
   shortage of economics teachers.
There was a lively response. One speaker pointed out that the
recent proliferation of link courses reflected the enormous change
in the status of schools compared with further education colleges
that had taken place in the last decade, with enormous improvements
in the facilities offered in further education. He felt it a great
pity that link courses were generally confined to the less able, who
also happened to be the pupils who undertook most practical work, to
which further education facilities tended to be particularly well
suited. He wanted to see further education colleges offering
courses designed for Advanced level pupils in order to eliminate the
need for small, uneconomic sixth form sets in schools. This sug-
gestion prompted another speaker to point out that schools ought to
help each other by exploring possibilities for inter-school link
courses. He felt that the existing financial climate would oblige
schools to accelerate the trend to link courses in an attempt to
optimise use of resources.

Other speakers were not slow to point out the difficulties encountered in running link courses. All too often the links were
extremely tenuous. One speaker admitted to being soured by his
experiences: unwanted pupils dumped on unready colleges; pupils
following unsuitable courses run by staff some of whom possessed
qualifications which would not permit them to be employed in secondary schools in Scotland; almost total lack of liaison between
principal and head teacher, and between lecturer and teacher.

Not everyone felt inclined to put the majority of the blame for
any débâcles on the further education colleges. As one speaker
stressed, institutions did not respect each other, and some schools'
approach to link courses was arrogant and condescending. Between
one sector and another there existed hostility and suspicion. Some
speakers felt that schools had much to answer for, and spoke of
schools in which, in their view, pupils were treated oppressively
with absurd behavioural restrictions imposed upon them. In such
schools, they contended, the more liberal treatment meted out to
pupils on their weekly visits to further education establishments
was anathema in the eyes of the school authorities, who found reason
to end the link. Others deplored the cynical despatching of
troublesome school classes to unsuspecting colleges.

It was comforting to learn of successful schemes, and their

success was for unremarkable reasons: careful planning and continuous co-operation between enthusiastic people who liked and trusted each other, and whose respective institutions had facilities to offer that were genuinely needed by the other party. Successful link courses mentioned included courses in mechanised accounting, computer studies, retailing, typewriting, catering and engineering. Nobody was able to cite a link course involving further education students coming into a school, but the possibility was welcomed as desirable.

The five issues for discussion posed by Mrs Noble were touched upon briefly by one speaker. His views were

1 In the absence of an economics specialist in the school, the responsibility for curriculum planning in Mode 3 and non-examination courses lies with the further education college.

2 Link courses would increase the opportunity to study economics.

3 Link courses would provide an opportunity to improve the quality of the economics studied.

Nobody demurred at these views, despite ample opportunity to do so, and nobody at all was prepared to attempt answers to discussion points 4 and 5. But other questions were raised too. How could schools expect to attract and retain economics teachers if sixth form classes, however small and uneconomic, disappeared? What were the implications for headmasters' salaries of courses which might make further education more attractive than school to seventeen-year-olds? And, above all, what steps could be taken to improve relationships between different sectors of education? Perhaps, as one speaker suggested, co-operation on CEE courses offers the most likely immediate focal point for progress with link courses involving the teaching of economics.

POSTSCRIPT
Robert Wilson

Fundamental questions such as those posed by Keith Robinson in his
introduction have no one simple answer. For educational philosophers and researchers there is, perhaps, ample time to reflect
before attempting a sophisticated reply. The practising teacher
enjoys no such privilege, and for the young teacher embarking on his
teaching career there may not be an opportunity so much as to pose
the questions. The decision that economics should be taught to less
academic pupils at the later stage of the secondary school may well
have been taken for him in his particular school, not because of any
passionate belief by those in authority in the virtues of the
subject matter, but perhaps merely because classes 5X, 5Y and 5Z
still have two blank periods on their weekly timetable and the young
economics graduate needs his timetable filling out a little in the
name of equity. In such circumstances it is fairly common for the
novice teacher to be told that he is being given 'a free hand',
which may well be the very last thing that he wants, since he feels,
probably correctly, that both he and his subject will be assessed on
his initial performance.

It appears to me that 'Extending Economics within the Curriculum'
offers something of value to all teachers and not least to those
placed in the above predicament. First of all, it offers a fair
degree of comfort. Implicitly recalled in the papers produced by
practising teachers are moments, maybe even months, of failure and
frustration. Richard Winsor admits to having generated boredom
amongst his pupils; Dorothy Davidson implies that some of the
visits she arranges are not wholly successful; Pamela Morrison
states quite starkly that to obtain written work from some pupils in
her school is almost impossible; Jenny Wales does not seek to deny
that some of her pupils are merely longing to leave school notwith-
standing her efforts; Harry Ramsay concedes that he was unable to
generate enthusiasm amongst all his pupils; and Leslie Orton refers
to persistent absenteeism and occasional discipline problems. And
yet what is patently obvious to anyone who has met with and talked
to each one of these particular teachers is just how singularly well
suited they are to their chosen profession, and how, without exception, they appear to have learned to accept times of failure with
the same equanimity as times of success - a formula for survival if
ever there was one.

   Second, scattered among the pages are some good ideas suitable
for adapting, refining, extending or just plain plagiarising. The
teachers' answer to Keith Robinson's second question is well nigh
unequivocal. Almost without exception, the contributors suggest
that content should reflect the experiences and interests of the
pupils, and that method should place a premium on active pupil
participation. Diluted Ordinary level economics courses are unacceptable to staff if only because they are demonstrably unacceptable
to less academic pupils. There is less unanimity on exactly what to
put in their place. Not every teacher would accept Pamela
Morrison's view that in schools where 'early leavers' predominate
'any course that is to be successful needs to concentrate on the
bits of knowledge and the kinds of skills that will help them to get
decent jobs' (is this true of music, speech and drama, art and
craft?). Nor, for that matter, would every teacher of the 'early
leavers' be inclined to the level of self-deprecation experienced by
Linda Thomas when she felt that she had succeeded only in amusing
and entertaining her charges. Yet there is a fair amount of common
ground and common activity, and as a result fewer children now leave
school unaware of the existence of the major financial and economic
institutions which will have a direct bearing on their own lives,
some obtain a grasp of the major economic forces at work, and a few
admit to having enjoyed the economics lessons. At the time of
writing, there appears to be a movement in the direction of integrated courses and the subject-specialist appears to be in some
danger of loss of identity and diminution of status. In Scotland,
economics teachers are officially 'in surplus' and the number of
economics graduates admitted for training is to be halved. It would
appear that the effective answer to Keith Robinson's second question
will be provided for the rest of the 1970s not by teachers, nor by
researchers, but by the Treasury. In such Spartan times, teachers
will be obliged to seek ways and means of running their courses
comparatively cheaply, and the perspicacious reader will find useful
hints on parsimony among these pages. For those obliged or disposed
to participate in schemes involving co-operation with other departments, Angus Taylor's paper is replete with sound advice.
   Third, the papers bear testimony to the fact that at least some
of the research and development work in economics education urged by
Raymond Ryba in 1974 (in 'Curriculum Development in Economics', ed.
D.Whitehead, Heinemann, London, 1974, chapter 18) has indeed begun
to take place. For the teacher who is floundering on by trial and
error, the indications are that he can look forward to a considerable increase in the amount of literature available to him for
perusal. Whether it will support what he is doing, and whether it
will be couched in terminology which is readily intelligible is less
certain - I am more optimistic with regard to the former than the
latter.
   Two things are absolutely certain. The first is that the circumstances in which teachers of economics perform their professional
duties are going to change markedly in a short period of time as
certain trends are accentuated and other trends are reversed. The
rate of staff turnover may well decelerate (which has implications
for course continuity, team-teaching, etc.), the maximum size of
school may well decrease (which has implications for the range of

subjects offered and for the number of separate subject disciplines allowed to exist), the dates on which 'early leavers' are able to leave may well be more flexible (which has implications for course planning in terms of duration, content and method), and the form of '16 plus' public examinations may well be drastically revised. The second certainty is that whilst all this is taking place, a gener-ation of schoolchildren will undergo a once-in-a-lifetime experience of full-time education and teachers will have to continue to do what they can for them. And what target might teachers set themselves with these 'early leavers'? Surely this: to provide a course for 'early leavers' which is 'sufficiently successful' (Pamela Morrison's term) and 'worthwhile' (Linda Thomas's term) as to make both the parents of the more academic pupils, and the more academic pupils themselves, clamour for access to it. That would be progress indeed.

INDEX